Also by Vanessa May

Sociology of Personal Life (2011, Palgrave Macmillan)

Connecting Self to Society

Belonging in a Changing World

Vanessa May

palgrave
macmillan

First published 2013 by
PALGRAVE MACMILLAN

Palgrave Macmillan in the UK is an imprint of Macmillan Publishers Limited, registered in England, company number 785998, of Houndmills, Basingstoke, Hampshire RG21 6XS.

Palgrave Macmillan in the US is a division of St Martin's Press LLC, 175 Fifth Avenue, New York, NY 10010.

Palgrave Macmillan is the global academic imprint of the above companies and has companies and representatives throughout the world.

Palgrave® and Macmillan® are registered trademarks in the United States, the United Kingdom, Europe and other countries

ISBN: 978-0-230-29286-4 hardback
ISBN: 978-0-230-29287-1 paperback

This book is printed on paper suitable for recycling and made from fully managed and sustained forest sources. Logging, pulping and manufacturing processes are expected to conform to the environmental regulations of the country of origin.

A catalogue record for this book is available from the British Library.

A catalog record for this book is available from the Library of Congress.

Typeset by Aardvark Editorial Limited, Metfield, Suffolk

*In memory of Eva May (1938–2007),
who gave me my first and safest
sense of belonging*

Contents

Preface

I can trace the beginnings of this book project to 2001, when I moved from Finland to England. For the first year or so after the move, it felt as though my identity had lost its moorings. This led me to a fascination with (and awakened my sociological imagination towards) the relationship between self and society, and in particular with how our sense of self is rooted in particular settings. Not just people and cultures, but also physical places and material objects. It was the small things in my new environment that seemed to unsettle me the most, such as the buildings that were so unlike Finnish ones, and the street signs that were slightly (yet somehow significantly) different. Trying to decipher the unwritten codes of English behaviour also felt like a chore at times.

In my previous work I had focused on narrative identities, on how we weave our identities from a cultural toolkit of stories and frameworks. But the sense of dislocation I was experiencing seemed to have little to do with the narrative I told about myself, which had not changed that much between my last day in Finland and my first days in England. Instead, it seemed to be more about the social and material world through which I navigated daily. In the coming years, I tried out various concepts to get at this puzzle sociologically, but none of them seemed quite adequate.

Then, while teaching a module on 'Self and Society', I came across Savage et al.'s (2005) work on belonging, as well as a chapter by Jenkins (2008) on 'Symbolising belonging'. I had finally found a concept that seemed to encompass the different dimensions of my own experiences. By then I was settled in England, with a permanent job and a feeling of having put down some roots here. I felt as though I understood how things worked and was familiar with the look, feel, sound and smell of my surroundings. And I found that this sense of belonging was actually even harder to explain, perhaps because by then I took this feeling for granted. I have continued to explore these issues within my undergraduate sociology module 'Self and Society' that I have taught at the University of Manchester, and I would like to thank my students over the past four years for their part in this process.

The following people also deserve my sincerest thanks, and their influence can be seen on the pages of this book. Gemma Edwards gave helpful comments on an early draft of a paper that formed the basis for this book. Sarah Wilson's paper at the Turning Personal conference in 2009 first got me thinking about sensory belongings, and I would like to thank her for continuing to inspire me with her work and for her friendship. Carol Smart, Jennifer Mason, Stewart Muir, Christian Greiffenhagen, Dave Cutts and David Morgan have, in various conversations, kindly indulged my obsession with belonging and provided me with new ideas and references to pursue.

I feel fortunate to be a part of Realities at the Morgan Centre at the University of Manchester, which has always been an exceptionally collegial, supportive and fun working environment. For this I am grateful to my Morgan Centre colleagues who include many of the people already mentioned, as well as Nicola Allett, Wendy Bottero, Hazel Burke, Katherine Davies, Anna Einarsdottir, Janet Finch, Brian Heaphy, Sue Heath, Vicky Higham, Petra Nordqvist, Paul Simpson, Dale Southerton, Becky Tipper and Sophie Woodward. I hope they can identify a particular 'Morganite' approach that reflects the inspiring intellectual environment I have had the pleasure to be part of.

I would also like to thank the audiences at the following conferences for their helpful comments on various papers related to belonging: Turning Personal, Vital Signs 2, and the British Sociological Association 2010 and 2011 Annual Conferences. My thanks also go to Professor Elianne Riska at the Swedish School of Social Sciences, University of Helsinki and Dr Sirpa Wrede, also at the University of Helsinki, who twice invited me to Finland to present my ideas to a very friendly and supportive audience.

I also extend my thanks to Anna Reeve at Palgrave Macmillan. This is the second book we have worked on together, and I have always received excellent guidance and support from her, for which I am very thankful. I am also grateful to the two anonymous readers who provided helpful feedback on an earlier version of the manuscript, and to Maggie Lythgoe for her keen editorial eye.

My personal thanks go to Mark for everything (plus one cat); Tony, Patrick, Minni, Sebastian and Francesca for roots past, present and future; Joan and Jim Hampson for welcoming me into their family with countless Sunday lunches; and Maria Aretoulaki who has been crucial to my sense of belonging in Manchester. Roona Simpson and Shelley Budgeon have always remembered to kindly enquire 'How goes the book?' and then patiently listened to my long-winded explanations of what was done, what was still to do, and how long I expected all of this to take.

I dedicate this book to the memory of my mother Eva May who taught me just about everything I know about the art of writing and gave me the safest possible sense of belonging while growing up.

Part 1

Self and Society in Social Theory

Introduction

1

Why belonging?

Where do you feel you belong? Is it amid the busyness of a large city or in a quiet rural spot? Do you feel a sense of belonging in the country in which you live? Why is that? Do you have specific groups of people you belong with? Are these people similar to you and in what way? How you answer these questions says something about *who* you are and your relationship to other people, as well as about your background. It is these connections between self and society that are the focus of *Connecting Self to Society*. Belonging, which I define as the process of creating a sense of identification with, or connection to, cultures, people, places and material objects, is one of the ways in which these connections manifest themselves. Furthermore, I suggest that belonging acts as a kind of barometer for social change: significant changes in our surroundings are reflected in a fluctuation in our sense of belonging.

Belonging can also be characterized as feeling at ease with one's self and one's social, cultural, relational and material contexts. We come to understand who we are partly on the basis of where and with whom we belong, which is why belonging is of fundamental importance to the self. Belonging has been defined by many as a basic human need (Baumeister and Leary, 1995; Melucci, 1996; Calhoun, 2003a, 2003b). But belonging is more than just an individual feeling – it is, at times, a fiercely contested social and political issue that has tangible consequences. In contemporary multicultural Britain, for example, there are heated public debates over who can or has a right to belong, with consequent impacts on people's citizenship rights and their ability to successfully claim a sense of belonging. Thus, an individual's sense of belonging is affected by collectively negotiated understandings of who 'we' are and what 'we' stand for, and who gets excluded as the 'other'.

On the face of it, the words 'I belong' seem to be quite straightforward. And indeed, whenever we turn on the television or radio, read a newspaper or talk to people, we are likely to hear one version or another of an account of how some person or group does or does not belong. But despite its ubiquitous nature, the concept of belonging remains curiously undertheorized by social scientists, with a few notable exceptions (for example Miller, 2003; Antonsich, 2010; Yuval-Davis, 2011; May, 2011a). This is perhaps because it is such a taken-for-granted concept, as my colleagues and I found in a recent research project.[1] When we asked our research participants whether or not they belonged, many of them merely stated 'yes, I belong', without really being able or willing to expand on that statement (May and Muir, 2011). But such commonsense, taken-for-granted phenomena deserve critical analysis because despite their deceptive appearance of being 'natural', they are shaped by social forces.

This chapter introduces some of the key themes of this book, namely a view of both self and society as relational, that is, as constituted in the social interactions between people. Following on from this, if we adopt the view that society is the result of human interaction, then social change must be understood as the result of changes in how people interact with each other. This is why, I argue, it is important to examine social change from the perspective of the person. The concept I use to do this is 'belonging', which directs our attention to the multi-dimensional and complex connections and disconnections that people experience with their surroundings, and the people, places, objects and cultures that exist within these.

A relational view of self and society

A key theoretical starting point in *Connecting Self to Society* is the relational view of the self. In a nutshell, the **relational self** means that rather than the self being something innate, something we are born with, it emerges in relationships with and in relation to other people. (Terms in bold are explained in the Glossary at the end of the book.) As children, we gain an understanding of self because our parents and other significant people *tell* us who we are or who we should aspire to be. In this process we learn to invoke similarity *and* difference: I am like her because we both grew up in Finland and I am unlike him because I like techno rather than baroque music. This process of identification is a two-way one: we identify *with* (self-identification), while others identify us *as* (categorization) (Jenkins, 2000: 7–8). And because identification always involves others (who we identify with and who categorize us), it is a *relational* process. In understanding selves as relational, that is, as connected to other people as well as culturally and socially embedded, I will also be using the concept of 'personal life' as developed by Smart (2007).

Not only is *Connecting Self to Society* based on the premise that the self is relational, but society is also seen in relational terms, drawing inspiration from Simmel's (1950) and Elias's (1991) arguments that society is not a 'thing' but rather the dynamic product of interactions and relationships between individuals. Society can be viewed as a set of relationships between three 'orders': the individual order of what goes on in people's minds; the interactional order of what goes on between people; and the institutional order, that is, 'patterned, organized and symbolically-templated "ways of doing things"'

(Jenkins, 2000: 10). I suggest that society is also made up of individuals' relationships with their material environment. These different orders do not exist in isolation, rather they are experienced by individuals as part of one 'enmeshment' (Mason, 2010). For example, we use our bodies to think and move, and to interact with other bodies, while the environments in which we do these things are organized in particular ways, both in terms of physical layout and expected patterns of behaviour.

Thus, we find ourselves in the domain of everyday life and people's everyday interactions, habits and practices, which help (re-)create **social order**, that is, a particular way of doing things and thinking about the world. This leads us into the field of phenomenology, a sociological tradition that is interested in the way people make sense of the world and go about the business of everyday life. Following this train of thought through to its logical conclusion, it is possible to say that our relationship with the surrounding world is not only crucial to our sense of self, but is also a building block of society. Furthermore, I argue that belonging is one of the more significant forms that this relationship takes. And because our relationship to the surrounding world is multifaceted, so is our experience of belonging. It therefore makes sense to examine three aspects of belonging: relational (between people); cultural (the institutional order); and material (space and objects). These three facets of belonging are not separate 'things' but overlapping, interlocking orders of experience. How a person feels about the space they are in is partly influenced by the relationships they have with the people in that space and by the 'cultural content' of that space. So, for example, I might feel more at home if I go to a minimal techno night with my best friend and other like-minded people than I would attending a formal champagne breakfast with 'posh' people I do not know that well.

It is worth noting here that the 'self' I mainly refer to in this book is a Western one, although in places I will discuss alternative conceptions of the self. Our contemporary notions of 'self' have a historical genesis encompassing the Greco-Roman concept of the person as a free individual, Christian ideas of the soul as something within us and indivisible, **Enlightenment** notions of our equal capacity to think and make choices, and Victorian ideals of the free, self-determining subject and universal justice (Gergen, 1999; Burkitt, 2008: 5–6). The Western habit of distinguishing between 'inside' (where our feelings and ideas reside) and 'outside' is also of a particular time and place. Although our own notion of self is so ingrained as to appear inescapable and universal to us, as though the self 'just is', the ancient Greeks did not use the term 'self' as a noun with the indefinite article 'a', while the Buriats in Siberia view the self as made up of three souls (Taylor, 1989: 111–14).

Understanding social change

From the start, one of the central interests of sociology has been how **social change** affects our sense of self. Understanding the effects of social change remains crucial in a globalized world characterized by rapid economic and social transformations. Major structural upheavals, such as the current economic crisis, affect not only national economies and big businesses, but also the everyday lives of people who might face unemployment or homelessness, for example. Changes such as those brought about by migration, **deindustrialization**, urban regeneration schemes and technological advancements have an impact on where we live, who we live among, where and how we work, and how we go about our daily lives.

It is fairly usual for sociologists to think of the macro-level of, for example, the economy or the labour market and the micro-level of individual lives as two separate spheres, as though these 'really' exist, and as though these analytical concepts 'are self evidently meaningful in the experience of living' (Mason, 2011a: 79). For example, social change is generally described in structural and macro-terms such as 'industrialization', 'urbanization', 'postindustrial society', 'globalization', 'gender relations', 'the labour market' and so on. These are then seen to act on the lives of individuals. Yet, as Honneth (1995) and Mason (2006) point out, these macro-processes do not happen 'out there', but are taking place in the everyday lives of people. This is why it is important to examine everyday life, although it might, on the surface, seem too mundane to warrant much attention, if we are to understand social change:

> Each and every day we make ritual gestures, we move to the rhythm of external and personal cadences, we cultivate our memories, we plan for the future. And everyone else does likewise. Daily experiences are only fragments in the life of an individual, far removed from the collective events more visible to us, and distant from the great changes sweeping through our culture. Yet almost everything that is important for social life unfolds within this minute web of times, spaces, gestures, and relations. It is through this web that our sense of what we are doing is created, and in it lie dormant those energies that unleash sensational events. (Melucci, 1996: 1)

One of the ways in which sociologists have studied the impact of social change is to focus on macro-change such as **globalization**, and how this requires individuals to adapt. I suggest that taking people's experiences of belonging as the starting point provides an alternative to this kind of top-down structural theorizing. Jennifer Mason (2006) has argued for the need to find new and creative ways of studying social reality in order to transcend the micro–macro divide that has traditionally existed within sociology so as to improve our ability to explain what is going on. The macro and the micro are interlinked and sociologists must find ways of holding both in sight when trying to understand social change. Because belonging is a manifestation of the connection between self and society, a focus on belonging allows us to examine the mutual interaction between social and individual change.

Beginning our investigation of social change at the level of people's everyday experiences allows us to understand

> why, for us and so many others, things no longer 'add up': why it is that our routine gestures no longer are what they have been even in the recent past as we interact with different people, as we pass from one life ambit to another at work, at home, on holiday, or alone in solitude? (Melucci, 1996: 1)

In other words, finding explanations as to why people experience shifts and fluctuations in their sense of belonging helps us to understand not only what is going on in individual people's lives, but also what is going at the aggregate level of society.

Why 'belonging' rather than 'identity'?

In many ways, this book is about identity, about who we are. But it is also about much more than identity. I propose that understanding people's sense of self through the concept of belonging does something very different from theories of identity. These entail studying individuals through their member-ship in **identity categories**, such as ethnicity, gender or class, thus isolating these different facets of identity for closer examination. Alternatively, these identity categories can be understood as intersecting, as in the case of **intersectional** theories of identity, which argue that ethnicity and gender intersect and can have a cumulative effect, as in the case of minority ethnic women who can face discrimination because they are non-white *and* women (Crenshaw, 1991).

The risk that sociologists take when they use identity categories as their start-ing point is that they enter into a circular logic, whereby the identity category or a combination of categories are seen as defining the person; consequently, that person's life is explained by their membership in this category. Elsewhere (May, 2004), I have used the metaphor of a lens in relation to the category 'lone mother' as a way of explaining why such explanations are unsatisfactory. If the starting point of a study is the category 'lone mother', then 'lone moth-erhood' becomes the lens through which a woman's life is interpreted. Thus, lone mothers' health problems or poverty are explained by the fact that they are lone mothers, and if their children do badly at school, this is also seen as 'caused by' their mothers' marital status. But there are other ways of studying these women's lives, such as taking the woman's biography as a starting point, in which case it is the woman's background and social location, as well as general attitudes towards lone motherhood, that are used to help explain her experience of being a 'lone mother'. It is important, therefore, not to reduce people to the categories that social scientists use:

> Social science too often just ends up with whatever category it starts with. If you study gay couples, then it is hard not to conclude with regard to sexu-

ality. While, as far as I can tell, being gay has no particular bearing on any other generalisation one would make about these individuals ... most of the diversity that is found ... does not reduce to sociological categories or labels. (Miller, 2008: 291–2)

As Calhoun (1999: 225) says, the prevailing rhetoric of identity posits 'singular, integral subjects', not the people with multiple solidarities and hybrid identities that we find if we examine them through their sense of belonging. Constructing a sense of self is both an individual process, for example the choices we make regarding with whom and where we wish to belong, and communal – the choices others make about rejecting or accepting us. It is these decisions that help shape who we are. Most people experience a sense of connectedness to not one but several groups, places and cultures: the self 'is constrained by overlapping, various communities, each of which is itself changing. Such plurality is the norm, not the exception' (Griffiths, 1995: 93).

Calhoun (2003b: 558) goes on to argue that 'too much gets tossed out along with the genuinely specious notion that ethnicities, nations, or other social groups are internally homogeneous, sharply bounded, and self-subsistent'. Elsewhere (May, 2010), I have argued that sociologists should approach categories (such as identity categories) with caution and critically explore how these categories have emerged, what uses they are put to and how people who are duly categorized react to this categorization.

The category 'lone mother' is a good example. It is a category used by laypeople and sociologists alike to bundle people together and interpret their life experiences through the fact that they are 'lone mothers'. In doing so, the mistake that is often made is to assume that everyone in this category is alike because they share membership of the category 'lone mother'. In order to avoid making such assumptions, it is better to begin any exploration from the perspective of women who are categorized as lone mothers, and to explore the effects this categorization has on their lives, as well as the extent to which they identify or disidentify with this category, and why. This is perhaps even more pressing an issue when the meanings attached to these categories are stigmatizing, and when such identity categories can be used to control or marginalize groups of people (May, 2010). This has happened, for example, to lone mothers, non-heterosexuals, ethnic minorities and women.

Identity categories also render people somehow flat or two-dimensional. In categorizing people, we apportion bits of them into social categories that are often mutually exclusive and do not take into consideration the possibility of varying and multiple feelings of affinity and connectedness. For example, a person with dual British and Finnish citizenship may feel particularly British in some contexts, but more Finnish in other contexts, and at other times may feel both British and Finnish. To ask a person to categorize themselves as British, Finnish or British Finnish involves a fixed 'categorical logic of identity' that denies such complexity and 'movement of and between categories' (Probyn, 1996: 9). In addition, these categories are not able to capture the complexity of being a person, which involves not only negotiating social categories such as nationality, but simultaneous relationships with cultures, people and the material world. Like Probyn, I suggest that it is better to use the concept of 'belonging' rather than 'identity', because belonging:

> captures more accurately the desire for some sort of attachment, be it to other people, places, or modes of being, and the ways in which individuals and groups are caught within wanting to belong, wanting to become, a process that is fuelled by yearning rather than the positing of identity as a stable state. (Probyn, 1996: 19)

What do we belong to, then? Probyn borrows the concept of 'heterotopia' from Foucault to argue that our field of belonging is not made up of distinct categories that act as receptacles for individuals and things. Instead, she directs our attention to the embodied experience of belonging, which allows us to retain a complex view of the self as not made up of two-dimensional identity categories but as a fully rounded being who can experience belonging on many different and, at times, contradictory dimensions:

> The sights and sounds of the spaces in which I sometimes belong are integral to the ways in which I live and think belonging ... Heterotopia designates the coexistence of different orders of space, the materiality of different forms of social relations and modes of belonging. (Probyn, 1996: 10)

Furthermore, I have chosen to focus on belonging rather than identity because this better befits a relational view of the self. Whereas 'identity' begins from the separate, autonomous individual, 'belonging' focuses on what connects people to one another.

The concept of belonging helps us to move beyond the familiar terrain of theories of identity because it foregrounds other sites of identification such as the sensory and material aspects of the world, and the role these play in our sense of self. Thus, this book is about connections and relationality, not just with other people, but also with places and material objects. It is our relationships with these different dimensions of the surrounding world that help create our sense of self:

> people ... strive to create relationships to both people and things. These relationships include material and social routines and patterns which give order, meaning and often moral adjudication to their lives; an order which, as it becomes familiar and repetitive, may also be a comfort to them. (Miller, 2008: 296)

The phenomenological approach adopted in this book focuses our attention on people's embodied experiences of and connections with the world, and to the mutual relationship between the social and the self. The emphasis is on the interconnectedness of the different spheres of life, how they are experienced and made sense of by people. The aim of such an approach is to avoid producing two-dimensional or top-down accounts of self and society that are severed from lived reality (Smith, 1987: 129–30, 132). Instead, *Connecting Self to Society* seeks to understand how people make sense of themselves within a complex world that offers them multiple and sometimes contradictory points of connection. These keep shifting and changing, and in responding to these shifts in their everyday practices, individuals help generate further social change.

Thus, *Connecting Self to Society* examines an issue that is of fundamental importance to individuals and to society, namely the role that belonging plays in connecting self and society, and particularly how belonging can be used to shed light on the impact that social change has on our sense of self.

The structure of this book

Part 1 explores various ways in which sociologists have accounted for the relationship between self and society, and the impact of social change on the self. Chapter 2 explores the origins of sociological thought in relation to self and society by discussing the works of Marx, Durkheim and Weber, the 'founding fathers' of sociology. All three provided 'contrast theories' (Thorns, 2002), in which modern societies were contrasted with premodern ones, and conclude that developments in modernity threatened the self and social cohesion. Echoes of these theories can be found in two dominant accounts within sociology, the psychosocial fragmentation thesis and the individualization thesis, discussed in Chapter 3. Both accounts explore the effects that a 'loss of tradition' has had on the self. According to the psychosocial fragmentation thesis, we are left with fragmented and vulnerable selves, while according to the individualization thesis, this loss of tradition has increased people's ability to choose their own life paths and to act reflexively. The problem is they both take a top-down approach, by beginning from 'loss of tradition' as a 'social fact' that individuals have had to adapt to.

Chapter 4 introduces an alternative approach, which begins with the understanding that self and society are relational and any study that tries to understand social change must begin with the relationships people have with each other and their surrounding material and cultural world. Chapter 5 brings together three sociological traditions – phenomenology, the sociology of everyday life, and the sociology of personal life – that do just this. All three posit that society must be understood from the point of view of individuals' everyday engagements with the world, and that personal lives are embedded in social, cultural and relational contexts.

Part 1 lays the groundwork for a relational study of people's everyday engagements with the surrounding world. Part 2 focuses on belonging, a concept that allows us to do this in a multifaceted way. Chapter 6 discusses in more detail what belonging is and how it is attained, as well as casting a critical eye on the assumption that belonging is necessarily positive. Chapters 7–9 focus on the three key sources of belonging: belonging to culture is explored in Chapter 7; belonging to people forms the subject matter of Chapter 8; and Chapter 9 explores the significance of place and material objects to our sense of belonging. Concluding thoughts are presented in Chapter 10. Throughout, I will discuss empirical examples from existing studies of how people make sense of these various forms of connectedness and relationality.

Note

1. The Inter/generational Dynamics project, which was part of Realities, a 'node' of the ESRC National Centre for Research Methods (2008–11). The project team comprised Jennifer Mason, James Nazroo, Stewart Muir, Vanessa May and Anna Zimdars.

Where It All Began: The Sociological Classics

2

Introduction: from traditional to modern selves

The aim of this book is to understand how self and society are interlinked and how social change impacts the self. In Chapters 2 and 3, I present some key sociological theories that have explored this link. These theories are generally understood to form the 'canon' in sociology, from the 'founding fathers' Karl Marx, Émile Durkheim and Max Weber through to the Frankfurt School, the individualization thesis and feminist theorizing on the self. Many of the theorists you will encounter in this and Chapter 3 are ones you are likely to find in most sociology textbooks on the self. I focus on particular aspects of their work, namely what they had to say about the nature of the relationship between self and society. For more in-depth discussions of each theorist, and for a more nuanced account of the complexity of their theorizing, I refer the reader to the references cited in the text.

A central concern of sociology is the impact that social change has on the self. Indeed, it could be argued that sociology exists as a discipline thanks to the profound social changes that were experienced in the wake of **industrialization**, when societies shifted from 'traditional' to 'modern'. Most areas of human life were affected as the old feudal power structures disappeared and capitalism flourished, and as increasing numbers of people moved into the rapidly growing cities to work in the new factories. Changes in the way production was organized led to an increasingly complex division of labour between the many new occupations that emerged. In time, the old feudal class structure was replaced by a division between capitalists, who owned the means of production, and workers, a division that brought with it new social inequalities. A clearer distinction was also drawn between 'home' and 'work', with the 'private sphere' of the home becoming a distinctly feminine place, while the 'public sphere' became classed as male territory.

The 'founding fathers' of sociology – Marx, Durkheim and Weber, whose works are explored in this chapter – were keen to understand these changes. All three focused on nascent capitalism and concluded that it had a negative impact on people's sense of self: Marx conceptualized this as **alienation**, Durkheim as **anomie** and Weber as 'living in an iron cage'. Each argued in their own way that the capitalist system not only creates difference and distance between people but also means that people feel their lives are governed by forces outside themselves over which they have little control. Thus, the founding fathers were somewhat pessimistic concerning the impact of modernity on the self; and as I will go on to explore in Chapter 3, similar accounts about the detrimental impact of social change on individuals and communities have since repeatedly surfaced within sociology.

Marx on alienation

I begin by examining Marx's account of how the forces of capitalism had come to alienate people not only from society but also from themselves. Marx was interested in explaining the structure and evolution of societies and the main focus of his work was on the impact the emergence of industrial capitalism in the early 1800s was having on society. Marx belonged to the revolutionary wing of the so-called 'Manchester School of political economy' (Thorns, 2002) – he aimed not only to theorize what was going on under industrial capitalism, but also to contribute to the overthrowing of the capitalist system.

In *The German Ideology*, Marx examined how people organize themselves into social groups, for example based on social class, and argued that by doing so, they produce the social frameworks in which they live. These frameworks provide a range of possible selves that we can be, such as a worker or a capitalist (Burkitt, 2008). Furthermore, Marx argued that the position within society that an individual is born into largely helps determine the life this individual can lead, in terms of affluence or occupation for example. According to Marx, because humans define themselves mainly through their labouring activity, their sense of self-worth is tied up with their labour (Morrison, 2006: 121). For Marx, then, it is our position within the division of labour that gives us our identity, and changes in the 'mode of production', that is, who owns and controls the tools, the labour and the finished product, are likely to lead to new identities and new class conflicts.

The one concept Marx developed in his work (based on Hegel's original work on this concept) that is particularly pertinent to the question of the self is that of 'alienation'. Marx first developed this concept in *Economic and Philosophic Manuscripts*, published in 1844, where he argued that changes in how labour was organized had led to workers being alienated not only from their labour and the products of this labour, but also from themselves. In traditional societies, most production took place on a relatively small scale, where farmers and craftspeople tended to own their 'means of production', that is, their own labour and their tools, as well as what they produced. Industrialization meant that production shifted into factories owned by capitalists, and the emergent money economy meant that the value of things, including labour, was measured in monetary terms. Workers did not own their own labour but sold it for a wage, nor did they own the products they helped produce. This meant that the capitalists reaped the financial benefits of their wage labour by paying workers a low wage and selling the end product at a profit.

Marx ([1844]1970: 72) argued that production had become an 'activity of alienation' for workers, and labour no longer acted as the basis of self-definition but was '*external* to the worker, i.e. it does not belong to his essential being'. The product of the worker's labour also became an 'alien' object. Marx ([1844]1970: 70) noted that

> the more the worker spends himself [sic], the more powerful the alien objective world becomes which he creates over against himself, the poorer he himself – his inner world – becomes, the less belongs to him as his own.

Work no longer acted as a source of self-affirmation but had become a mere means to an end to satisfy basic needs (Morrison, 2006: 122, 124). Marx and Engels developed the concept of alienation further in *The German Ideology*, published in 1846. They argued that the increasing division of labour and specialization meant that each person had a 'particular, exclusive sphere of activity, which is forced upon him [sic] and from which he cannot escape' if that person wishes to keep their livelihood (Marx and Engels, [1846]1977: 54).

Hochschild (2011: 31–2) argues that Marx was mistaken in assuming that the processes described above automatically mean that workers become alienated from the things they make, noting that people engage with emotional work in order to remain attached to their 'precious symbols of self', including the fruit of their labour. People use various strategies in order to counteract the processes of alienation, and have 'become brilliant at avoiding estrangement' and thus 'regulating capitalism from the inside'.

Marx also proposed that individuals were becoming alienated from their fellow human beings because life had become one of competition, and an unfair one at that for workers (Morrison, 2006: 126). The end result of this, according to Marx, was that individuals begin to feel that their 'society is not of their own making and that it no longer reflects their being or their nature, but instead appears to be alien and thus stands over and against them' (Morrison, 2006: 120). The irony that Marx and Engels pointed out was that this 'alien power' was, in fact, the product of people's own actions; in creating ever more sophisticated divisions of labour, they were unwittingly generating the conditions for their own increasing alienation. According to Marx, alienation could only be averted if humans were able to freely associate and be self-determining rather than be governed by laws that were, under a condition of alienation, perceived as external. Marx predicted that the class struggle that was taking place between workers and capitalists would eventually lead to a new collective identity among workers, which would spark a revolution that would overthrow capitalism (Burkitt, 2008: 18).

A short interlude: from *Gemeinschaft* to *Gesellschaft*

Marx was by no means the only sociologist of his time to be interested in the shift from traditional to modern societies. Tönnies published *Community and Society* in 1887, drawing the by now famous distinction between *Gemeinschaft* (community), which according to him characterized premodern societies, and *Gesellschaft* (society) which had become prevalent within modern societies. Tönnies depicted *Gemeinschaft* and *Gesellschaft* as two diametrically opposed systems. While life in *Gemeinschaft* is intimate and private, *Gesellschaft* is characterized by public life because of the shift from home or household economy to trade economy and from agriculture to industry (Tönnies, [1887]1963: 33, 78, 93).

Gemeinschaft is built on love, understanding and agreement, that is, a unity of will. There is an organic basis to relationships that are based either on blood ties (kinship *Gemeinschaft*), locality (neighbourhood *Gemeinschaft*) or commonality of mind (friendship *Gemeinschaft*) (Tönnies, [1887]1963: 42). Relationships in *Gemeinschaft* are characterized by frequent physical proximity and contact. In contrast, *Gesellschaft* is an 'artificial construction of an aggregate of human beings [who] are essentially separated in spite of all the uniting factors' (Tönnies, [1887]1963: 64–5). People living in a *Gesellschaft* remain separated because there is no a priori unity, no common will: 'here everybody is by himself [sic] and isolated, and there exists a condition of tension against all others' (Tönnies, [1887]1963: 65). *Gesellschaft* is characterized by individuals' negative attitude to each other and lack of generosity. These people remain 'independent of one another and void of mutual familiar relationships', while any social cohesion is based on mutually advantageous exchange (Tönnies, [1887]1963: 76).

Tönnies's theories have had a significant influence within sociology. For example, Durkheim identified some similarities between the theory he was developing on the shift from mechanical to organic solidarity and Tönnies's distinction between *Gemeinschaft* and *Gesellschaft*. Durkheim was also keen to distinguish his own work from that of Tönnies by saying that the organization of modern societies was no less 'natural' than that of traditional ones (Durkheim, [1887]1972). Some years later, in reply, Tönnies ([1896]1972) defended his own position by writing a rather damning critique of Durkheim's book *The Division of Labour in Society* ([1893]1984).

Durkheim on anomie

Durkheim's work spanned a number of interests, including the rules of sociological method, religious life, collective representations, and the impact of the shift to modern society on how individuals organized in society, forms of social cohesion and solidarity. Durkheim advocated a historical comparative method in sociology, with the aim of uncovering social laws. Durkheim adopted a realist perspective, according to which social realities exist outside individuals and affect their lives. He viewed society as an organism, a thing (contrary to Weber, who is discussed below), thus constructing a dichotomy between self and society. Durkheim saw society as made up of **social structures**, which he described as consolidated ways of acting that function as external constraints over the individual (see **structuralism**). In other words, social structures exist independently of individual consciousness and society is not the mere sum of individuals, but has its own reality (Lukes, 2010). In *Elementary Forms*, Durkheim ([1912]1965) argued that collective representations such as religion, ideals and values develop into 'partially autonomous realities' (Bellah, 2010: 19) that are institutionalized as various forms of 'culture', which then influence social change.

According to Durkheim, social structures are substantial and have powers over people, for example by imposing limits on action in the form of duties and obligations (Morrison, 2006: 152–3). Durkheim saw categories of thought as 'existing prior to the experience of any single individual', but these categories were historically contingent – that is, they differed from one society to another rather than being universal (Burkitt, 2008: 19). According to Durkheim, society comes before individuals, who cannot exist separately from it, which is why he argued that it was 'defensible to focus on society without taking into account the individual's separate attitudes and dispositions' (Morrison, 2006: 153). So although Durkheim does talk about the mutual existence of individual and society, he does so from a structural viewpoint.

There are some similarities in Durkheim's and Marx's approaches. Like Marx, Durkheim was interested in the effects that the increasing division of labour, brought about by industrialization, had on self and society. He also saw that selves are 'characterized by their place in the division of labour', such that our self becomes dependent upon our talents, the job we do and our social status (Burkitt, 2008: 19). Durkheim argued that the emergence of individualism was one of the consequences of industrialization. He posited that a differentiated society with an advanced division of labour leads to individual variation (Bellah, 2010; Münch, 2011: 94). In effect, according to Durkheim, human beings gain their individuality thanks to society.

In *The Division of Labour in Society*, published in 1893, Durkheim talks of each society as being of a particular psychological type. Societies are created by individuals coming together and creating a commonality to which, to some extent, they conform. Societies are bound together with the help of (positive) solidarity, of which Durkheim distinguishes two types: mechanical and organic. According to Durkheim, primitive societies exhibit **mechanical solidarity**, while the more civilized and developed a society is, the closer it comes to **organic solidarity**.

Mechanical solidarity is solidarity by similarity that 'links the individual directly to society without any intermediary' (Durkheim, [1893]1984: 83) and can be found in simpler societies where all members of the group share the same common beliefs and sentiments. This type of society can only be strong if the shared beliefs and interests outweigh those held by the different people individually. It therefore follows that the stronger this type of solidarity is, the weaker the individual personality: 'In societies where this solidarity is highly developed the individual ... does not belong to himself [sic]; he is literally a thing at the disposal of society' (Durkheim, [1893]1984: 85). Durkheim called this type of solidarity 'mechanical' as an analogy for the 'cohesion that links together the elements of raw materials' (Durkheim, [1893]1984: 84). The second kind of solidarity – organic solidarity – exists in more complex societies that are characterized by a highly developed division of labour, where each group performs a different function and where an individual 'depends upon society because he [sic] depends upon the parts that go to constitute it' (Durkheim, [1893]1984: 83). The shoemaker is only good at making shoes, and needs the farmer to produce the food they eat and the builder to build the houses they live in. Durkheim called this form of solidarity 'organic' because it resembles that of a biological organism – each organ within the body has its own special functions and the survival of the body depends on each of these (Durkheim, [1893]1984: 85).

Similar to Marx, Durkheim saw this new division of labour as 'fundamental to the creation of different self-identities' (Burkitt, 2008: 18) because organic solidarity requires that individuals are different from each other. Durkheim argued that the more people there are, the more likely they are to end up in competition with each other over the same resources if they are all alike. So he proposed that it is only 'natural' that when societies grow in size, people start to differentiate themselves from each other. This is one way of ensuring peaceful neighbourliness because it means that instead of everyone pursuing the same objective, 'the soldier seeks military glory, the priest moral authority, the statesman power, the scientist professional fame' (Durkheim, [1893]1984: 209). But this social differentiation, if it goes too far, can also be a source of social disintegration or a state of anomie, according to Durkheim ([1893]1984: 294). Anomie means that individuals place too high a value on themselves above others and become isolated from each other, without social solidarity or social values to give meaning to their lives. In other words, individuals no longer feel they belong to or are part of society because the shared norms that bind people to each other have eroded (Morrison, 2006: 183; Crossley, 2006: 14–15).

Durkheim ([1897]1989) further developed the concept of anomie in his book *Suicide*, where he argued that the state of anomie could lead people to commit suicide. He noted that suicide could not be explained with the help of personal motives alone; there were also social causes to suicide. How else could we explain the fact that suicide rates vary from country to country? Durkheim concluded that the explanation to this variation could be found by examining the degree of social regulation and social integration, that is, the strength of social bonds, in these countries. In societies with weaker social restraints, individual wants were less regulated and were likely to be out of kilter with needs. Durkheim proposed that individuals experiencing this imbalance between wants and needs were prone to feeling a sense of disappointment and despair.

And these individuals, who were in effect in a state of anomie, were more likely to commit suicide, or 'anomic suicide' as Durkheim termed it. (For a further discussion of the concept of anomie, see Bernard, 2010.)

Burkitt (2008: 20) identifies one central problem in theories such as Durkheim's that take social structures as their starting point, namely that because categories of thought are taken as a given, such theories are unable to address how these categories are developed. The theories of Simmel and Elias, which will be discussed in depth in Chapter 4, are better suited to answering such questions because they examine the simultaneous and mutual development of individuals and social structures. Durkheim also did not pay attention to *how* an individual develops the capacity to understand the collective rules that help make up social structures, nor does he account for the microrelationships that are involved in this process. Thus, we can see that Durkheim's theory is somewhat devoid of social actors. With the help of Mead's theory on the development of the relational self, I will argue in Chapter 4 that people do not follow rules as the result of external 'structures' exerting their influence, but that it is in human interaction that individuals come to adopt the attitude of their group.

Weber on the strictures of rationalization

Whereas Tönnies and Durkheim were concerned with the impact of social change on social cohesion and thus individuality, Weber focused on the development of a new rational way of organizing life. His work spanned topics such as the development of Western civilizations, religion and economy. Morrison (2006) describes Weber's body of work as fragmented, partly due to the ill health he suffered, which meant that his work was often interrupted. Consequently, it is not as easy to identify overall themes in Weber's writings as it is with Marx and Durkheim. Whereas Marx focused almost solely on the economic sphere (therefore being critiqued for 'economic determinism'), Weber argued that this was not enough because the (highly interconnected) political, religious and legal spheres must also be included in order to understand and explain social change (Morrison, 2006: 277).

Weber is generally known as the father of *Verstehende* sociology, an interpretive sociology that aims to understand the meanings that social actors attribute to their actions and experiences. According to Weber, it is not enough to merely observe social action, it must also be understood from the perspective of social actors (Morrison, 2006: 354). Rather than seeking universal social laws, sociology should be explaining by interpreting. In direct opposition to Durkheim, Weber argued that society is not an organic whole that exists over and above individuals (Poggi, 2006: 36–7). The social contexts in which we are situated are constituted by other individuals rather than by structures existing over and above us (Poggi, 2006: 37). This book, for example, which draws heavily on **social constructionism**, is indebted to Weber's *Verstehende* sociology, as will become apparent in Chapters 4 and 5.

One theme in Weber's work that is particularly relevant to the study of the self is the rationalization process, which he argued was influencing all spheres of society. Rationalization allowed humans mastery over the world, and was characterized by technological rules calculated to produce profits, democratic law replacing absolute monarchies, and the adoption of universal legal principles (Morrison, 2006: 280). One of the questions Weber asked was what type of person such a world would produce (Kalberg, 2005).

In *The Protestant Ethic and the Spirit of Capitalism* published in 1904, Weber examined the growing influence of Protestantism on how individuals organized society and how they behaved, in essence giving rise to capitalism. Weber identified a number of key elements of Protestantism that spread to all aspects of life and consequently enabled modern capitalism to flourish. These included the denunciation of worldly asceticism, which meant that it became morally acceptable to accumulate wealth. In addition, Protestantism espoused a belief that worldly activity was a way of proving one's faith to God. Hard work was elevated, while wasting time was seen to be:

> the first and in principle the deadliest of sins ... Loss of time through sociability, idle talk, luxury, even more sleep than is necessary for health, six to at most eight hours, is worthy of absolute moral condemnation ... [Time] is infinitely valuable because every hour lost is lost to labour for the glory of God. (Weber, [1904]1992: 157–8)

This hard work was expected to be productive also in the sense of producing wealth as 'a sign of God's blessing', and was not to be used for 'idleness and sinful enjoyment of life' but in a rational and utilitarian fashion (Weber, [1904]1992: 163, 172). In other words, the accumulation of wealth was acceptable, but not the heady consumption of material goods that this wealth could buy: 'The inevitable practical result is obvious: accumulation of capital through ascetic compulsion to save' (Weber, [1904]1992: 172). A person was only 'a trustee of the goods which have come to him [sic] through God's grace' and, as such, must 'give an account of every penny entrusted to him' (Weber, [1904]1992: 170).

What started out as a religious ethic of ordering one's life according to a rational plan so as to best serve God was to become the basis for what Weber called the 'spirit of capitalism'. One of the hallmarks of capitalism is that it 'seeks profit rationally and systematically' (Weber, [1904]1992: 64) by, for example, adopting bookkeeping and various efficiency measures such as strict timekeeping. Weber proposed that living one's life in such a rule-bound, bureaucratic way (as opposed to following a more 'natural' rhythm) had an alienating effect on people, because individuals felt like cogs in a machine where their lives were ordered based on abstract rules rather than person-centred thinking and where they were reduced to performing repetitive tasks that distanced them from their work (Kalberg, 2005: 4). He described this as 'living in an iron cage'. Weber argued that as societies become more bureaucratized, they will become increasingly 'closed, stagnant, and ossified ... suffocating alike the orientation of persons to values and individual freedoms' (Kalberg, 2005: 34). Bureaucratic society is devoid of compassion, dominated by the impersonal calculation of interests and advantage; a 'closed, rigid and inward-looking society devoid of noble ideals, pluralistic and competing values' (Kalberg, 2005: 35).

Thus, Weber expressed concerns over the increasing rationalization and bureaucratization of society. In *Economy and Society* ([1922]1968), he further discussed the dehumanizing effect of bureaucratic decision-making, which is devoid of emotions and treats people as 'cases' rather than as individuals. Weber was quite pessimistic about the future in this respect. Poggi (2006) and Kalberg (2005) note, however, that there have also been waves of opposition towards this rationalization process, and that Weber's predictions were too bleak; despite standardization, there is also plenty of heterogeneity and invention. Weber was more pessimistic about modernity than Durkheim, nor did he believe in a social-ist revolution as the solution to the alienation that resulted from ordering lives according to the principles of rational and bureaucratic thought. In fact, Weber viewed socialism as merely another form of bureaucratic governance, which would have the same impact as other forms of bureaucracy; here his prediction was rather accurate, as subsequent experiences in the Soviet Union proved.

According to Weber, the autonomous individual was under threat from the increasing standardization of activity. Contrary to Marx, Weber argued that everyone in modern societies was being affected, not just workers (Kalberg, 2005). He proposed that in order to attain selfhood, individuals must 'take back the power and responsibility to freely choose their own values and actions' (Burkitt, 2008: 21). But Weber also identified positive features in industrial capitalism, such as dynamism, which counteracted bureaucratization, and in some respects welcomed the new era, noting the positive consequences of an emphasis on personal liberties (Kalberg, 2005: 3).

Burkitt (2008: 21) notes that Weber's theory has some key flaws, namely that he exaggerated the impact of Protestantism in Europe and overestimated the extent to which asceticism became the ideal. Indeed, as Burkitt (2008: 22) points out, if the ascetic self was as predominant as Weber argued, contempo-rary consumer culture, where individuals are encouraged to consume increas-ing amounts of goods at ever-increasing speeds, would not have been possible.

Conclusion

For the sociological classics, the main aim was to understand and explain the impact of industrialization and urbanization on self and society. Although the accounts examined above diverge in many ways, and have given rise to quite different sociological traditions, they share one thing in common: they depict a shift from a relatively cosy (and some would say romanticized) society charac-terized by homogeneity, stability and unity to one of heterogeneity, uncertainty and disconnection. This shift was said to have left people trapped in an alien-ating and bureaucratized world.

Echoes of these early interpretations of the impact of social change can be seen throughout the history of sociology. Fast-forward to the latter half of the twentieth century and the early twenty-first century, and we encounter theorists who have offered gloomy accounts of the impact of mass production, consumer culture and deindustrialization, which are said to have transformed us into conformist, other-directed, self-obsessed, helpless and fragmented persons, which, in turn, is eroding trust, social cohesion and community. Thorns (2002: 25–6) critiques such 'contrast theories' for creating a dichotomy of two polar opposite types, which are abstractions and simplifications of the real world and lack historical depth. Such romanticized depictions of 'lost' communities ignore the inequalities that existed, and overlook the fact that conformity and stability were often the result of power and oppression, not choice and consensus. In Chapter 3, I return to such contrast theories and explore why they have remained so popular.

The Loss of Tradition: Diminished or Reflexive Selves?

3

Introduction

Chapter 2 explored how the founding fathers of sociology accounted for the impact the emergence of industrial capitalism and urbanization had on the self. Since then, Western societies have continued to experience changes. Class relations have slowly transformed thanks to workers' rising wages and standard of living. Technological developments such as the increasing use of electricity allowed industrial production to be organized on a mass scale. Industrialists, most famously Henry Ford, calculated that in order to ensure that workers were able to afford these mass-produced goods and have the time to use them, they had to increase workers' wages and reduce working hours (Soja, 2000). This gave rise to 'leisure time' as well as the newly affluent worker.

And so a new consumer culture was born. By the middle of the twentieth century, even 'average' people could afford to own their own home and buy consumer goods such as cars and washing machines, which had previously been luxury items only available to the rich upper classes. Western countries experienced a major economic boom after the Second World War (1939–45), and a new wave of globalization swept across the world as people from the former colonies moved to countries such as the UK and France to fill labour shortages, and eventually settled there (Shaw, 2000; Chamberlain, 2006).

But in the 1960s, companies found that they could no longer increase their profits as before, and sought new ways of securing these returns by, for example, moving production to countries where labour was less unionized and therefore cheaper. As the production of goods shifted to countries such as China, countries in the West went through a period of deindustrialization. This led to major socio-economic shifts, including mass unemployment, particularly in heavily industrialized regions and cities (Short, 2004). Western countries have since developed into 'postindustrial' societies, characterized by a large service sector and a knowledge economy that is largely based on high-end financial services and information and communications technology companies (Soja, 2000). The 1980s saw a widespread deregulation of markets, the aim of which was to make it easier for money and goods to move across national borders in search of increased profitability.

In the current era of globalization, large transnational companies are financially more powerful than many small nation states, footloose capital moves rapidly in search of profit, and improved production technologies mean that mass production can react quickly to consumer demand and operate on a 'just in time' basis (Dürrschmidt and Taylor, 2007). Much of the world is now governed by a neoliberal agenda, whereby privatization and 'free markets' are valued in the name of the unfettered operation of big business. This remains true even after the 2008 financial meltdown, which is proving to be the deepest recession experienced since industrialization, and is widely understood to have been caused by the recklessness of the financial markets.

Since the beginning of the twentieth century, there have also been significant advances in gender equality, bringing about women's increasing participation in the public sphere of work and politics, with consequent shifts in the gendered division of labour in the home. Especially since the Second World War, mores and values as well as legislation around family life and sexuality have changed, to the extent that commentators are either bemoaning the 'downfall' of 'the family' (Popenoe, 1993) or the emergence of 'brave new families' or 'families of choice' (Stacey, 1993; Weeks et al., 2001). What is certain is that there is an increasing diversity in the way Western people organize their personal relationships and living arrangements.

Below, I introduce two types of sociological account on social change that have come to dominate the discipline. Both focus on the so-called 'loss of tradition', whereby a distinction is drawn between societies of old – that is, premodern societies – and late modern societies that emerged during the twentieth century. The first account, the **psychosocial fragmentation thesis** (Adams, 2007), argues that this loss of tradition has led to people becoming isolated, fragmented, narcissistic and vulnerable. The second, the **individualization thesis,** maintains that the conditions of **late modernity** have increased people's capacity for reflexivity.

Both sets of theories posit that particular types of society produce a particular type of person. In doing so, they offer a top-down explanation that prioritizes social structures as the driving force behind either psychosocial fragmentation or increased reflexivity: society changes and individuals have no choice but to adapt to this change. I identify three major problems with these theses, namely in the distinctions they draw between the past and the present and between social structures and the personal, as well as their depictions of selves as monadic, that is, essentially disconnected. As an antidote to these approaches, I present a relational view of self and society in Chapter 4.

Vulnerable, fragmented selves

Proponents of the psychosocial fragmentation thesis have largely focused on the impact that consumer culture, particularly the mass production and consumption of goods, has had on the self. Whereas Durkheim had spoken of the increasing differentiation between individuals, Max Adorno, Theodor Horkheimer and Herbert Marcuse – all three associated with the **Frankfurt School** of critical thought – argued that the increasingly advanced social, economic and scientific systems had led to the mental and personal impoverishment of people. The Frankfurt School was critical of liberal capitalism and Enlightenment thinking, arguing that these led to the privileging of instrumental rationality (and here we can see echoes of Weber's concern over the rationalization process), which in turn acted to repress individuals (Heaphy, 2007: 30). The Frankfurt School had emancipatory aims, wishing to free individuals from the increasing pressure to conform to a technological rationality in the service of efficiency and productivity. Adorno and Horkheimer ([1944]1997: 36–7), for example, argued that conformity was expected of people who had become mere cogs in a machine or oarsmen yoked in the same rhythm.

In constructing their argument, Adorno and Horkheimer ([1944]1997: 120) focused particularly on what they called the culture industry, that is, mass media and the arts, which 'now impresses the same stamp on everything':

> Pseudo individuality is rife: from the standardized jazz improvisation to the exceptional film star whose hair curls over her eye to demonstrate her originality. What is individual is no more than the generality's power to stamp the accidental detail so firmly that it is accepted as such. (Adorno and Horkheimer, [1944]1997: 154)

Similarly, Marcuse argued that mass production had led to cultural homogeneity. Think, for example, of entertainment produced by the mass media. It may feel as though you have a wide range of different music styles or films to choose from, but, according to Marcuse (1964: 14), these products are more alike than they are different and 'carry with them prescribed attitudes and habits, certain intellectual and emotional reactions which bind the consumers more or less pleasantly to the producers'. In other words, these mass products indoctrinate us into a way of life, leading to one-dimensional thought and behaviour that fall in line with the rationality of the system. As Adorno and Horkheimer ([1944]1997: 133–4) put it, the culture industry numbs people into willing dupes who buy into, actively partake in and play along with the rules of the system that enslave them and, consequently, they cannot see beyond the conditions of their existence.

Adorno and Horkheimer's as well as Marcuse's theories can be critiqued for **determinism** (Adams, 2007: 18), that is, for depicting individuals as passive beings who are freely moulded by various social forces and authorities – the state, the elites, the culture industry. No account of resistance and creativity is offered; indeed, they seem to be saying that resistance is futile because what we think of as resistance is, in actual fact, mere conformity to the rule.

Another take on the impact of consumer culture can be found in the works of David Riesman, Christopher Lasch and Frank Furedi. All three argue that contemporary society has left people without moorings and overly involved with superficialities (such as consumption) and with what other people think about them based on these superficial characteristics. In *The Lonely Crowd* (1961, originally published in 1950), Riesman proposed that each society exhibits a dominant social character and that industrialized societies are dominated by an 'other-directed' social type of person who is shallow, friendly, uncertain of themselves, and who requires approval from others. This latter point, Riesman felt, was particularly true of the USA. The other-directed type wants to be popular and valued by their peers, which entails being constantly attuned to signals from others as to which goals are the desired ones at any particular time (Riesman, 1961: 21). Other people, and our wish to be liked and accepted by others, become our main source of direction in life (Riesman, 1961: 22).

Adams (2003) critiques Riesman's argument that the other-directed person was a product of a particular time only. Adams argues that there have always been important elements of other-directedness in people – this is because, as will be examined in Chapter 4, our sense of self is relational, that is, constructed in relationships with and in relation to others. According to Adams, it is, therefore, not possible to identify a time when other-directedness was not an important part of our character.

In writing *The Culture of Narcissism* (1978), Lasch was influenced by Riesman, in that he used a similar language of psychological fragmentation. Like Riesman before him, Lasch (1978: 34) proposed that each society produces a distinct personality structure that dominates: 'Every society reproduces its culture – its norms, its underlying assumptions, its modes of organizing experience – in the individual, in the form of personality.' Lasch (1978: 4) argued that Americans have retreated to 'purely personal preoccupations' and are convinced that 'what matters is psychic self-improvement', thus retreating from politics and collective life. Strengthening this turn inward is also the prevailing belief that the world is a dangerous place with an uncertain future (note that Lasch wrote this book during the Cold War years, when fears of a nuclear holocaust were widespread). This perception of society as a dangerous place leads to an ethic of self-preservation, which replaces the Protestant ethic of self-improvement, while therapy replaces religion and communities as our source of security, support and advice (Lasch, 1978: 7, 53).

According to Lasch (1978: 10), these social changes have bred a narcissistic personality structure. The narcissist is fundamentally insecure and needs others to validate their self-esteem. Lasch (1978: 50) proposed that there is little choice in the matter for us, because narcissism is the appropriate response to contemporary social conditions:

> Narcissism appears realistically to represent the best way of coping with the tensions and anxieties of modern life, and the prevailing social conditions therefore tend to bring out narcissistic traits that are present, in varying degrees, in everyone.

There is little room for agency in Riesman's and Lasch's theories, and they can be critiqued for ignoring the ways in which people creatively reject and appropriate the demands of others to their own means (Adams, 2007: 21). We do not always do what we think others expect of us.

Lasch (1978) identified therapy as a key source of security for people, replacing community and religion. In *Therapy Culture*, Furedi (2004) examines the increasing importance of therapy in more detail, arguing that what he calls a 'therapy culture' is in danger of rendering us helpless victims. According to Furedi, the role of religion and shared moral norms has declined as a source of meaning in life, leaving a gap that therapeutics promises to fill. Whereas previously people would have found informal solutions to their problems with the help of family and friends, now they turn to the 'so-called helping professions' (Furedi, 2004: 99), for example in relation to parenting, relationships and careers.

Furedi also proposes that the demise of politics has transformed formerly collective grievances into emotional problems that require personal solutions such as therapy, rather than collective ones such as social activism. According to Furedi, this emphasis on individual identity distances us from each other, and with the erosion of community, we are increasingly forced to rely on our individual resources. Furedi (2004: 144) argues that our 'I' identity that separates us from each other has become stronger than the 'We' identity that binds us together. Our attachment to others is fragile and our obligations towards and expectations of each other are confusing. Therapeutic culture feeds this individualization by portraying individual autonomy not in terms of responsibility towards others but towards oneself, which further acts to distance people from each other.

There is intense cultural concern directed at our emotions, and we are urged to 'get in touch with ourselves' and 'express ourselves' in order to manage our emotions (Furedi, 2004: 30, 34). People have come to think of themselves in terms of emotional wellbeing, which is generally seen to be under threat. As a result, we feel emotionally vulnerable, prone to depression and stress-related illnesses. Thus, there is a widespread belief that we are not capable of managing all aspects of our everyday lives without professional help (Furedi, 2004: 98). Many common experiences, such as bereavement or giving birth, are now couched in terms of risk of trauma or psychological illness, while therapeutic concepts such as stress, anxiety and addiction have become part of our everyday vocabulary. These 'ready-made therapeutic explanations' for our troubles are systematically offered as a way of making sense of distress, and individuals confronted with the ordinary troubles of life are now 'routinely advised to seek professional advice and counselling' (Furedi, 2004: 107–8, 113). Indeed, *not* seeking professional help is, at times, seen as symptomatic of illness or moral failing (Furedi, 2004: 37).

Furedi argues that therapy culture leaves people more prone to perceive themselves as ill, and powerless in the face of these illnesses. Yet, we can ask, as Adams (2007: 26–7) does, whether Furedi is merely perpetuating what he criticizes, that is, rendering people into helpless, passive victims. Furedi also fails to provide a more complex account of therapeutic culture – surely, as Adams says, there must be both 'winners' and 'losers', that is, people who are empowered by therapeutic culture as well as those who are rendered powerless by it.

Were things so good in the past?

The theories discussed here are but a sample of works that are part of what Adams (2007) terms the psychosocial fragmentation thesis. According to Frow (2002: 632), this virtually theological discourse on **modernity** depicts contemporary life as 'the loss of significant totality, the fall into repetition'. Such nostalgic views of the past have, according to Chase and Shaw (1989: 6), been an implicit and recurring trait of sociological work on modernity, where the present is 'unfavourably contrasted with some putative property found in the past', leading to 'analyses of modern times which have weighed them and found them wanting' and 'culturally or politically deficient'. Similar nostalgic accounts that juxtapose contemporary society with the world we have lost and that we hope to redeem have also been readily picked up in popular debates.

Chase and Shaw (1989: 8) highlight that the assumption that selves in the past were more 'whole' or 'integrated' is ahistoric, ignoring the brutality of past societies. They argue that although accounts that contrast 'now and then' seem attractive, this does not necessarily make them true:

> The temptation was to conjure up a past defined not by the painstaking investigation of the historical record but by positing a series of absences, of negatives. If we now have *Gesellschaft*, there must have been *Gemeinschaft*; if our consciousness is fragmented, there must have been a time when it was integrated; if society is now bureucratised and impersonal, it must previously have been personal and particular. The syntax and structure of these ideas makes them superficially attractive but this appeal is no warrant for their veracity. (Chase and Shaw, 1989: 8)

Such 'contrast theories' (Thorns, 2002) are appealing because they chime with nostalgic yearnings for 'a simple and stable past as a refuge from the turbulent and chaotic present' (Lowenthal, 1989: 21). This nostalgia is not something that only contemporary people are affected by. For example, the Victorians expressed 'regrets for preindustrial rustic calm' and viewed the Middle Ages as a time of 'a shared and ordered spirituality lacking in their own tawdry, secular, individualistic times', where selfish individualism reigned and made selves divided, fragmented and unsatisfying (Lowenthal, 1989: 21; Stafford, 1989: 35). Does this not sound similar to how people in our time talk about, say, the 1950s, a period that is often presented as a golden age of social cohesion and stability? And it is likely that people in the 1950s looked back at another 'golden age':

> The diverse goals of contemporary nostalgia do have one point in common. They mainly envisage a time when folk did not feel fragmented, when doubt was either absent or patent, when thought fused with action, when aspiration achieved consummation, when life was wholehearted; in short, a past that was unified and comprehensible, unlike the incoherent, divided present.

Significantly, one thing absent from this imagined past is nostalgia – no one *then* looked back in yearning or for succor. (Lowenthal, 1989: 29)

A nostalgic view thus depicts past societies as providing a more secure or predictable existence for the majority of people (Stafford, 1989: 33). This is an idealized world lacking in usury, greed and corruption; where workers were not exploited; where life was simple, wholesome and meaningful; and where people were psychically whole, before being fragmented by the alienating effects of the division of labour as depicted by, for example, Marx and Durkheim (Stafford, 1989: 42–3):

If one word is wanted to sum it all up, that word is *organic*, with its connotations of naturalness and integrity. Of course, this composite image of pre-commercial society is a myth, a construct; sober historians know that reality was never so rosy. (Stafford, 1989: 43)

I return to this issue of 'contrast theories' below by exploring further reasons why they appear so convincing.

Reflexive and individualized selves

A somewhat different type of account from the psychosocial fragmentation thesis began emerging in the 1990s and has come to be known as the 'individualization thesis', also called the 'extended reflexivity thesis' or the 'reflexive modernization thesis'. This by now equally canonical interpretation highlights the new freedom that people have to choose who they are and who they associate with. Whereas the psychosocial fragmentation thesis depicts the erosion of old routines and certainties as a threat to our psychological wellbeing, theorists such as Giddens and Beck see potential here for being liberated from old structures and for increased individuality that is chosen rather than prescribed. The 'old' social categories such as class, gender and ethnicity no longer determine who we are as they did in the past. In Giddens's (1991) terms, our lives have become disembedded from tradition and old contexts. Consequently, people now face both the new freedoms and the new challenges or uncertainties that this reflexivity entails. The two individualization theorists who are examined here are Anthony Giddens and Ulrich Beck.

Giddens is one of the foremost sociologists working in the UK today. He is best known for his work on structuration (a theory in which he tried to bridge the structure–agency divide), **reflexivity** and globalization and for his political theories concerning 'the third way'. Here, I focus on his theory of the reflexive self as developed in *Modernity and Self-identity* (1991), where he argued that becoming disembedded from tradition and old contexts has meant that individuality has gained some new distinctive qualities. Most importantly, the self has become a reflexive project because it is no longer given (for example by 'old' categories such as social class or gender) but created by ourselves in a reflective manner. Giddens does not mean to say that people in the past were not reflexive, rather that reflexivity has become a central element of modern social life. In traditional cultures, transitions such as that from child to adult were clearly staked out and accompanied by formalized rites, for example rites of passage to manhood or womanhood (Giddens, 1991: 79). In contrast, in late modern societies, the self has to be constructed as part of a reflexive process where individuals make choices about who they want to be, thus creating their own biographies. Many aspects of our lives, such as relationships and sexuality, have become more malleable and 'plastic' (Giddens, 1992). In other words, there are fewer pre-given ways of being. Giddens points particularly to the ways in which women's lives have changed as a result, with advances in education, new opportunities to seek waged work, and no longer having to endure unhappy relationships.

Creating one's own biography requires strategic life planning because we are faced with a puzzling diversity of options and possibilities (Giddens, 1991: 2, 85). To help choose between these, we turn to impersonal expert knowledge systems such as therapy, which offers not simply a means of coping with novel anxieties, but is also an expression of the reflexivity of the self (Giddens, 1991: 5, 33–4). It is worth noting the similarity of argument with Furedi (2004), in terms of why a therapy culture has gained such a key role in contemporary society. But unlike Furedi, Giddens does not see the increasing importance of therapy in a negative light.

One critique of Giddens's work has been that despite his focus on the body and on relationships, the self is depicted as a disconnected and disembodied being (Crossley, 2006: 22–3; Smart, 2007). Chapter 4 goes on to explore a different kind of self, namely a relational self who emerges out of and exists within webs of relationships, while Chapter 9 explores the embodied sensory engagement of the self with the material world.

The second individualization theorist I discuss is Beck, who, like Giddens, has been interested in exploring the effects of globalization on society and individuals (namely individualization). He has written about cosmopolitanism, and, together with Elisabeth Beck-Gernsheim, he has examined the nature of contemporary love and relationships. Beck and Beck-Gernsheim (1995), like Giddens, identify women's liberation from the traditional constraints of gender as the driving force behind many of the changes that have taken place in relationships. In *Risk Society* (1992), Beck argued that globalization has led to the loss of old certainties, leaving people to craft their own biographies. Beck is, however, more cautious than Giddens in his pronouncements regarding the freedom for manoeuvre that people have and points out that with increased institutionalization and standardization of, for example, the educational system and the labour market, our lives are now structured according to new institutional biographical patterns (Beck, 1992: 131–2).

Beck (1992) argues that we live in a risk society where nothing is set in stone, everything can change. Old certainties, such as the role religion played in explaining the world, are lost, replaced by a new awareness of risk. The proportion of our biography that is open and must be personally constructed is increasing:

> Life, death, gender, corporeality, identity, religion, marriage, parenthood, social ties – all are becoming decidable down to the small print: once fragmented into options, everything must be decided. (Beck and Beck-Gernsheim, 2002: 5)

People have a variety of different lifestyles to choose from, which compels them to be agents of their own life planning. Whereas in the past, the opportunities and dangers of life were predefined, in contemporary societies individuals must interpret these for themselves (Beck and Beck-Gernsheim, 2002: 4). In other words, we must make choices about our identity based on our own risk assessment rather than on ready-made formulae that would tell us how to live our lives. The result of this choice is that people construct reflexive, elective or do-it-yourself biographies instead of living out socially prescribed ones (Beck, 1992: 135, 1994: 15). For example, people with the same income level or the same educational background can choose between different lifestyles and identities. So, it is no longer possible to determine a person's personal outlook, family position, social and political ideas or identity merely on the basis of their social position. Consequently, Beck concludes that social class has become a 'zombie category', which is 'dead but still alive' (Beck and Beck-Gernsheim, 2002). In other words, although the term 'social class' is still in use, it has, in fact, lost its relevance and explanatory power.

What is different about Beck's analysis compared to that of Giddens is that he offers a fuller account of the ways in which our lives continue to be shaped by external forces. In other words, individuals are not completely free to choose their identities because their lives are led within social institutions such as the labour market and the educational sector (Beck, 1992: 90). Traditional ties have partly been replaced by these secondary agencies and institutions, which stamp the biography of the individual (Beck, 1992: 131). Our lives are now partly shaped by our entry into and exit from the educational system, by the sector in which we work, by changes in laws such as recent increases in the statutory retirement age in many European countries, or by economic cycles. The latter has become particularly evident in the wake of the global financial crisis that erupted in 2008, as the lives of countless individuals have been affected by job insecurity, redundancy, a drop in real incomes and house repossessions.

This is not, however, a simple question of one set of old regulations or norms being replaced by new ones. Beck and Beck-Gernsheim (2002: 2) argue that the significant shift that has taken place is that individuals must now supply these norms for themselves and 'import them into their biographies through their own actions'. They call this situation where we have increasing freedoms yet are curtailed by new forms of standardization and social controls one of 'precarious freedoms' (Beck and Beck-Gernsheim, 2002: 16).

The gendered and classed limits of reflexivity

Given that the individualization thesis highlights the particular impact that reflexive modernization has had on women's biographies, it is worth pausing for a while to consider feminist responses, particularly to the claims over the weakening of traditional norms around gender and the decreasing relevance of social class. This section provides some understanding of the contribution that **feminism** has brought to the study of the self.

The individualization thesis can be critiqued for overemphasizing the reach of reflexivity when, in fact, the position of the self-reflexive individual who has the freedom to construct their own biography is a privileged one that not all have the resources to attain (Lash, 1994). It could be said that the reflexive individual is an idealized version of a white, middle-class man, and an identity that is not within easy reach for those who are non-white, working class or women. Adkins (2004) argues that not everyone has the same ability to exercise reflexivity over the constitution of their gender and sexuality, and that it is important to distinguish between winners and losers in terms of reflexivity – women in particular being losers because femininity is, in many ways, a fixed category. Gender identities are 'less amenable to emancipatory processes of refashioning' (McNay, 1999: 95) than the individualization thesis purports because they are fashioned at an early age and are, in many respects, beyond rational control.

Feminists have also shed light on the somewhat contradictory developments whereby women have both gained some new freedoms, but also become subject to new inequalities. Despite continuing differences in men and women's ability to attain reflexive selves, it is clear that the lives of women in Western countries have changed dramatically in the past century or so, with many important rights gained in relation to voting, citizenship, marriage, education, property and more, and with concomitant improvements in gender equality. Although it would appear that women now 'have it all', the picture is more complicated than that. Shelley Budgeon (2011), for example, notes that the ideals of individualization converge with those of **neoliberalism**, and urges us to be critical of post-feminist claims that women have been successfully liberated from traditional femininity, are independent and have access to a wide array of choices. Although such claims may chime well with feminist goals of women's autonomy, Budgeon brings to our attention the conceptual slippage that is at work, whereby what is often being promoted is a neoliberal ideology of 'choice' and 'self-determination' that plays into the hands of free-market values.

Rather than a disappearance of structures that shape our lives, Budgeon points to the complex ways in which these structures are being reconfigured, in different areas of life. The 'new femininities' that have emerged exert contradictory expectations and pressures on women, offering subject positions that are rife with tensions because they require women to enact aspects of both traditional femininity, for example in terms of appearance, and masculinity, such as educational and occupational success. Budgeon notes that women are still expected to be physically attractive and heterosexual in order to present a 'successful' self. Some 'individual choices', such as being a lesbian, remaining single or childless, or being a feminist, can act to curtail a woman's chances. Thus, women must 'play along' with the general rules of the game and can only be empowered within certain regulated norms. The rhetoric of unfettered 'choice' masks these structural, regulatory boundaries that women (must) live with and within.

Furthermore, mobility in terms of gender performance is linked to further axes of inequality such as class and ethnicity. In other words, white men have more leeway in choosing how to perform masculinity, while the choice of femininities available to working-class women are more restricted compared to middle-class women and so on (Adkins, 2004). Skeggs (2004: 176) highlights the importance of social class by pointing out that to become the 'risk-taking, enterprising, mobile, reflexive, individualistic self' depicted by the individualization thesis requires the ability to mobilize assets, which in turn rests upon 'access to the right resources'.

It is important to recognize that the current dominant ideology of neoliberalism creates new inequalities where those seen to lack the requisite skills to be autonomous subjects are deemed 'failures' (Budgeon, 2011). Thus, if one is stuck in a dead-end job with little chance of improving one's lot, it is likely that this is seen as one's own fault, rather than as the result of systemic inequalities that mean that some individuals, such as working-class non-white women, do not necessarily have access to the resources that would enable them to be self-determining, autonomous individuals who fully engage with the markets. Blaming the victim in this manner weakens solidarity, because personal troubles are *not* seen as political problems that we are collectively responsible for or that require collective action to redistribute resources.

Walkerdine et al.'s (2001) longitudinal study of working-class and middle-class girls in the UK provides us with an idea of what these resources might consist of. They argue that despite claims about the 'death of class', the gap between working-class and middle-class women in terms of education, career and income has widened. Yes, women have made great strides in education, but it is mainly middle-class women whose educational chances have improved. Walkerdine et al. found that the pathways of working-class girls were very different from those of the high-achieving middle-class girls, who were told from the start that their destiny included higher education and a professional career, and who attended better quality fee-paying schools. While middle-class girls were encouraged by their parents and teachers to excel academically and were taught the skills to become the autonomous and rational individual befitting the new world order, working-class girls did not have such a set path in front of them, and even intelligent working-class girls did not receive the same encouragement from teachers as middle-class girls with equivalent school success. For the many working-class girls who did do well in school, the transition into higher education, and the social mobility this would have provided, remained too big a leap to take. But while middle-class girls become the embodiment of the bourgeois rational subject, they do so at a price – Walkerdine et al. found that behind the academic success of many middle-class girls lay a whole host of anxieties that were not being addressed, because these anxieties were out of kilter with the rational subject these girls were meant to embody:

> the entry of middle-class girls into masculine norms of rational academic excellence comes at a price. It is not achieved easily and indeed is produced out of the suppression of aspects of femininity and sexuality. In that sense, in our view the discourses of 'girl power', which stress the possibility of having and being what you want, provide an ideal that is almost impossible to live up to, and through which young women read their own failure as personal pathology (Walkerdine et al., 2001: 178)

Walkerdine et al. (2001) argue that the class system is undergoing transformation, not eradication. Class is not just an economic category, but is deeply implicated in the 'production of subjectivity' and is 'written on the body and mind', such that we all (to an extent unwittingly) give off and are good at reading small 'class difference signs' (Walkerdine et al., 2001: 24, 26). This idea will be further explored in Chapter 4 in relation to Bourdieu's theory of habitus. What we can take from this is that there are clear limits to self-invention, as evidenced by the continuing inequalities in education and the occupational opportunities that follow.

I now discuss three critiques that can be made about the psychosocial fragmentation thesis and the individualization thesis, namely that they present a dichotomy between past and present; they depict the self as a monad; and they draw too stark a distinction between personal life and social structures.

Have things really changed so much?

What unites the psychosocial fragmentation and the individualization theses is their depiction of the past and the present as distinctly different. Past societies are characterized by stable and clearly identifiable social structures that strongly determined individual lives, which were consequently more predictable than contemporary lives (Williams, 1977). In contrast, when social theorists turn their gaze to the society of their day, what they see is flux, uncertainty and risk that unsettle any such moorings, securities or certainties. As a result, they end up depicting the present as fluid and in the making, and as somewhat chaotic and formless (Burkitt, 2004: 220).

Why is it, then, that the past so easily appears as fundamentally different to the present? When thinking of our predecessors, we tend to view their behaviour as lacking in freedom in contrast to the behaviour of contemporaries. This is because the world of predecessors is over and done with (Schutz, [1932]1967) and, consequently, it appears as more fixed than the present or the future, which seem fluid and unknown. Furthermore, people tend to distinguish between past and present thought: past thought presents itself to us as finished and explicit, which is very different from how we experience thinking in the present, which to us feels 'more active, more flexible' (Williams, 1977: 129). The past appears complete and stable, and any change and flux that was experienced by our predecessors has been ironed out of this picture. It could thus be argued that interpretations of a stable past are partly based on this optical illusion created by our temporal perspective.

Barbara Adam (1996: 135) critiques the dualism of such 'before-and-after analyses of fixed states, established retrospectively', and proposes that tradition has not been replaced by 'reflexivity, disorder, flux and uncertainty', but that these coexist, which is why it is their 'mutual implication' that should be the focus of social theory. In other words, social scientists should remain attuned to how traditions survive, although often in changed form. Furthermore, Thompson (1996) argues that such analyses are based on the misconception that traditions are fixed and pre-given, when in fact they are always open to change and flexible. In sum, traditions have not disappeared, but remain important features of contemporary societies, although their content and function may have shifted (Thompson, 1996: 94).

Perhaps a more accurate account of past and present would be one where sociologists acknowledge that, at any time, 'the only certainty is uncertainty' and 'the only constant in our lives is change' (Chase and Shaw, 1989: 8). This is true of even the most basic things such as the environment in which we live, which is never static but constantly undergoing what Gibson (1979) calls 'ecological events', that is, changes in plants, animals, water and land. These can be slow or fast, perceptible or imperceptible; nevertheless, we are living in an ever-changing and shifting world.

The psychosocial fragmentation and individualization theses posit 'tradition' as something external to us. In other words, they reify 'tradition' into a 'thing' that exists independent of our actions. An alternative approach is to consider traditions as something that come alive through our everyday actions. Thus, traditions can be defined as repeated actions that have come to be perceived as 'the way things are done around here' (cf. Bourdieu, 1979). Traditions are constantly being enacted and refashioned by us, and they never stand still. This constant refashioning also means that 'tradition' has *never* fully prescribed people's behaviour, although it may seem as though it has when we look back in time. Again, this is merely an illusion created by hindsight.

Another key component of the psychosocial fragmentation and individualization theses is that they either bemoan or celebrate the disappearance of certain types of identity. Wiley (1994) critiques such accounts for failing to distinguish between the generic self and the particular identity. He sees *the self* as denoting something universal in human nature, 'characterizing all human beings in the same generic way, at all times and places' (Wiley, 1994: 1), such as our ability to be rational, to think in an abstract manner, to use language and so on. Wiley (1994: 1) presents *identity* as something historically specific rather than a universal feature of human nature that allows us 'to recognize individuals, categories, groups and types of individuals'. These identities, which often originate from institutions and have historically specific traits, are often mistaken for universal human nature.

One of the best examples of this is sexuality. The idea that sexuality is a basis of identity did not emerge until the nineteenth century, yet nowadays it is thought of as universally 'true' (Weeks, 1991). People in contemporary Western societies assume that sexuality 'just is' a cornerstone of a person's identity, and may find it difficult to imagine this not being the case. What this example shows us is that identities (or identity categories) are historically contingent; they have a historical genesis, and are therefore not permanent. As Wiley would argue, taking the emergence or disappearance of such historically specific identities as evidence of the reinvention or demise of human kind amounts to a category mistake, whereby particular identities are mistaken for something innately, universally human. The qualities of specific identities are not the essence of human nature, whereas personhood is, according to Wiley (1994: 2):

> It is a mistake to say that identities are trans-historical and universal, but it is also a mistake to say that personhood and selves are not. The selves are generic human structures, and the identities, any one of which may or may not be present, are distinct from and inhere in these structures.

While some would, in turn, critique Wiley by saying that the notion of personhood is also socially constructed (Morgan, 2011a), the point remains, namely that perhaps the theorists who argue that the disappearance or appearance of certain identities means a fundamental change in human nature are making the category mistake that Wiley has pointed out. A different perspective allows us to see that, in fact, because self and society are interdependent (as I shall argue in Chapter 4), and because change is inherent in both, no identity – or, indeed, society – can be considered as 'better suited' to humankind. Rather, they should be viewed as interlinked products of their time, and judged accordingly.

Monadic selves

The second characteristic that the psychosocial fragmentation and individualization theses share is that they depict a monadic self that is solitary and separated from other people. Stafford (1989: 44–5) argues that this 'myth of a society of isolated, sovereign individuals, each a self-contained centre of consciousness, desire and purpose, each motivated by self-interest, forming relationships with others which are artificial and contractual' was constructed during Victorian times in opposition to the myth of 'the happy and organic Middle Ages'. Such a monadic view of self is now the dominant one in the West (Burkitt, 1991). Gergen (1999: 118) calls this 'the ideology of the self-contained individual', which, as he points out, is problematic because it does not help explain how we come to understand each other. If we are all isolated behind our individual masks, how can we ever come to know, let alone trust, other people? There are also important consequences for the social sciences, which, if they embrace this view, end up depicting self and society as 'two opposing entities which are fundamentally divided', making it difficult to envision the links between them (Burkitt, 1991: 1).

It is no surprise therefore that theories based on the assumption that selves are monads end up depicting inherently isolated people separated by metaphorical thick walls and masks, whose relationships are always under threat. It is important to remember that this 'ideology of the individual' is a particularly Western one that is not without its ideological undertones (Esteva and Prakash, 1998). The contemporary dominance of neoliberal thought, for example, rests on the idea of the self-sufficient individual. Stafford calls this monadic self a myth because humans can never be fully self-contained, even when alone; instead, 'the very fibre of their being is constituted by relationships they have, or have had, with others' (1989: 44; cf. Burkitt, 1991; Gergen, 1999). Adopting such a relational view has important theoretical consequences for how we envision the link between self and society. Rather than something that has to be created through effort and struggle, it is built in because self and society exist in a mutual relationship. Such relational theories are examined in more depth in Chapter 4.

Thing-like structures

My third critique of the individualization and psychosocial fragmentation theses is that they adopt a structuralist view by distinguishing 'social structures' and 'the personal' as two separate and inherently different spheres. Social structures are depicted as semi-permanent fixtures that exist over and above people, imposed upon them and determining who they fundamentally can be – either fragmented or reflexive (Williams, 1977; Burkitt, 2004: 212). Conversely, the personal is equated with 'everyday life', which is then constructed in essentializing terms, that is, as existing in and of itself (Sandywell, 2004: 174). Contrary to this perceived difference between 'social structures' (the official sphere) and 'the personal' (the unofficial sphere), they are, in fact, more similar than such views allow, interdependent and permeable, each affected by the other (Williams, 1977; Burkitt, 2004; Sandywell, 2004). This point will be explored in more detail in Chapters 4 and 5.

Williams (1977: 128) has argued that depicting society as a fully formed whole – in contrast to our day-to-day experiences that lack this sense of being a finished product – is linked to the habitual separation between the personal and the social. It is because we experience the two as different, one as fixed and the other as malleable and shifting, that we view the individual and the social as two distinct spheres:

> If the social is always past, in the sense that it is always formed, we have indeed to find other terms for the undeniable experience of the present: not

only the temporal present, the realization of this and this instant, but the specificity of present being, the inalienably physical, within which we may indeed discern and acknowledge institutions, formations, positions, but not always as fixed products, defining products. And then if the social is the fixed and explicit – the known relationships, institutions, formations, positions – all that is present and moving, all that escapes or seems to escape from the fixed and the explicit and the known, is grasped and defined as the personal: this, here, now alive, active, 'subjective'. (Williams, 1977: 128)

This is part of a broader **ontology** (view of reality) that Gardiner (2000: 18) calls 'atomist-rationalist'. It is one that views the world as a reified, thing-like being, rather than an evolving process (see, for example, Durkheim's realist perspective). We reduce the world to that which is observable and quantifiable ('empirical facts'), but in doing so we simplify and impoverish reality. We end up viewing the world not as a complex whole but rather as isolated elements of 'self' and 'society', which seem static rather than constantly in transformation. It is perhaps no coincidence that this view of reality, which emerged at the time of industrialization, characterizes much sociological theorizing.

Conclusion

The psychosocial fragmentation thesis and the individualization thesis examined in this chapter tend to privilege the social because they posit that particular types of society produce particular types of person. I call this a top-down approach, which may seem a bit counterintuitive when it comes to the individualization thesis, given that its focus is on reflexivity and self-invention. However, despite its emphasis on the agency of the individual (a freedom from social structures as it were), the core argument of the individualization thesis is that it is *late modern societies* that have produced more individualized and reflexive people.

This chapter has also shown that there is a long tradition within sociology of presenting individuals as bounded, separate and atomistic entities rather than as inherently relational (Burkitt, 1991; Gergen, 1999). In the psychosocial fragmentation thesis, people's connection to each other is not seen as something in-built but as something that must be upheld. As a consequence, this connection to others can be seen as inherently fragile and at risk, which helps explain the doom-laden tone of the accounts of diminishing social cohesion. In turn, the individualization thesis exaggerates the individuality of people at the expense of relationality (May, 2011b).

The purpose of Chapters 2 and 3 has been to set the scene by discussing how some key sociological traditions theorize the self, and why it is important to look beyond this canon for alternative approaches to understanding the relationship between self and society. The remaining chapters present a view of social reality as one of 'enmeshment' (Mason, 2010) that does not posit dualisms such as personal/social and everyday life/social structure. After all, these are only concepts that sociologists have developed as a way of making sense of the world, and we should not assume that they exist 'out there' as tangible realities, or that they are ways in which people make sense of their everyday experiences. I propose that instead of taking such abstract concepts as our starting point, it is better to begin from people's lived experiences. Doing so means that we view society not as a thing but as created in interaction between people. Equally, people exist embedded in social contexts and gain a sense of self in relationships with others. Such relational views of self and society are explored in more depth in Chapter 4.

The Relationship Between Self and Society

4

Introduction

Chapter 3 ended with the observation that the psychosocial fragmentation and individualization theses can be critiqued for their depiction of selves as isolated monads and 'society' and 'self' as two separate entities. This chapter explores theories that see the self as inherently relational and focus on the interconnections between the social and the self. I will argue that such an approach is necessary in order to fully appreciate the impact that social change has on our selves.

There are three theorists in particular who offer a good grounding for the ensuing discussion, namely Georg Simmel, Charles Horton Cooley and Norbert Elias, who urged sociologists to adopt a relational approach to the study of self and society. All three are influential figures within sociology, but have not gained quite the same canonical position as Marx, Durkheim and Weber. Simmel's writings have only relatively recently begun to receive more attention, perhaps partly because rather than developing a grand narrative about modernity, his focus lay on fragments of existence (Heaphy, 2007: 23). I propose that it is exactly this focus on fragments that renders Simmel's theories useful for studying social change as it emerges in everyday personal life. This is because, from the point of view of the person, social change often lacks overall coherence and only becomes visible in a piecemeal manner. The grand narratives of social change, such as those told by Marx, Durkheim and Weber, can usually only be told with the help of hindsight.

Simmel's work shares with Durkheim a focus on differentiation and individualization, with Marx a focus on the money economy and alienation, and with Weber the growth of instrumental rationality – and like the other three theorists, he was also rather pessimistic about modernity. Yet what distinguishes Simmel is his interest in sociality, that is, the impact that modernity had on how people interacted with and related to each other.

Like Simmel, Cooley and Elias also highlighted the role of the individual when seeking explanations for the relationship between self and society. Cooley shared with Durkheim an interest in a 'group mind', that is, the existence of a consciousness beyond the individual. But unlike Durkheim, for whom the origin of this mind was in the collective, Cooley argued that any collectively shared norms originated from the individual (Jenkins, 2008: 57). For Elias, what bound people into society, and the mechanism whereby people ended up following the rules and norms of society, was their interdependence. In other words, people exist within networks of relationships within which they are, to various degrees, dependent on other people, and it is partly because of this dependence that we tend to try to act in a way that does not offend significant others (Crossley, 2006: 24).

In sum, Simmel, Cooley and Elias proposed that self and society cannot be understood independently of each other because neither can exist without the other: society is made up of individuals (and more specifically, the relationships between individuals), while individuals are inherently social, that is, gain a sense of self in a social context. Several theorists have since echoed these ideas, including Craig Calhoun (2003b), who also speaks of the social as constituted through the actions of persons and, in turn, the social as constitutive of the personal. If individual and society are mutually bound up in this way, it is necessary to conclude that they cannot be viewed as separate entities but as aspects of the same thing:

> A separate individual is an abstraction unknown to experience, and so like-wise is society when regarded as something apart from individuals ... In other words, 'society' and 'individuals' do not denote separate phenomena, but are simply collective and distributive aspects of the same thing (Cooley, 1902: 1–2)

Thus, when distinguishing between individual and society, we are not seeing separate things but the same thing from different points of view: a general or an individual point of view (Cooley, 1902: 2). As Simmel (1950: 7–9) points out, if we view the world up close, we see individual persons and their characteristics, but as we move further away, our perspective changes so that the individuals disappear and what we see instead is society. We interpret this as seeing two separate entities, but both are, in fact, views of the same thing seen differently depending on our distance from it. Elias (1991: 19) warned against thinking of either society or the individual as more important than the other or as 'single, isolated substances'. Instead, he advised sociologists to examine the relationship between them, 'to start thinking in terms of relationships and functions'.

Elias (1991: 19) compared society to a house, saying that we cannot understand the shape of a house by examining individual bricks independently of their relations to each other, and, conversely, we must understand the structure of the whole if we are to understand the relationship between the individual parts. Looking at each individual separately one after the other tells us little about society because the whole may be structured or organized in a way that is not apparent in the parts (Cooley, 1902: 3). This means that when examining individual lives, we must always do so in relation to the broader social context, lest we misunderstand or only partially understand what is going on (Cohen, 1982a: 15).

I now explore what a relational view of society entails; what it means to say that the self is relational; and how these two interrelated points influence how we can understand social change.

A relational society

Approaches that privilege the social, such as the psychosocial fragmentation and individualization theses, depict society as a thing that exists 'out there' separate from individuals and that impinges upon individual lives in particular ways. As discussed in Chapters 2 and 3, such approaches also characterize social structures as fixed *things* that mould our lives. Yet, there is another way of looking at society: Simmel (1950: 9–10) depicted society as an event, as something that individuals *do*, rather than a concrete substance. To emphasize this aspect, he sometimes used the term 'sociation' instead of 'society', thus highlighting interaction as a key element of the social. By doing so, Simmel captured the dynamic nature of society (Goodstein, 2002: 228). Furthermore, he argued that sociologists should not confine themselves to studying large social formations alone because less conspicuous forms of relationship and interaction are also significant (Simmel, 1950: 9). Simmel (1990: 174) proposed that the 'interaction between individuals is the starting point of all social formations'.

In other words, social structures such as 'the family' or 'social class' are not 'things' that 'really' exist, but are the result of individuals interacting with each other in a particular way. The reason why 'the family' might feel as though it exists 'out there', separate from these interactions that constitute it, is that what we know as 'family' has become a seemingly permanent and universal way in which people organize their relationships, and has therefore become crystallized as an easily definable social structure that has assumed a logic and independence of its own (Simmel, 1950: 9).

Another reason why we so easily end up thinking of social structures as things that have volition is because we tend to personalize 'social collectives' such as 'the state', 'the nation' or the 'working classes' 'as if they were real persons known in indirect social experience' (Schutz, [1932]1967: 198–9). Social structures are highly complex networks, yet 'when we speak of any collectivity as "acting", we take this complex structural arrangement for granted' and think of it as though it were an individual acting consciously (Schutz, [1932]1967: 199). This helps explain why we end up thinking about 'society' as an entity that exists 'out there' that acts in a conscious and goal-oriented manner. An alternative way of looking at social structures is one that sees them as coming into being in our everyday interactions. I now turn to explore the work of Garfinkel (1967) who argued exactly this: that social order is not simply 'there' but is made.

Social order in the making

The ethnomethodologist Harold Garfinkel wanted to understand how social rules are created through talk and interaction. Social order is the product 'of action and interpretation by actual women and men' and 'an accomplishment of members of society' (Smith, 1987: 90). **Ethnomethodology** is interested in making the familiar world 'strange' by problematizing taken-for-granted assumptions and activities. This requires suspending one's everyday assumptions in order to be able to see the processes by which people manage to create a shared sense of order.

Garfinkel (1967) argued that reality is accomplished rather than merely experienced – what we understand as social structures do not exist out there in and of themselves, but come into being thanks to people behaving in particular, often patterned, ways. An example of this is how people accomplish 'gender', as discussed by Garfinkel in his famous study of Agnes, a male-to-female transsexual. Garfinkel focused on the work Agnes had to do in order to 'pass' as a woman, and how this work was part of the process through which members of society 'produce stable, accountable practical activities, *i.e.*, social structures of everyday activities' (1967: 185). In other words, this is work that *everyone* must do in order to accomplish a successful performance as a member of the gender category 'woman' or 'man'. This work, however, remains 'seen but unnoticed' (Garfinkel, 1967: 180): we *see* each other's gender performances in that we routinely categorize people as either men or women, but we *do not notice* the work that goes into a successful performance. Rather, we take this performance for granted because we feel it is only 'natural' that men and women behave in particular ways. It is by examining the work done by people like Agnes, who cannot automatically claim membership of a social category but have to consciously work at a successful performance, that the familiar becomes strange and the creation of social order becomes particularly noticeable.

This social order that we accomplish in our everyday interactions offers us a sense of familiarity, predictability and comfort. As will be discussed in more detail in Chapter 6, these are all cornerstones of a sense of belonging, although generally not visible as such until they are absent. Garfinkel (1967) asked his students to perform 'breaching experiments' to see what happens when this shared tacit agreement over the nature of social reality is breached. He asked students to behave as though they did not know how they were supposed to act in social situations. For example, students would quiz interlocutors as to the precise meaning of what they were saying. A simple question such as 'How are you feeling?', rather than eliciting the usual response of 'I'm fine, thanks', would lead to a lengthy and increasingly fraught exchange, as the student replied 'What do you mean? My mental or physical state?' and so on.

By upsetting people's expectations as to what 'normally' happens in such situations, Garfinkel's students were able to make visible just how much the smooth running of everyday social life depends on these minute acts of 'indexicality', where we use shorthand expressions that act as indices of 'what we really mean'. These breaching experiments also revealed just how important it is that social interactions run more or less predictably according to certain tacit rules. Chapter 6 explores the significance of these shared understandings and ways of behaving for belonging, and why breaches in them can lead to a sense of not belonging.

What are social structures?

What Garfinkel's work teaches us is that social structures should not be viewed as entities but as sedimented practices resulting from fixing 'in geographical space and in codified language the relational forms and activities of the past' (Burkitt, 2004: 220). In other words, if enough people behave in similar ways for long enough, this becomes identified as 'this is how things are done', and becomes codified in language. For example, a man and a woman who live in the same house and have children together have come to be known as a 'family'. This fixing can have both material manifestations, for example single-family housing, and intangible consequences, such as feeling a special sense of affinity with particular people because they are 'family' (Young, 2005: 20).

Understanding 'family' to consist of a (married and heterosexual) couple and their (biological) children who live together has become sedimented to the point of appearing 'natural', that is, the only conceivable way of organizing intimate lives. Consequently, there are strong **social norms** associated with areas of life connected to family such as sexuality, intimate relationships and parenting. These norms shape how people think, evidenced by the virulence of some of the debates around lone motherhood and same-sex marriage, and how they act, evidenced by the number of couples who get married or cohabit.

We recognize such social forms more easily when they are articulated and explicit. There are a number of religious edicts and state laws regulating family life that set out quite clearly the 'rules' of family life. These also help make this social form appear 'fixed' and permanent. Social structures are meaningful in people's lives because they 'constitute the historical givens in relation to which individuals act and which are relatively stable over time' (Young, 2005: 20). You and I conduct our everyday lives in the context of such sedimented ways of thinking and doing things (de Quieroz, 1989; Burkitt, 2004). Williams (1977: 130) points out that social forms only become a part of social consciousness if they are 'lived, actively, in real relationships'. It is this aspect that I now examine, namely how social structures and norms become a part of our lived lives and, ultimately, our sense of self.

Cooley and Mead on the relational self

The relational view of the self posits that humans are relational beings rather than isolated individuals, and that individuals gain their sense of self in relationships with and in relation to other people (Burkitt, 1991). As the historian Edward Carr (1961: 25) said:

> As soon as we are born, the world gets to work on us and transforms us from merely biological into social units. Every human being ... is born into a society and from his [sic] earliest years is moulded by that society. The language which he speaks is not an individual inheritance, but a social acquisition from the group in which he grows up. Both language and environment help to determine the character of his thought; his earliest ideas come to him from others. As has been well said, the individual apart from society would be both speechless and mindless.

We learn to distinguish ourselves as a person, and to appreciate how we are different from or similar to other people, while other people continuously reflect back to us who we are. Feminists such as Griffiths (1995: 132) have highlighted that human relationships and language are central to the construction of a self, which can therefore never be a singular individual. I now turn to the work of two theorists who have heavily influenced such relational accounts of the self, Charles Horton Cooley and George Herbert Mead, who were both representatives of the American pragmatist tradition of philosophy, which was concerned with the practical outcomes of human behaviour (Jenkins, 2008: 57).

Cooley and the 'looking-glass self'

Cooley (1902: 149) proposed that the self is inherently social and that we need others in order to have a sense of self. Even the *idea* of the self is a linguistic phenomenon, which requires a shared culture and language to exist. Furthermore, it is not possible to use language without thinking of other people, because we have learned it in contact with others. In addition, our self can never be completely distinct from other persons because our mind includes thoughts about others, and our self-feeling includes the people with whom we identify most (Cooley, 1902: 92). And even when we do *not* identify with others, they are an integral part of our self, because we think of ourselves not only in relation to those whom we resemble, but also those whom we are different from (Cooley, 1902: 96–7). So, a self contains *distance from* as well as *closeness to* others, and there is 'no sense of "I" ... without its correlative sense of you, or he [sic], or they' (Cooley, 1902: 151).

In addition, Cooley (1902: 152) argued that how we believe others perceive us is important in terms of how we see ourselves: 'in imagination we perceive in another's mind some thought of our appearance, manners, aims, deeds, character, friends, and so on, and are variously affected by it'. He famously developed the notion of a 'looking-glass self' to conceptualize this. There are three elements to the looking-glass self: how we think others perceive us; how we imagine they judge us on the basis of this; and the resultant self-feeling, for example pride or shame (Cooley, 1902: 152). According to Cooley, we strive for a positive judgement by others, although not necessarily in a conscious fashion. Yet, the moment we fall into disgrace, we become acutely aware of just how important other people's perceptions of us are to our sense of self (Cooley, 1902: 177).

As Carsten (2000: 698) notes, having one's story listened to is an important part of the process of constituting a self. A concrete example of the relational self comes from Zingaro's (2009) study of self-disclosure of sensitive or traumatic personal experiences, which highlights the importance of how others *hear* our stories, and how this then has an effect on how we feel about ourselves. Those whose disclosures have 'gone wrong' speak of the vulnerability, hurt and frustration they felt as a result. In other words, it is important that what we tell about ourselves is *heard* in the right way, that other people take notice of and give value to who we say we are:

> we will always be accountable to others in dialogue, but the way this is usually expressed is in terms of credibility: if the story seems unbelievable, or the audience does not seem to believe her, then the teller has a need to prove something, not necessarily to corroborate the details of the story but to prove herself a credible witness. (Zingaro, 2009: 134)

I argue below that being seen as a 'credible witness' rather than someone who fabricates stories is important, because we wish to be seen as *moral* and morally accountable members of society.

Melucci (1996: 29) proposes that in order to 'have' an identity, we require intersubjective recognition, to be acknowledged by others. This, in turn, entails membership in a group. Others must perceive us and recognize us as a self, because we can only feel we are 'real live persons' when we 'are experienced as such by another' (Laing, 1965: 119). This is felt keenly by toddlers who may get distraught if their mother leaves the room, because they believe that they cease to exist when their mother cannot see them. Having a self thus presupposes a relationship and dialogue with others (Laing, 1965: 139).

Mead and the generalized other

Cooley's influence can be seen in **symbolic interactionism**, such as in the work Mead, who argued that human consciousness emerges in interaction (Jenkins, 2008: 57, 64). In *Mind, Self & Society*, Mead (1934) provided a detailed account of how our selves are created in interaction with others, but also how society emerges out of these relationships. Mead depicted a two-stage process where children first develop a sense of 'I' (the inner self), before they gain a sense of a more social 'me'. As a result of this process, children acquire the capacity to imagine how others see them.

At first, a child has no sense of being a separate being from her mother (or main carer). But eventually the child develops a sense of separateness, a sense of self, which Mead called the 'I'. In this first stage of development, a child is able to imagine how individual people see her and judge her behaviour. The child is able to do so because she receives constant feedback from her parents, who encourage her when she behaves appropriately ('What a good girl you are!') and scold her when she does something she is not supposed to ('Stop that, that is naughty!').

Mead proposed that, with time, as we become socialized, we also develop a sense of a social self he called the 'me'. In this second phase of development, the child is also able to imagine not only what specific people, such as her parents, think of her, but also how a 'generalized other' might see her. By **generalized other**, Mead meant a more abstract notion of the social group. By coming to understand how this 'generalized other' might see her, the child is becoming aware of social norms held in the society she belongs to and, to a degree, assumes this set of social attitudes. By internalizing the social attitudes of the group, the child develops the ability to evaluate her own actions in light of the group's norms. No longer do the parents have to remark on everything their daughter does – the child begins to do this internally for herself. Although the generalized other is a fairly abstract notion, it is the product of ongoing encounters between individuals – in other words, the generalized other does not exist 'out there' in and of itself, but is realized in interaction (Jenkins, 2008: 63).

Thus, as part of the process of acquiring a sense of self, a person takes on the attitudes and language of her community as part of herself. Collective under-standings and our connection to others become an in-built part of our selves; indeed, 'the self' would not exist without these:

> That which we have acquired as self-conscious persons makes us ... members of society and gives us selves. Selves can only exist in definite relationships to other selves. No hard-and-fast line can be drawn between our own selves and the selves of others ... The individual possesses a self only in relation to the selves of the other members of his [sic] social group; and the structure of his self expresses or reflects the general behavior pattern of this social group to which he belongs, just as does the structure of the self of every other indi-vidual belonging to this group. (Mead, 1934: 164)

We can see this relational sense of self in the making through the example of Emily. Emily was the daughter of two New York academics, who (perhaps controversially) decided to audio record Emily's bedtime monologues when she was aged 21–36 months, and subsequently allowed a group of researchers to analyse these recordings. Each recording began when Emily's parents were saying good night to her, and continued with Emily talking to herself after her parents had left the room.

These recordings offer a prime example of how a child is socialized into 'appropriate' behaviour. Emily's interactions with her parents just before bedtime were interwoven into her monologues, and it is here that regulation turns into self-regulation (Watson, 1989). At one period, Emily went through a phase of separation anxiety, and was reluctant to allow her father, who usually tucked her into bed, to leave the room. Her father would first coax and then command her to settle down and go to sleep. After being left alone, Emily would talk to herself, using the same expressions and intonation as her father. She would also describe 'her present experience (going to sleep) in terms of a general social reality, by recounting the same event occurring at the same time for "everybody", a shared rather than a private reality' (Watson, 1989: 279). In other words, Emily was situating herself within the world of people, representing her own experience among those of others, and she accomplished this through a process of internalization, where 'the individual perspective of the unsocialized child becomes the social perspective of the child in a social world' (Nelson, 1989: 284). She was becoming a *social* being who was aware of others and who understood how events are socially organized. Emily was learning to see things not simply from her own point of view, but to understand how events are interpreted by others in her group (Nelson, 1989: 285).

It is important to note that although Mead focused on the parent–child relationship as crucial to a child's development of a sense of self, parents and adults are not the only social bonds that matter in this process – peers also play an important role. Based on a study involving Brazilian children and young people aged 10–17 years, de Castro (2004) found that they constructed important notions of difference and sameness among themselves. Similarly, Mauthner (2005) and Edwards et al. (2006) have found that sibling relationships are important in this process of gaining a sense of self. As Davies (2012) argues, siblings can construct their sense of self in relation to each other, for example one being labelled 'the naughty one' one while the other is seen as 'the good one'.

It is also interesting to consider how technological changes might affect the nature of our 'looking-glass self' or the 'generalized other'. Facebook, for example, has become 'a crucial medium of visibility and public witnessing' onto which we project our self, and which mirrors this back to us such that 'the truth about yourself is revealed to yourself by what you post on Facebook. On Facebook, you find out who you are' (Miller, 2011: 179–80). In this way, Facebook could be envisaged as a new form of 'generalized other', which gives us a sense not only of who we are, but also who we ought to be (Miller, 2011: 180). According to Miller (2011), the contemporary compulsion to put things under a general public gaze means that the flight from community that Tönnies and Furedi wrote about is, in fact, not taking place.

An important aspect of identity or self is that it does not originate from within but from our interactions with other people. As such, our sense of self is firmly rooted in collective understandings of what it means to be, for example, a man or a woman, middle class or working class, someone who listens to opera or someone who is into indie music, and how such a person should behave. As a result, our 'self' always reflects the group(s) we belong to.

Becoming a moral self

The process whereby children learn how to become competent members of a group or society is called **socialization**. One step in this process, as discussed above, is to internalize social norms, which means not only learning to behave and present oneself in an acceptable manner, but also coming to judge one's own behaviour in light of these norms. When children are being instructed in how to behave, they are also being told what kind of person they are expected to be (Burkitt, 2008: 62). It is in this dialogue that children become aware of the social rules of interaction and what constitutes acceptable behaviour, as well as coming to comprehend other people as 'concrete others' and understand their viewpoint. The feminist philosopher Seyla Benhabib (1992: 189–90) reminds us that we are children before we are adults and that the nurture, care and responsibility that others show towards us is essential if we are to develop into morally competent, self-sufficient individuals. In sum, we are 'called into being' as moral selves who are accountable for our own actions (Shotter, 1993).

Both Williams (1977: 117–18) and Benhabib (1992: 51) note that this process of socialization is not an abstract one, but takes place in specific institutions and settings, such as within families and in school, and that our relationships with other people are an important part of this process. Each institution selects and enforces its own range of meanings, values and practices. There is no one single overpowering 'way of doing things', instead we have access to several perspectives and must negotiate a mix of, at times, contradictory expectations. That is, there are several 'generalized others' we can draw upon (Crossley, 2006).

So, it is important to examine the relational self not as something that is fully determined by social context, but as a mixture of unique individuality and social shaping. As individuals, we enjoy some degree of creative autonomy where 'we merge cultural and parental influences, normative social orders and other ingredients, which we add as we go along' (Miller, 2008: 295). Thus, we are not merely carbon copies of each other, but neither are we fully free to be whoever we wish to be. This is evident in the patterning of traits and lifestyles. There is an organizing principle at work in each society that helps shape who we become (Miller, 2008: 203). I explore this organizing principle in more detail below in relation to Bourdieu's notion of habitus.

The moral self is not a moral geometrician who merely copies abstract universal rules to situations, but rather an embodied and affective being who exercises moral imagination and has the capacity to think of how the various possible actions will be understood by others (Benhabib, 1992; Shotter, 1993). In doing so, the self is actively engaging with the social, and changes it if it must. I return to this point in the last section of this chapter examining social change. In other words, we are not simply rule-following animals – we are also *moral beings* who evaluate our own actions and take responsibility for them. All our actions 'must be performed with an awareness of how they will be *judged by others*' (Shotter, 1993: 94):

> To be a person and to qualify for certain rights as a free, autonomous individual, one must also be able to show in one's actions certain social competencies, that is, to fulfil certain duties and to be *accountable* to others in

the sense of being able to justify one's action to them, when challenged, in relation to the 'social reality' of the society of which one is a member. Being someone in this sense is a rhetorical achievement. (Shotter, 1993: 192–3)

Numerous empirical studies have found that people do indeed tend to construct a 'moral' self and to convey to others that they know and respect shared social norms or moral imperatives (for example Ribbens McCarthy et al., 2000; Presser, 2004; Green et al., 2006; May, 2008). Convicted criminals, for example, may wish to use various narrative strategies, such as denying responsibility or denying harm, to convince others that despite their breach of the law, they are persons with moral integrity (Presser, 2004). In a study of how women who had contemplated divorce accounted for their decision to either divorce or remain married, I found that while there is a moral impera-tive according to which a 'good' mother must put her children's wellbeing before anything else (cf. Ribbens McCarthy et al., 2000), what constitutes 'a child's best interests' is not clear-cut. There were traces of different and, at times, contradictory moral norms, such as 'divorce is wrong because it is harmful to children' and 'warring parents can do more harm to their chil-dren than divorce does' (May, 2008). As moral selves, people navigate their way through this thicket of prescribed actions by weighing up their various options and the possible outcomes of these (see also Smart and Neale, 1999; Ribbens McCarthy et al., 2000). By doing this, they are signalling to others that they are aware of the group's norms and hold themselves accountable to these. In other words, they are making a claim for membership in and belonging to a group.

Bourdieu on habitus

Another way to examine the relationship between self and society is to utilize Bourdieu's theories on how social class distinctions come about and are lived. He was reacting against theories of social class that not only constructed static variables such as economic wealth, occupation and education, but also claimed that there is a linear relationship between the socioeconomic status of people and their class position. In *Distinction* (1979), Bourdieu argued that people do not merely 'have' the resources to attain a particular class identity, such as money or education, they must also be able to mobilize these in the context of social relations. So, in order to fully understand how class operates, it is vital to study practices, that is, what people *do* to realize their class identity.

The key concepts that Bourdieu used to explore how social class is prac-tised are **social field** and **habitus**. Bourdieu (1979: 124) argued that society is 'socially ranked geographical space', which he conceptualized in terms of 'social fields'. A field is a combination of space and interaction – there can be different kinds of interaction going on in the same place, and interactions of the same type can occur in more than one place. A person's social field is made up of the various situations and contexts they move through. Depending on our social position in a specific social field, we internalize particular 'durable, transposable dispositions' – habitual ways of being in and seeing the world – that form our habitus (Bourdieu, 1979: 72).

Because our habitus reflects a particular field, we feel at home in that field and fields similar to it. We feel a sense of bodily comfort and ease in this place and in the social situations within it. In a field where we 'feel at home', we have a 'feel for the game' (Bourdieu, 2000). We know how to behave, how to comport ourselves, what to say and so on. In fields where we do not have this tacit knowledge, where we do not have a feel for the game, we feel ill at ease.

Habitus also allows us to classify or categorize other people, for example according to taste (from vulgar to distinguished). We experience a sense of affinity with people who share our habitus (or one similar). It is this similarity in habitus that lies behind our ability to make sense of other people and their behaviour, and this harmonization of our habitus also means that there is no need to explicitly coordinate our activities – it happens as though by itself, 'naturally'.

Why, then, do we have a need for such systematic dispositions? One reason, according to Bourdieu (1977: 76), is because situations present themselves 'with an urgency and a claim to existence excluding all deliberation'. In other words, we rarely have time to stop and consider our motivations and interests and to weigh these against likely outcomes. Instead, we resort to:

> a whole body of wisdom, sayings, commonplaces, ethical precepts ('that's not for the likes of us') and, at a deeper level, the unconscious principles of the *ethos* which, being the product of a learning process dominated by a determinate type of objective regularities, determines 'reasonable' and 'unreasonable' conduct for every agent subjected to those regularities. (Bourdieu, 1977: 77)

Bourdieu (1977: 78–9) noted that people tend to see their own habitus (ways of thinking and acting) as 'natural', like 'second nature', as though it has always been there. This is because we suffer from 'genesis amnesia', that is, we cannot remember how our habitus developed. Habitus is so deeply ingrained in us that it operates largely in an unconscious fashion, such that much of our behaviour feels 'intentionless'. In other words, we are not consciously aware that we are, in fact, making choices because we are not aware of the possibility of behaving differently. In addition, people tend not to be aware of how their habitus (their position in social space and the consequent internalized dispositions) shapes their perspective of the world (Bourdieu, 1979: 171–2). Habitus can, therefore, be seen to contribute to a sense of belonging, which, as I will argue in Chapter 6, is often achieved when we can go about our lives without consciously thinking about whether or not we belong, when we can take our selves, the world around us and our place in it for granted.

Goffman on presenting an acceptable self

So far, I have examined theories of how we develop our individuality in interaction with other people, and how we come to internalize shared social ways of thinking which then guide our action. Here, the focus turns to how these shared cultural repertoires are used in everyday interaction. The key theorist in this matter is Erving Goffman, who, rather than focusing on the social psychology of the development of the self, or how we become people who are able to apply social rules, took the existence of these rules as given, as well as individuals' ability to employ them in everyday interaction. Instead, he was interested in *how* social interaction was patterned.

Goffman viewed social life as a performance and in *The Presentation of Self in Everyday Life* (1959) employed metaphors from the world of theatre – such as roles, scripts, props and stages – to describe this performance, the aim of which is to keep 'face' through impression management. In other words, we try to perform acceptable selves. Individuals attempt to control the impressions they give to others in order to appear competent and of sound character (that is, moral) in particular social situations and to avoid painful emotions such as shame and guilt (Scheff, 2006; cf. Shotter, 1993). For example, we dress differently for different occasions. If I were to attend a formal funeral wearing the worn and paint-splattered clothing I use while doing DIY, I would probably be giving the impression that I am not very competent in terms of respecting the gravity of the occasion. You might also try to maintain a certain degree of expressive control, for example by not yawning too openly during lectures.

Yet, there are times when our expressive control slips, for example when we burp during a dinner with prospective in-laws. This threat to a successful performance of an acceptable self leads to attempts to save our performance. Goffman called this 'face work' that the performers engage in. Goffman also argued that helping others keep 'face' through the use of tact is a key social rule. So, for example, if a person stumbles while walking down the podium at their graduation, audience members might engage in tactful inattention by looking away and pretending not to have noticed.

Smith (1987: 90–1) critiques Goffman for only studying the effects of how the everyday world is organized, that is, how people behave in particular situations. Similarly, Garfinkel (1967) noted that Goffman's theories only help us understand the 10 per cent of human action that takes place within the realm of consciousness, whereas 90 per cent of our action is unconscious. The early work of feminist philosopher Judith Butler (1990, 1993) can help us complement Goffman's work on this matter. Butler focused particularly on gender, using the term 'performance', by which she means something different from Goffman's 'presentation'. Whereas Goffman's presentations of self seem somewhat self-consciously done, Butler argues that our sense of self is so deeply ingrained through countless iterations of thinking and behaving in particular ways that these come to feel 'natural' and, to an extent, beyond conscious thought.

Butler (1990) argued that not only do we perform culturally accepted versions of gender – such as sitting like a girl – and through these performances come to acquire our gender identity, but that our performance *creates gender itself*. Thus, gender, as it is expressed by the human body, does not originate from within, but by performing gendered ways of thinking and doing, these become inscribed on a person's body and thinking. Gender norms become sedimented over time due to the repeated performance of socially established meanings in relation to gender; for example, that women wear skirts and men wear ties. Consequently, we come to see, speak and perform 'male' and 'female', and to understand these performances as 'natural'. One aspect of human behaviour that is somewhat missing in both Butler's and Goffman's theories is the fact that not everything is rule governed – as will be discussed below, there is always a degree of improvisation at play in human interaction (Jenkins, 2008: 92–3).

It is also important to consider the emotional aspect of presenting a moral self. The way we are brought up – for example, admonished when we 'misbehave' – means that feelings of, for example, pride and shame are connected to these presentations of self (Scheff, 2006; cf. Cooley, 1902). This is not to say that everyone feels the same emotion in a similar situation, but, nevertheless, pride and shame are fundamental emotions that, to an extent, reflect a person's social status. For example, a sense of belonging to a particular social class is emotionally charged, as shown by Sayer (2005) and Skeggs (1997). According to Sayer (2005: 211), the issue of class in the UK is 'morally problematic because of its arbitrary relationship to worth, virtues and status, and this is why it is a highly sensitive subject'.

Cynical performers?

Another criticism levelled at Goffman's theory of the presentation of self is that it presents people as cynical performers. Who is to know whether this performance is in any way genuine? The question of whether Goffman's concepts convey a sense of 'contrived insincerity' has been the focus of some debate (Tseëlon, 1992: 117). Kenneth Gergen (1999: 78), for example, argues that Goffman presents a cynical view of people:

> Goffman's analysis suggests that just beneath the surface of our actions there is a manipulative agent who is continuously conning others. Sincerity itself is just another con, which might even succeed in duping the actor.

This is perhaps too one-sided a reading of Goffman's work, who did also talk about helping others save face, which, in turn, requires some amount of trust between people. Helping others save face can also be seen as a form of altruism, where social actors are not concerned with 'conning others' but with helping others manage a successful presentation of self. Furthermore, the argument that Goffman's selves are merely cynical performers rests on the notion that there is such a thing as a 'true' self lurking behind these performances. Tseëlon (1992) argues that Goffman was postmodern before his time: he was not interested in the relationship between 'surface' and 'inner' reality. In fact, perhaps these two are indistinguishable. Tseëlon poses the question: was Goffman challenging the distinction between 'the real' and 'the staged'? I return to this question of 'inner' and 'outer' in Chapter 9 in relation to Daniel Miller's work on different conceptions of the self that can be found in Europe and Trinidad.

Garfinkel's (1967) comments on Goffman's work are helpful here. Although Garfinkel agrees with Goffman that individuals are involved in 'impression management', he says that this does not provide a sufficient explanation of what is going on. Impression management à la Goffman implies that it is enough for individuals to play a role in an acceptable fashion and to be accepted by others as what they present themselves to be. In Agnes's case, for example, it should, according to Goffman, have been enough that her work to 'pass' as a woman was successful in any particular situation. Garfinkel argued, however, that there was more going on than that because what she was aiming for was *being* a 'normal' woman. Garfinkel was, in effect, saying that it *does* matter to people whether or not their presentations of self are genuine, because we are not only 'performing' to an outside audience, but to our selves (and our internalized generalized other). Garfinkel's point has been borne out by subsequent research. For example, Mason-Schrock (1996) noted in his study of transsexuals that it is of utmost importance to be able to construct a coherent narrative about one's gender identity that *feels real* rather than one that merely convinces other people.

The 'moral self' discussed above is also a useful concept to explore in connection with this question of whether 'performing' equals duping others. People do not merely learn to 'perform' in a fashion that is acceptable to others; rather, in the process of internalizing the group's values or norms, it becomes important for individual subjects to *be* morally acceptable members of that group (Shotter, 1993). This is because people come, at least to some extent, to accept shared norms and to evaluate *their own actions* in light of these norms. Thus, it is not enough to behave *as though* one were adhering to shared understandings of what is appropriate, it is also important that these actions *reflect one's value system* – which is in accordance with that of other people in the group. In other words, there is a general tendency to want to be accepted by one's social group that is not simply a question of superficial conformism. Rather, acceptance matters to people on a *moral* level and has an emotional impact, as I will discuss below. And, as shall be further explored in Chapter 6, this acceptance is a prerequisite if we are to gain a sense of belonging among other people.

The decision that many of us are faced with in the course of our everyday lives is how much we are willing to adjust in order to be accepted in a group. For example, many women have probably experienced a situation that Griffiths (1995) describes, namely finding oneself laughing at sexist jokes in male company so as not to be seen as lacking a 'sense of humour'. Such experiences are familiar to people who have membership in conflicting groups and who might have to play down aspects of their selves in order to 'fit in'. For example, working-class people in middle-class occupations can find that they have to change their accent, the way they dress, their tastes and their mannerisms in order to be accepted, which can lead to feelings of inauthenticity (Griffiths, 1995: 117). Empirical research indicates that presenting a self that feels inauthentic comes at a price, as people may feel a sense of ambiguity and discomfort at having to 'hide' aspects of themselves (for example Rogaly and Taylor, 2009).

New twists in the presentations of self?

Here, I wish to explore the impact that developments in information and communication technologies (ICTs) have had on the self. I am particularly interested in the emergence of social networking sites (SNSs), which have become extremely popular worldwide in the space of a decade. SNSs afford new ways to present the self – for example by creating an online persona via status updates and photographs on Facebook or by commenting on the world via Twitter – and researchers are beginning to investigate the links, overlaps and differences between offline and online selves (Enli and Thumim, 2012). It would seem that although the general understanding is that online presentations of self are carefully constructed and not necessarily an exact match with who that person is offline (cf. Walther et al., 2001; Ellison et al., 2006; Gershon, 2011), the online persona is also expected to reflect the offline person in many important respects.

When we examine presentations of self online, we must also take into account what kinds of presentations are possible on the various SNSs. Facebook, for example, offers a fairly rigid framework within which we can present our self and, according to Gershon (2011: 867), encourages its users to become 'neoliberal selves' who 'manage themselves as flexible collections of skills, usable traits, and tastes that need to be constantly maintained and enhanced'. Constructing a profile on Facebook means engaging the reflexive techniques of self-management that are encouraged by neoliberalism. The self becomes a metaphorical business: the more skills and alliances one has, the better. In essence, the self becomes a 'brand', and Facebook does indeed seem to be blurring the boundaries between 'personal' and 'commercial', as 'the lines between private identity and public persona, corporate sponsor and individual producer, user and consumer are hopelessly blurred' (Hearn, 2008: 212). This is not to say that every Facebook user subscribes to a neoliberal agenda, or is engaged in shameless self-promotion, as people use SNSs very differently. However, as sociologists, we should remain mindful of the underlying logics according to which new ICTs operate, and the kinds of selves they 'hail' or encourage (cf. Butler, 1990; Hall, 1996).

While SNSs have been critiqued for contributing to a narcissistic culture of self-promotion, Livingstone (2008) reads them somewhat differently. The self that is presented on Facebook, for example, is not necessarily disembedded.

Using Mead's (1934) distinction between the 'I' and the 'me', Livingstone argues that social networking engages the social 'me' that is connected to a peer group rather than the private 'I'. In addition, the norms of the peer group will influence how someone uses SNSs, because one of the reasons why people use these sites is to feel connected to a 'real' or 'virtual' group of like-minded people.

Social change

So far this chapter has explored relational accounts of both society and the self. It is now time to bring these two together in order to see how they could help us understand social change. As has been discussed above, people are born into a world that is already structured and that presents them with ready-made prescriptions as to how to behave and think. As social beings, individuals are always, to an extent, bound by the social conventions of their time and behave accordingly – which accounts for continuity in social relationships and structures: 'Being "social" involves being inescapably determined by, dependent on, and committed to other people, patterns of social organization, and culture' (Calhoun, 2003b: 558).

Internalizing rules is, however, not merely a question of copying behaviours like automatons, but of showing intellectual and volitional control. Behaving 'properly' is a conscious act of demanding a certain kind of behaviour of ourselves rather than unconsciously copying what others do (Shotter, 1993: 112). Bourdieu (1977) also warned that although human behaviour is always, to a degree, regulated by habitus, it cannot be explained by mechanistic stimulus-response models, whereby behaviour is directly reduced to pre-established models or structures. That is, our context does not determine our habitus but shapes it, and in each social interaction there is a degree of improvisation at play (Bourdieu, 1977: 78). So, habitus is practical (and situated) reason rather than mere reflex.

In other words, we are not mere puppets, but react to our social context with reason, as is apparent in situations where 'habit' breaks down or is not possible, such as when we are thrown into an unfamiliar situation. For example, when entering a café in a foreign country, you may be unsure as to whether you can choose your own seat, whether the waiter will come and get your order or whether you are meant to go up to the bar to order your drink, whether you are meant to pay at the bar, when the waiter brings your drink or when you leave, and whether you are meant to leave a tip. In such situations, we must consciously reflect on our behaviour in ways that we would not necessarily do in familiar situations where our habitus is in harmony with the social field (Brubaker and Cooper, 2000). The important thing to remember is that even then, we are using reasoning, although we may not necessarily be aware of it because it feels as though we are acting 'naturally'.

It is this interaction between the social and the individual that leads to social change because people do not simply copy past behaviours but must adopt a certain degree of spontaneity, improvisation and creativity in applying these rules of social interaction. Shotter (1993) notes that we are not handed a rule-book that would tell us how to behave in any given situation, and we rarely have a predetermined mental plan of how we will act in particular situations. Instead, we use our knowledge of social rules to judge what is required of us, depending on who we are interacting with and where, and to apply what, to us, feels like the appropriate rule for each situation. Bourdieu called this having a 'feel for the game'. For example, if we are at a nightclub with friends, we are aware that the rules of interaction are somewhat different than at a family dinner with elderly relatives. Others then make the moral judgement of whether our behaviour is acceptable or not (Burkitt, 2008: 59–62).

As Crossley (2006: 89) notes, when weighing up a potential course of action, we hold imaginary dialogues with our generalized others in which we antici-pate possible reactions to what we are about to do. In these internal dialogues, we can challenge existing rules, and if we feel that we have constructed a persuasive reply to potential criticism, or do not care about this criticism, we can act out this challenge in practice. This means that we are not passive lumps of clay whose actions are determined by rules. Individuals shape the social context in which they live, either individually or collectively, and can generate new perspectives. Thus, in our interactions, we (re)produce the similar and the typical, but also the individual (Elias, 1991).

It is rare, however, that a single person can affect change on a social level. Social structures are the aggregate result of many individual interactions and change only as the result of 'the confluence of many individual actions within given institutional relations' (Young, 2005: 20). Such social change can rarely if ever be reduced to the conscious intentions of one person or group of people (Elias, 1991; Young, 2005: 20). Bourdieu (1977: 72) speaks in similar terms of 'habitus' as 'collectively orchestrated without being the product of the orches-trating action of a conductor'. Furthermore, social change cannot be predicted because it is the combined result of individual people reacting to new situa-tions in, to some degree, idiosyncratic rather than completely patterned and predictable ways (Bourdieu, 1977: 73; Elias, 1991: 63–4). Thus, there exists a constant and complex loop between individual (inter)action and social change, both affecting each other in somewhat unpredictable ways.

Conclusion

In this chapter I have argued for a relational view of self and society. Such an approach views selves as constituted in social interaction, in relationships with and in relation to other people, both those who we identify with and those who we define as 'other'. These relationships are thus fundamental to our selves. This means that selves are always connected to others, even if that connection is felt as difference and distance from others. Similarly, a relational view of society entails that society is not a 'thing' that exists in and of itself, but is constantly in the making in the interactions between people. Furthermore, I argue that society is constituted not only of how people relate to each other, but also their relationship to their material environment and to more abstract or symbolic notions such as 'society', shared cultural norms, traditions and values.

In other words, self and society are mutually constitutive and cannot exist without each other. Consequently, change in one leads to change in the other. My argument is that since belonging is one of the ways in which we connect with the surrounding world, an important way in which this change is experienced (at least initially) is as a shift in our sense of belonging. In practice, this can lead to a change, however subtle, in how people think and behave, which then generates further social change. In other words, there is a constant loop between self and society, both influencing each other, and neither remaining static. How individuals respond to the social is key in this process. Chapter 5 explores sociological approaches that try to understand the social through the perspective of the person.

Everyday Personal Life 5

Introduction

In Chapter 4, I argued for a relational view of self and society that depicts these as interlinked, with social change taking place as people react in new ways to existing social structures, traditions and the like. Any attempt to understand this process requires a dynamic approach that begins with the individual. In this chapter, I develop such a framework, drawing inspiration from phenomenology, the sociology of everyday life and the sociology of personal life. Central to all these is the argument that because the social – structures, institutions, norms and so on – is created in the interactions between people, any sociological study should begin from these interactions, that is, from everyday life.

The chapter begins with a discussion of phenomenology, which understands social reality as something that is created through thought and action, rather than as something that is given. Smith (1987) argues that sociologists must, therefore, take everyday life 'as a problematic', that is, focus on *how* it is constituted and by whom. One approach that does this is the **sociology of everyday life**, which is interested in how people engage with pre-existing social structures in both regulated and creative ways (de Certeau, 1984). But in doing so, it tends to erect a boundary between the 'structural' and the 'everyday', whereas in Chapter 4 it was argued that a relational approach to self and society tries to do away with such boundaries. This is why I also draw on the **sociology of personal life,** which understands human life as comprising interconnected spheres, and selves as connected to other people as well as culturally and socially embedded (Smart, 2007). The chapter ends with a discussion of why it is important to keep the embodied dimension of everyday life in focus.

Phenomenology

Phenomenology is interested in the relationship between the person and the world, seeing the two as existing in a reciprocal relationship. Heidegger ([1926]1962), the 'father' of phenomenology, developed the concept of 'being-in-the-world'. He argued that the notion of 'being', or 'the fact that things exist at all', is a key, taken-for-granted aspect of life (Relph, 1985: 16). Laing (1965: 19) noted that we tend to have a sense of this totality in our everyday lives, while it is only through existential thought that we can begin to comprehend our being-in-the-world.

In going about our everyday lives, we try to make sense of the world around us and develop a meaningful understanding of it. We tend to view the world as something that *is*, as 'completely constituted, to be taken for granted' (Schutz, [1932]1967: 36). Similarly, we tend to view objects and actions as inherently meaningful – as opposed to something we give meaning to. This is what Schutz calls our 'natural attitude'. Yet the world is never complete but constantly emerging and reconstituted through this very act of giving meaning to it (note the similarities with ethnomethodology, discussed in Chapter 4). In addition, experiences do not *have* meaning in and of themselves; 'meaning does not lie *in* the experience' (Schutz ([1932]1967: 69–70). Instead, experiences only become meaningful when we reflect upon them and *give them meaning*. Thus, we *make* the world meaningful to us, yet because we do so from within our 'natural attitude', we are not aware of this process. Schutz says that it requires effort to 'bracket' our natural attitude and turn our attention to how we 'make' the world.

Smith (1987: 118, 123–4) emphasizes that people work together 'in concrete actual situations' to reach a shared understanding of social reality through a 'concerting or coordination of activities'. When giving meaning to things and events, this meaning does not emerge from within us, but is constructed in interaction with others. We share a common environment to which we attribute shared meaning. Thus, an object with four legs and a seat only becomes a chair when it is named as such and when we develop a shared understanding of this object as something we can sit on:

> The social construction of reality is precisely that of creating a world we have in common. It is the work of continually accomplishing a world that does exist as a reality that is the same for me as it is for you. Where you see chair, I see chair. Or if I do not recognize that strange humpy lumpy object as a chair, you tell me 'that's a chair' and I know then how it works as an object coming to hand or rather to seat ... Its capacity as chair arises as you announce its social organization, and we both then know how to enter it into the concerting of our joint work of having a cup of coffee and a conversation together. (Smith, 1987: 125–6)

We use these shared understandings to categorize things, events and people and to make sense of what is going on around us. Think, for example, of how you know the difference between a wedding and a funeral. You may use what people are wearing, their facial expressions and the type of music that is playing as clues to what is going on and how you are expected to behave. After identifying a situation as a funeral, you are likely to modify your behaviour accordingly by not appearing too jolly. What is important is that the other people attending the same event are likely to reach a similar conclusion and coordinate their activities accordingly. Such acts of interpretation are based on our past experiences, which constitute our stock of knowledge of the world, how it is ordered and how things function. We use this stock of knowledge or 'what we know' to make sense of the here and now (Schutz, [1932]1967: 81–2, 84). Schutz (1964: 73) also called this the 'stock of recipes' or 'cookbook knowledge' that we use to 'deal with the routine matters of daily life'. These 'schemes of interpretation', which are handed down to us 'by ancestors, teachers and authorities' and learned through experience, operate, in effect, like guides to situations (Schutz, 1964: 78, 95). With the help of such 'stocks of recipes', we are able to interpret a social situation on the basis of its 'key ingredients', such as who we are interacting with and in what kind of space, as in the funeral example.

Our schemes of interpretation are so ingrained in us that they feel 'natural'. We come to think of many aspects of social reality as 'this is just how things are' without realizing the *social* origins of our particular view of that reality (see Bourdieu's 'genesis amnesia' in Chapter 4). However, the socially constructed nature of reality becomes more apparent if we look back in time and notice that the meanings that are attached to experiences shift across time and cultures. For example, what 'family' means has changed considerably over the past few centuries. Yet, in any historical period, people will think that their understanding of 'family' is just how things are – 'this is what family *is*' rather than 'this is what family is understood to be in my culture'.

In going about our everyday business, we rely on the familiarity of things and our ability to take the world for granted. Many of us take it for granted that everyone around us will understand what our gender is, or that strangers in the street will not engage us in lengthy conversation. These unwritten 'rules' for how the world should work rarely enter into our conscious mind but they bring stability and predictability to social interactions, because they enable people 'to recognize each other's actions, beliefs, aspirations, feelings, and the like as reasonable, normal, legitimate, understandable, and realistic' (Garfinkel, 1967: 173). It is these taken-for-granted and therefore unnoticed aspects of social reality that phenomenology is particularly interested in examining.

An everyday world structured by power relations

Our everyday lives take place within broader social, economic and political processes, yet phenomenology has been critiqued for not taking these power relations into account (Tilley, 1994: 26). To develop a critical understanding of the everyday, it is not enough to merely observe and describe what people do, because people's actions are not independent of the wider sociohistorical setting and must therefore be interpreted in light of the asymmetrical power relations of which they are part (Gardiner, 2000: 7). The shared understandings that people operate under are not neutral, rather they reflect the power relations they are the product of. This is because dominant groups in society have more power in terms of defining social reality and to have their definition stick – in other words, these groups are the ones who are more likely to define the discourses that constitute our view of the world (Foucault, 1977). Bourdieu (1979) defined this capacity to shape how the world is understood as 'symbolic capital': some social groups have more influence over, for example, what is considered 'good taste'.

In other words, the everyday world 'cannot be accepted as simply "at hand" without need of any further explanation' (Schutz, [1932]1967: 222). As Felski (2002: 617) notes, we should not adopt a 'wide-eyed acceptance of what is, nor to treat the everyday as a transparent or self-evident category'. There is a need to problematize everyday life, 'to expose its contradictions ... and to raise our understanding of the prosaic to the level of critical knowledge' (Gardiner, 2000: 6). We should be careful, however, not to assume that 'ordinary' people are 'cultural dopes' (Gardiner, 2000: 7) or 'naive, credulous, and blinded by ideology', nor that theorists are the only ones who are 'able to see things as they really are' (Felski, 2002: 617).

A key theorist of the everyday is Dorothy E. Smith (1987), much of whose work has centred around the issue of how sociologists produce knowledge, in other words, **epistemology**. Smith was one of the early 'standpoint feminists', whose criticism against traditional 'malestream' sociology was that it created abstractions that were far removed from how people lived their everyday lives, and that it excluded and marginalized women's experiences (Griffiths, 1995; Gardiner, 2000). This was because the producers of such knowledge, that is, men, assumed that others are much like themselves, but the end result was the creation of knowledge that was 'systematically exclusionary and distorting' (Gardiner, 2000: 184). Smith wanted to create instead a 'sociology for women' to redress this imbalance. In her view, it matters whose viewpoints gain precedence in the creation of knowledge because knowledge and power are closely connected. In addition, she proposed that although it is now commonplace to believe that 'experts' have access to 'the truth' and create knowledge that is 'objective', there is no such thing as a definitive or value-free account of social reality. All accounts 'must rely on a process of creative interpretation, by which we exclude certain factors, highlight others, and use rhetorical figures or tropes to authorize a given version of events' that is based on a particular framework of understanding the social world (Gardiner, 2000: 186–7). All accounts are, therefore, only partial and reflect a particular standpoint.

Smith proposed that it is important to understand the social world from the standpoint of different individuals (Griffiths, 1995: 59–60), and argued that viewing the world from the standpoint of women brought to light the existing 'relations of ruling', namely that the world is dominated by patriarchal and capitalist forces, which marginalize women's experiences. Because of their position within these relations of ruling, women have a bifurcated (divided) consciousness, whereby they are able to understand both the 'dominant' masculine form of knowledge and their own experiences as differing from this.

The irony is that Smith tended to discuss 'women' as one homogeneous group united by their shared gender, thus making the same mistake as 'male-stream' theory by assuming that the experiences of all women were similar to their own (Griffiths, 1995). Spivak criticized Western feminists for having ignored 'the specific social, cultural and historical circumstances of non-Western women's lives' and thereby denying the subjectivity of poor women living in the global South (Morton, 2007: 124, 138). Theorists such as bell hooks (1981) and Patricia Hill Collins (1990) have argued that the experiences of black and ethnic minority women diverged from those of white women, and called for a more nuanced understanding of how gender was inextricably linked to 'race' and ethnicity. The notion of 'intersectionality' (Crenshaw, 1991) was developed as a means of examining how these and other categories intersect in complex ways, such that, for example, a black working-class woman might feel that she has more in common with a black working-class man, who is similarly oppressed in terms of class and 'race', than she does with a middle-class white woman.

As noted in Chapter 1, these intersectional theories of identity are some-what unsatisfactory because they still operate on a logic that 'flattens' people into two-dimensional beings who are defined by their membership in identity categories, whereas the concept of belonging allows us to view people as having multiple and, at times, contradictory embodied connections with cultures, people, places and objects.

I now explore in more depth Smith's book *The Everyday World as Problematic* (1987), where she first developed in full her sociology of the everyday. She urged sociologists to go beyond surface descriptions of everyday practices to examine the underlying power structures and to 'critique existing social arrangements with an eye to transforming them' (Gardiner, 2000: 198). Smith (1987: 90) argued that in such surface descriptions, everyday life becomes divorced from the broader social relations that organize it and social structures become depicted as external 'things' that 'erupt' into people's lives, as though 'the two somehow existed alongside one another, largely independent except for occasional collisions'. Such an approach obscures the ways in which the everyday world is shaped by 'an *organization of social relations* that originate "elsewhere"' (Smith, 1987: 92, emphases added) and that are beyond the power and control of most people. So, although any sociological enquiry ought to begin from people's everyday experiences, this is not where it should remain, because the 'inner determinations' of the everyday 'are not discoverable within it' (Smith, 1987: 91).

In essence, Smith is saying that our lives are structured not by 'things' but by social relations beyond our immediate experience. Events seemingly intrude into people's lives, yet people are rarely aware of the origin of these events. For example, on the local level, we may notice old buildings being demolished and new ones being built, or jobs being lost. These locally visible developments are, however, the result of broader social processes, such as changes in the labour market brought on by globalization. Many aspects of our everyday worlds, such as our role as customers in supermarkets or the social organization of restaurants and cafés, are, in fact, the 'locally organized constituents of' the social relations of capitalism or the market (Smith, 1987: 158).

For Smith, it was important that sociologists 'begin with individuals as active subjects, engaged pragmatically in an endless series of everyday projects and accomplishments' and view people 'not only as "knowers", but as "doers", as skilled and accomplished members in tandem with others' who 'co-participate in the construction of a shared lifeworld' (Gardiner, 2000: 203). In other words, the patterning of life, that is, social order and social structures that shape our lives, does not come out of nowhere. Thus, although people's lives are shaped by processes external to their everyday world, these processes do not take place in some abstract level of 'society' or 'structure'. *All* processes take place *somewhere*, within the everyday world of somebody (Smith, 1987: 94). They are instigated by someone, involving social relations and the coordination of activities and meanings in concrete actual situations.

By focusing on the everyday world as a problematic, we begin to see the relationship between the 'microsociological' level of everyday life and the 'macrosociological' level of 'social structures' and 'society' (Smith, 1987: 99). The things that people do in their everyday lives (the micro-scale) relate to and are shaped by broader, macro-level patterns (Scott, 2009: 1) and vice versa. A sociology of everyday life 'seeks to relate the particular to the general, locate the concrete in the universal, and to grasp the wider sociohistorical context within which everyday practices are necessarily inscribed' (Gardiner, 2000: 208). Thus, when trying to understand the relationship between self and society, one of the best places to start is in everyday life. Green (2004: 50) argues, however, that because Smith begins with the micro-level of individual experience, she is not able to provide an accurate enough picture of the aggregate. For example, Smith cannot show whether most women do, in fact, have a bifurcated consciousness. It is for this reason that sociology cannot remain at the micro-level, but must also aim to understand aggregate developments, that is, the 'bigger picture'.

Sociology of everyday life

The category of the everyday is notoriously difficult to define because it 'is itself an unstable and difficult construct, which refers variously to a sphere of activity, a mode of temporality, or a mode of knowing or dealing with the world' (Frow, 2002: 630). One way of defining the everyday is as the routine and bodily praxis that is 'left over' beyond the 'superior' pursuits of politics, arts and science (Gardiner, 2000: 11). For Lefebvre ([1947]1991), the everyday was a somehow untouched 'natural' sphere where people can be 'real' and 'true', unsullied by (bourgeois) power and ideology (a notion that will be critiqued below). The aim of many theorists of the everyday has been to explore the everyday as a source for opposition towards the forces of capitalism, markets and the media.

A sociology of everyday life considers everyday life 'worthy of intensive study in its own right' (Gardiner, 2000: 207–8). The focus lies on apparently mundane practices and events, which allows us to appreciate how complex the minutiae of lived social relations are. Such an approach enables us to move away from such 'static sociological abstractions as "roles" or "structures"' and 'celebrates the intrinsic but oft-hidden promises and possibilities of ordinary human beings and the inherent value of commonsensical forms of thought' (Gardiner, 2000: 208).

Gardiner (2000) identifies two traditions within such everyday life studies: the first approach is based on the phenomenological and pragmatist traditions, drawing heavily on the work of theorists such as Schutz, Mead, Goffman and Garfinkel, who share the starting point that:

> investigators of the social world must articulate an interpretive understanding of how actors develop an 'insider's knowledge' of particular social processes and utilize this so as to act in a voluntaristic and creative fashion. (Gardiner, 2000: 231)

Borrowing from Garfinkel (1967), whose ethnomethodology was discussed in Chapter 4, Susie Scott (2009: 5) argues that it is important to make the familiar strange by 'bracketing out our prior assumptions about what is normal, natural and inevitable' in order to see familiar settings in a new light and to understand 'what lies beneath' seemingly innocuous social behaviour. Thus, studying the everyday means challenging taken-for-granted assumptions about the world. Sociologists studying the everyday tend to be interested in rules, routines and regular behaviours, which again means 'going beyond the surface of the immediately observable, digging deeper to identify the meanings behind it' (Scott, 2009: 5).

The second tradition within sociology of everyday life is a Marxist approach with political and emancipatory goals, such as the work of Lefebvre. In *The Critique of Everyday Life* ([1947]1991), Lefebvre was optimistic about the potential for transformation by noting that a Marxist analysis of everyday life could indicate 'what is possible' in terms of improving the quality of human life and bringing an end to alienation. But in later work he became less optimistic, 'stressing the recalcitrance of everyday life to revolutionary change and its susceptibility to bureaucratic restructuring' (Gardiner, 2000: 74).

I now discuss three aspects of everyday life that have been identified as worthy of study: first, the way in which the everyday world envelops both the 'official' and 'unofficial' spheres; second, how both the ordinary and the extraordinary are possible in the everyday; and third, everyday life as the site of possible change.

Different spheres?

There is a tendency to see 'the unofficial' or 'everyday' sphere as separate from 'the official' sphere. For example, Lefebvre distinguished between the everyday and the bureaucratic state apparatus, a division that, according to him, was the result of capitalism, which had led to a differentiation of social activities, such as the separation of family life and leisure from work (Silverstone, 2002: 766). Consequently, the self is now split between a public and a private self, while everyday life becomes a question of unconscious actions as human creativity is 'transformed into routinized and commodified forms' (Gardiner, 2000: 76). Lefebvre identified the centralized state, which in his mind caused 'human powers and capacities' to be 'increasingly transferred to an anonymous, bureaucratic apparatus', as key to this alienation (Gardiner, 2000: 77). Everyday life, where people experience the contradiction between these repressive qualities of modern society and 'genuine intersubjective community', offers a potential locus for transformation (Gardiner, 2000: 77).

Lefebvre thus posited the everyday as the site for 'emancipatory moments' that allow us to 'subvert the total commodification and homogenization of experience' through 'passion, non-logicality and the imaginary' that breach 'the utilitarian greyness of official society, overshadowed as it is by the logic of the commodity-form and an ethos of productivism' (Gardiner, 2000: 15). Silverstone (2002: 763) depicts the everyday as:

> a site for the toleration, indeed celebration, of ambiguity: a site for creativity and the transcendence – playful, political, or otherwise – of the constraints imposed by an increasingly dominant and strategic system of technological rationality, administrative order, and capitalist commodification.

In other words, Lefebvre offers the possibility of 'de-alienation' in the form of an emancipatory project that would liberate people from bourgeois ideology (Gardiner, 2000: 78).

Yet, such distinctions between 'official' and 'unofficial' spheres are unhelpful because they set up other oppositional categories such as 'private' and 'public', whereas in practice the boundaries between these are blurred (Edwards, 2011; Southerton, 2011; May, 2011c). As Burkitt (2004: 212) notes, it is important to remember that social structures do not exist over and above individuals. Although 'society' and 'individual' may feel like two separate entities (cf. Simmel, 1971a), these two spheres, which Burkitt terms the 'official' and the 'unofficial', are in fact interdependent and permeable, each affected by the other. Official rules establish codes of conduct and thereby affect how we act in our everyday lives. But our unofficial actions and expressed thoughts also exert a pressure on official rules, which, although they feel permanent, are, in fact, constantly albeit slowly changing. Thus, it is unwise for social scientists to present these as two distinctly different spheres.

Lefebvre has been critiqued for misleadingly depicting the everyday as a unified whole. Everyday practices occur in the context of dominant institutions, yet have no institution to represent them (de Quieroz, 1989). They are not organized wholes but repetitive fragments. In other words, there is no homogeneous set of everyday practices, nor a totality, and although they may in many ways resist dominant norms and power structures, they do not constitute a unified counter-culture nor a doctrine of change.

A detour into the sociology of personal life

As discussed above, the sociology of everyday life has been critiqued for separating the everyday and social structures. As a way of bridging this gap, I borrow conceptual tools from the sociology of personal life as developed by Carol Smart (2007). The term 'personal', which Smart (2007: 28) uses instead of the more atomistic 'individual', highlights the connectedness and social embeddedness of people's lives. Furthermore, Smart proposes that because memory and cultural transmission play an important part in our lives, people can be understood as 'embedded in both sedimented structures and the imaginary' (Smart, 2007: 29). This allows us to capture the role that 'traditions' and 'social structures', on the one hand, and creativity, on the other, play in people's lives. The sociology of personal life shares this interest in the role that both the fixed and the dynamic play in our lives with the sociology of everyday life, but helps us overcome the distinction between 'the unofficial' and 'the official' spheres that the sociology of everyday life somewhat unhelpfully erects. Personal life does not take place at only one level, but is 'lived in many different places and spaces ... and it forms a range of connections' (Smart, 2007: 29).

As discussed above, the boundary between private and public spheres is blurred. Personal life is not only shaped by but also shapes the public sphere. As individuals begin to behave differently in their everyday lives, this has an impact on the aggregate and on the public sphere (May, 2011b). For example, various social movements, such as the women's liberation movement, the civil rights movement and the gay liberation movement, have had a significant impact on legislation, which, in turn, has impacted personal life (Edwards, 2011). Therefore, a sociology of personal life does not merely concern itself with intimate relationships and 'the private', but is also interested in the intersection of a multitude of spheres as they come together in personal life. It not only examines the experiences of individuals, but also individual experiences in the aggregate, that is, collective behaviour and social structures. In addition, a personal life approach means examining life projects, and is therefore able to portray a sense of motion in people's lives, brought about by events such as unemployment or processes such as ageing that transform our lives (May, 2011b). A sociology of personal life is attuned to the dynamics of change, which means that it lends itself well to the study of social change.

The extraordinary everyday

The second aspect of the everyday that warrants attention is the fact that it comprises the ordinary, mundane and the routine, but also the extraordinary. This line of argument is inspired by the work of de Certeau (1984), who argued for a focus on the daily activities of people rather than on 'iconic' historical moments. According to de Certeau, the everyday is best viewed as actively constructed and produced. The everyday is made up of the ordinary, mundane, customary and commonplace things we take for granted and that often remain unnoticed. An interest in the everyday therefore means focusing on that which is familiar and habitual, and a mode of consciousness that is distracted (Harrison, 2000: 497; Felski, 2002: 607). Chapter 6 discusses how belonging, because it is based on habit and familiarity, can be seen as one such distracted mode of being in the world.

The everyday tends to be seen as the opposite to the exceptional or unusual, the events that disrupt the 'normal' running of things and because of their rarity become highly visible (Sandywell, 2004: 162). The relationship between the ordinary and extraordinary aspects of life is indeed one of the key foci of the sociology of everyday life. Lefebvre ([1947]1991), for example, points out the dangers of the mundaneness of everyday life, because it dulls the mind and pacifies people to the extent that they do not revolt against injustices.

There are, however, those who criticize such distinctions between the everyday and the extraordinary, arguing that these do not exist as two distinct and oppositional spheres (Felski, 2000; Frow, 2002). Sandywell (2004: 165, 174) argues that this dichotomy presents the everyday as ahistoric and static, while Ries (2002) notes that the extraordinary exists within the everyday. Everyday life encompasses both routine repetition of past behaviours as well as creative actions that help change what is regarded as 'commonplace' (McCracken, 2002: 147). Ries (2002: 733) proposes that even ritual, 'that realm of the extraordinary, liminal, upside-down, carnivalesque, transcendent – in fact enshrines nothing as much as the local practices of the everyday'. For example, in ritual celebrations such as Christmas or Diwali, the thing that many people fixate on is not so much the extraordinary (such as fireworks) but food – and in this way 'ritual celebrates everyday practices and values' (Ries, 2002: 733).

As mentioned above, the everyday is equated with the things we do routinely, the things we hardly pay any attention to yet which constitute the very fabric of our being. It is through repetition that an activity becomes routine, and in becoming routine, no longer needs to command our full attention:

> often as not, it will be something closer to inattention and distraction that will characterize the experience of routine. Indeed it would be precisely when an activity *becomes routine* for someone, that levels of concentration can be relaxed, allowing room for attention to be diverted to other things. (Highmore, 2004: 309)

Our daily lives are filled with routines: getting dressed, brushing our teeth, commuting to work, shopping, preparing and eating food, doing the washing, cleaning and so on. Disparaging statements about the dulling effects of mundane, everyday routine have a gendered element to them, as women are seen to be particularly 'weighed down' by routine – the routine of domestic housework for example (Felski, 2002: 613):

> It is women above all who embody repetitive time, whether equated with the mindless instinctual rhythms of biological life or the standardized

soul-destroying routines of capitalism. Repetition is seen as a threat to the modern project of self-creation and self-determination, subordinating individual will to an imposed pattern. And yet repetition is clearly vital to psychological development as well as the sense-making patterns of culture. (Felski, 2002: 613)

Routine can be experienced as draining and repressive but can also 'strengthen, comfort and provide meaning' and be creative (Felski, 2002: 28). Highmore (2004: 311) notes that 'routine can be experienced simultaneously as joyous and tedious, tender and frustrating'. Although everyday tasks may often seem mundane or banal, they can also offer 'enchanting encounters that work to provide creativity, emotional attachments, and prosaic pleasures' (Bhatti et al., 2009: 62), which can transform how we see the world and can therefore be a source of inventiveness, as discussed below.

The potential for change

The third aspect of the everyday that makes it of interest to sociologists is that it is in the ordinary and the extraordinary of everyday life that social change is made possible.

Everyday life is not a static or ahistoric finished product but is emergent, something that is forever fluid, dynamic, in the making and 'almost-not-quite' (Smith, 1987: 126–7; Harrison, 2000: 501; Sandywell, 2004: 165). Such an understanding of everyday life allows us to view social change not simply as a top-down process generated by 'extraordinary' events but as something that also results from our mundane 'ordinary' activities (de Certeau, 1984). Gardiner (2000: 19) argues that we can find 'embryonic forms of transformative social change within the hidden recesses of everyday life itself', especially in those moments when people become consciously aware of 'the ossified and reified structures of modern society'. Whereas ordinarily people take the world for granted, in such moments they problematize these taken-for-granted assumptions and 'thereby subvert the ideological and bureaucratic structuring of everyday life' (Gardiner, 2000: 19). This is because they 'can no longer rely on commonsensical notions and typified behavioural responses', but instead have to critically examine 'prevailing traditions and received ideas', which then makes them more receptive to 'alternative modes of being' (Gardiner, 2000: 20).

As Felski notes, de Certeau, rather than denigrating the everyday, points to its subversive potential to offer resistance to 'strategies of power':

> The quotidian is prized insofar as it resists the imposition of order, repetition, coherence; de Certeau writes of microresistances, clandestine creativity, evasions of the law, inventive ruses and subterranean refusals. (Felski, 2002: 612)

De Certeau distinguished between 'strategies' and 'tactics'. Strategies are undertaken by those with power, through which they 'seek to colonize a visible, specific space that will serve as a "home base" for the exercise of power and domination', while tactics are undertaken by those without power, and 'are dispersed, hidden and ephemeral, and improvised in response to the concrete demands of the situation at hand' (Gardiner, 2000: 172). Everyday life thus offers the possibility of resistance, partly 'because its very presence is not always registered by the panoptic gaze of bureaucratic power' and because its very 'messiness' means that it is unsystematic and unpredictable, which allows it to escape the grasp of the rational, bureaucratic sphere (Gardiner, 2000: 16). De Certeau therefore argued that we are not powerless – our room for manoeuvre is admittedly limited, but we do have creative ways of circumventing the system (Gardiner, 2000: 170).

McCracken (2002: 163) urges us to 'appreciate the everyday as the threshold between the ordinary and the extraordinary, between what is and what might be', while Gardiner (2000: 208) encourages researchers to remain 'attuned to the transgressive, sensual and incandescent qualities of everyday existence'. Others have also identified the creative potential of everyday life that contains 'subtle moments of creativity and festivity' (Rooke, 2007: 234), wherein lies the 'potential for things to be otherwise' (Harrison, 2000: 510).

Such tributes to everyday life run the risk of romanticizing it. Silverstone (2002: 764) reminds us that everyday life is not the haven that some propose it is: 'Everyday life is tough for most people most of the time.' The ambiguity offered by everyday life is not always a comfort but can be experienced as a threat 'in the material struggles of the everyday', where people 'battle against uncertainty and for clarity and confidence in the conduct of daily existence' (Silverstone, 2002: 763–4).

The mindful body

An important aspect of everyday life that has not been discussed in any depth so far is our bodily experience of it. For example, the phenomenological approach has been critiqued for its focus on the 'conceptual abstracted world' and for taking the material organization of the world for granted (Smith, 1987: 86). Smith (1987: 87, 89) argues that we must begin in the material world, which is 'where people are in the world' and therefore 'where knowledge must begin'. Our everyday life is multisensory and multidimensional, and always situated in space (Rodaway, 1994: 4). Everyday life is therefore always embodied, 'grounded in bodily experience and sensibility' (Silverstone, 2002: 764) and has its own particular (and familiar) smells, tastes and textures. This is why in theorizing everyday life, sociologists must pay attention to 'the sensate', that is, our embodied forms of knowing the world that are, to some degree, 'distracted' or 'on the edge of semantic availability' (Harrison, 2000: 499). I devote the rest of this chapter to exploring our bodily interactions with and embodied knowledge of the world.

Western thought has long been influenced by René Descartes's theory that the mind and body are two separate entities, with the mind (or soul) being able to exist even after the body perishes. This notion of a mind–body separation – otherwise also known as **Cartesian dualism** – has been challenged by many philosophers and social scientists. One theorist who has had a great impact on how contemporary sociologists view the body is the French phenomenological philosopher Maurice Merleau-Ponty. He argued that the body is not merely an object, but an affective subject (Merleau-Ponty, [1945]2002). This means that the body knows itself and the world through an active, embodied and reflexive engagement. In other words, we understand with our body as well as with our mind. Indeed, Grange (1985: 72) prefers to speak of 'flesh' rather than 'body' in order to highlight that our 'bodies' are living, not dead, and more than just density and mass. Flesh registers the environment through the various senses, it feels the world. The senses provide us with information about our environment on which we base our understanding of the world.

In other words, our consciousness or mind is not disembodied and does not exist separate from the body, contrary to what Descartes claimed. Burkitt (1999: 12) proposes that we are bodies of thought and that the mind – our perceptions, thoughts and feelings – can be seen as *produced by* our 'bodily action in the world'. We do not perceive the world 'from nowhere' but from within our bodies, the particularities of which shape our perspective. Take, for example, our sight. Our posture as upright animals with eyes at the front of our head means that the space in front of us dominates our consciousness (while our head conceals half of our environment), and we view the world in terms of horizontal-vertical (Grange, 1985: 72). In addition, the structure of the human eye determines which parts of the colour spectrum we can see (Lakoff and Johnson, 1999). Thus, our physical characteristics in part help shape *how* we perceive the visual world and *what* we perceive, and consequently what we make of our surroundings.

Gibson (1979: 111–12) also notes that each person has a field of view that is specific to them, and the nose, lips and cheek are part of this, as are other parts of the body such as arms, legs and belly. Any information we have about the environment 'is accompanied by information to specify the observer himself [sic], his body, legs, hands, and mouth', meaning that our perception of the external world is accompanied by self-perception, because 'to perceive the world is to co-perceive oneself' (Gibson, 1979: 141). In other words, whenever we perceive the world, we are also perceiving ourselves as part of it. Consequently, there is no mind–matter or mind–body dualism because the world and our perception of it are not separable.

Perceiving is thus both a physical and a mental act, entailing the reception of information and mental insight (Rodaway, 1994: 10–11). The body is not merely an object, but an intelligent, understanding being who acts skilfully and meaningfully (Crossley, 1995). A good example of this is driving a car. When we first learn to drive, we have to *think* hard about what we are doing: to work both the accelerator and the clutch not too much but enough, to press the clutch down while changing gear, to keep glancing at the rear-view mirror and wing mirrors, and so on. As time goes on, this knowledge of how to drive a car becomes *embodied*, part of our bodily memory and skill. And almost without noticing it, driving a car becomes something we can do without having to consciously think about how exactly we do it. We put the key in the ignition, turn it, and off we go. The important point to take from this is that our embodied ways of being are also a way of understanding the world. Bourdieu (1977) termed this our 'practical' knowledge of the world.

Haptic perception

If we experience the world through our bodies, then the senses are an important part of our 'being in the world'. Generally, the different senses – vision, hearing, taste, smell and touch – are considered as separate forms of perception, although, in reality, they interact, such that our perception of the world involves our whole body. The last remaining perceptual system, touch, has been called **haptic perception**, the original meaning of which is 'sense of touch'. In his definition of 'the haptic system' of perception, Gibson (1966: 99) included not only the skin that feels but the 'whole body, most of its parts and all of its surface':

> The haptic system, then, is an apparatus by which the individual gets information about both the environment and his [sic] body. He feels an object relative to the body and the body relative to an object. It is the perceptual system by which animals and men are literally in touch with the environment. (Gibson, 1966: 97)

Rodaway (1994: 41) refers to Gibson's haptic system when he talks of haptic or touch geographies that arise 'out of the tactile receptivity of the body, specifically the skin, and are closely linked to the ability of the body to move through the environment and pick up and manipulate objects'. The meaning of 'haptic perception' has been extended by Bruno (2002) to incorporate not only touch but also the other senses. In this understanding, haptic perception is sensory perception that involves the whole body and has been called 'a holistic way of understanding three-dimensional space' by O'Neill (2001: 3). It is important to view perception in this manner because it entails not merely the reception of a single stimulus from one source but is multisensual, such that the different perceptual senses interact (Rodaway, 1994: 11). We see, hear and smell things simultaneously and all this input goes towards our perception of an object or event.

It is by coming into embodied contact with people and things through 'touch, positional awareness, balance, sound, movement, and the memory of previous experiences' (O'Neill, 2001: 4) that we make sense of the context within which we live (Bruno, 2002: 253–4). The perceptual system is active: looking, listening, touching, smelling and tasting are more than just motor responses to sensory input, they are five modes of overt attention (Gibson, 1979: 244). We know our environment on the basis of our embodied movement through it:

> We know landscapes, in other words, because we go hiking in the mountains, because we drive through streets on the way to work, because we encounter landscapes continually in the course of going about our daily affairs. We know them because they reveal the state of the weather and the passage of the seasons, because they harbour the places of our memories, because they are the visible matrix of where we live. (Relph, 1985: 24)

Chapter 9 explores in more detail the role our sensory experience of the world plays in our sense of belonging.

Learning how to perceive

The world as we know it is not pre-given, but is the product of repeated embodied action (Varela, 1991: 172–3). Our perception involves innate elements (the basics of the fact that we can see, touch, hear and so on), but also learned elements (Gibson, 1966: 268; Rodaway, 1994: 11). This means that how and what we perceive is affected both by our physical senses and our individual training and cultural conditioning. As children grow up, their 'attention becomes educated to the subtleties of stimulus information' and they learn to perceive in particular ways, and this perception improves with experience (Gibson, 1966: 5–6, 269–70). In other words, our senses are not unmediated but socially shaped through cultural repertoires (Degen, 2008: 40). People from different backgrounds are likely to perceive and value their perceptions differently. We perceive through a 'cultural filter' that:

> reflects the shared values and taken-for-granted practices of a specific society (or sub-group within a society). In other words, we see, hear, smell, taste and touch the world through the mediation, the filter or lens, of our social milieu, the context within which we have become socialised, educated and familiarised. Even within one society, there are various subsidiary filters associated with the individual's socio-economic status, education, age and gender. Thus, the cultural perspective reminds us that perception is more qualitatively variable and creative than mechanistic stimulus-response models might suggest. (Rodaway, 1994: 23)

As children, we learn these perceptual priorities, that is, culturally accepted ways of looking, listening, smelling and touching that guide us to notice certain things and not others (O'Neill, 2001; Desjarlais, 2003). We have active perception, which means that we do not notice everything we perceive in terms of stimuli but notice what we orient ourselves towards (Gibson, 1979: 57). In other words, there is no 'pure' embodied experience somehow untouched by social conventions or social shaping (Young, 2005: 8). Thus, it is important not to lose sight of the social origins of our embodied being-in-the-world.

Tacit knowledge

Much of this sensory and embodied knowledge we have of the world cannot necessarily be expressed in words. We have both a cognitive and a precognitive experience of our surroundings and our tacit awareness of the environment precedes words (Gibson, 1979: 260–1). This means that our knowledge is, to a degree, unselfconscious and intuitive; we perceive more than we say.

Our action is, to a large degree, based on this tacit knowledge. For example, we might not be able to verbalize *how* we know that a table exists, or what a table *is*, but our knowledge is expressed in our actions of using a table as a table (Harrison, 2000). Felski (2002: 615–16) describes this as 'know-how', an instinctual way of knowing the world that we practise habitually, without much conscious thought. We have, for example, the know-how to catch a ball that is thrown towards us or to merge with traffic while driving a car. In fact, thinking about what we are about to do may, in such instances, impede the successful completion of our task – if we think too hard about catching a ball, we are more likely to fumble our catch.

As I argue in more detail in Chapter 6, this kind of unconscious knowledge of how the everyday world works plays an important role in our sense of belonging. It is when we can go about our daily tasks and interact with people without having to consciously think too much about it that many of us experience a sense of belonging. This tacit knowledge might become explicit if something changes in our surroundings. We might start to notice what we previously took for granted: that this place usually smells a particular way, that a building used to be there, or that the people who frequent our usual hangouts seem 'different' somehow. It is at this point, when we become consciously aware of a change in our surroundings, that we must start to rebuild our embodied knowledge of the world and adapt our embodied being to this change. In other words, we try to create a new sense of belonging. As noted above, many of these changes in our environment are linked to broader social changes, which is why a focus on people's changing experiences of belonging is a good way to study social change from the perspective of the person.

Conclusion

So far, we have established that self and society are mutually constitutive and interlinked – changes in one lead to changes in the other. This chapter has explored how a phenomenological approach might help us understand this link better, by focusing on the making of social reality, how it is constituted in the everyday rather than a given. This necessitates a sociology that begins in the everyday experiences of people, and that does not take these experiences as given, but understands them as embedded in and structured by relations of ruling that are not always immediately visible. It is also important to keep in mind that these experiences are embodied, but also that how we perceive the world is socially shaped.

What is still missing from the picture is a concept that captures this complexity. In Part 2, I argue that belonging is such a concept, because it enables an examination of the interlinked nature of self and society. In addition, belonging is a multifaceted and dynamic concept that allows us to explore the different aspects of human experience (cultural, relational and embodied) and the changes that occur in these. Part 2 is devoted to examining the different dimensions of the concept of belonging and the ways in which it captures the complex and dynamic connections between self and society.

Part 2

Self, Belonging and Social Change

Belonging: A Window into Social Change

Introduction

Part 1 examined different ways in which sociologists have explained social change and the impact it has on the self. Chapters 2 and 3 explored some rather pessimistic accounts of the effects that social changes – industrialization, urbanization, the rise of consumer culture and globalization – over the past 200 years or so have had on people's sense of self and community, and on social cohesion. According to the psychosocial fragmentation thesis, for example, people have become isolated, narcissistic and vulnerable, left to drift on their own without the safe framework of traditions to guide them or a sense of solidarity that would keep them connected to others. The individualization thesis claims the opposite: that the loosening of traditions has meant that we are now free to reflexively craft our own lives, that we now have the chance to be emancipated.

Both theses have been criticized for offering a somewhat static notion of past societies, as well as for depicting self and society as two separate entities. In addition, I have argued that the individualization and psychosocial fragmentation theses start from social change, and make claims about the harmful or liberating effects this has had on individuals, thus privileging the social. To rectify the last two points, Chapter 4 presented relational theories that focus on the relationship between society and self. I explored Cooley's (1902) and Mead's (1934) relational theories of the self, as well as the relational accounts of society offered by Simmel (1950) and Elias (1991). Garfinkel's (1967) portrayal of how this relational society emerges in everyday interaction, and Goffman's theory (1959) of how the relational self interacts with others were also examined.

Chapter 5 went in search of further conceptual tools that allow for a sociological study of the relationship between self and society that begins from the point of view of the person, turning to phenomenology, the sociology of everyday life and the sociology of personal life. Unlike the individualization and psychosocial fragmentation theses, the starting point for these approaches is that any sociological investigation must begin in the day-to-day experiences of individuals. Furthermore, these experiences cannot be taken for granted, but must be understood as embedded in broader structures of power. The important thing is that these structures of power are seen as (re-)created, challenged or discarded through human action. In other words, our everyday actions play a crucial role in (re-)creating the social and therefore in social change.

In Part 2, my aim is to convince the reader that belonging is a relational concept with the help of which social change can be studied from the perspective of everyday personal life. Belonging allows for a person-centred, dynamic and complex approach that understands people as active participants in society. This chapter begins by examining the nature of belonging and not belonging, and the significance that a sense of belonging (to a culture, a specific group of people or a place) has for our sense of self. I then explore three aspects of belonging that make it particularly suitable to the study of the interrelatedness of self and social change. First, a focus on belonging allows us to study the links between 'self' and 'society' from the point of view of the person and to examine how people engage with social structures in their everyday lives. Second, a sense of belonging is complex, encompassing our relational, cultural and sensory connections. Third, the concept of belonging lends itself well to the study of social change because a person's sense of belonging is dynamic and sensitive to change. In the ensuing discussion, examples from empirical studies on belonging from a wide range of disciplines including sociology, geography and cultural studies are offered as illustration. But first, let us consider how belonging could be defined.

Defining belonging

Although belonging is the focus of much research, few authors actually discuss at length what they mean by the concept. One exception is Linn Miller (2003), who offers one of the most comprehensive definitions of belonging. According to her, belonging is a feeling that affords 'a sense of ease or accord with who we are in-ourselves' and 'a sense of accord with the various physical and social contexts in which our lives are lived out' (Miller, 2003: 220). In other words, it is a feeling that tells us something about a person's connection to themselves and to the surrounding world of people, cultures and places. Ann Game (2001) proposes that a sense of belonging is inherently relational because it requires a mode of openness and a sense of connection with the world:

> To find our self, as we might typically say of belonging, is to find a self that is not a singular separate identity progressing through life's stages, but a self in connection. A sense of 'feeling solid within ourselves' comes with neither a turning in nor shutting out of the world, but with openness. (Game, 2001: 228)

Game's thoughts are akin to Cooley's (1902: 49–50) argument that humans have a capacity and a need for stimulus and company, which can only be set free if we communicate with other people. As he put it, alone we are like fire-works without a match, prisoners of our own trains of thought, whereas a good companion brings release and fresh activity. In a similar vein, Miller (2010: 132) and Douglas and Ney (1998) propose that communication is a basic need, and that it is therefore something we can feel bereft of.

It could be argued that belonging is an inherent capacity in people who have developed a sense of self, because this sense of self is partly based on who we feel similar to, that is, who we belong with. As Weeks (1990: 88) says: 'Identity is about belonging, about what you have in common with some people and what differentiates you from others.' Belonging is therefore not just any connection but *a particular kind of relation*, 'the sort of relation in which who and what we are is at issue' (Miller, 2003: 218). Belonging helps to make us who we are, although we are not always consciously aware of this (Miller, 2003: 217).

The above quote from Weeks also indicates that our sense of self is not only constructed in terms of similarity – it also needs an 'other' who is dissimilar to us (Hall, 1996). We know who we are partly on the basis of knowing who we are *not*. In other words, individual and collective identities are always constructed in relation to an 'other' through a process of 'othering', that is, defining a fundamental difference between self and other (Cohen, 1982a; Meinhof and Galasiński, 2005). Indeed, Cohen (1982a: 6) notes that in situations where different cultures come into contact, for example, this sense of difference is necessary if the cultures are to survive as distinct from each other. The alternative would be that the cultures merge together to become one.

This issue of drawing distinctions and boundaries, of 'othering', is a key concern in much of the sociological work on identity that has been carried out in the past few decades (Heaphy, 2007: 40). This body of work has focused on how certain identities (such as 'heterosexual') become established as the norm, while others ('homosexual') are marginalized, oppressed, excluded or silenced (for example Weeks, 1991). Identity can therefore be understood as produced through a process of categorization, that is, the drawing of boundaries between 'us' and 'them', thereby creating distinct categories of people (Hall, 1996). A focus on belonging makes it possible to interrogate how these categories operate in the everyday lives of people. For example, it is possible to explore the extent to which people utilize these categories to make sense of who they are and where they belong (May, 2010).

The need to belong

If belonging is what helps connect us to the world, and if we require this connection in order to gain a sense of self, the next logical step is to say that we have a need to belong. Indeed, there are theorists who argue this; for example, Maslow (1954) included belonging in his hierarchy of needs. The psychologists Baumeister and Leary (1995: 497) have suggested that 'human beings have a pervasive drive to form and maintain at least a minimum quantity of lasting, positive, and significant interpersonal relationships'. It is, of course, difficult to prove that such a need 'really' exists, but I propose that the fact that belonging is generally defined as something that is of crucial importance has significant consequences, because this influences how people interpret their experiences of (not) belonging. To paraphrase W.I. Thomas (1967), something that is defined as real has real consequences.

According to Miller (2003: 218, 222), we derive a sense of wellbeing from belonging, which she describes as a relation 'that is fitting, right or correct' and 'a mode or state of being that represents the ideal condition in which a human can dwell'. Game (2001: 228) portrays belonging in similar terms: 'It feels right, I belong, my body is comfortable here, it fits.' Despite the seeming importance that belonging has for wellbeing, this connection has not been researched that much. The empirical research that does exist shows that people who express a stronger sense of belonging also have better mental and physical health (Young et al., 2004; Krause and Wulff, 2005). A lack of belonging, in contrast, can lead to ill effects (Baumeister and Leary, 1995) – although we will explore not belonging in a slightly more critical fashion below.

Furthermore, Baumeister and Leary (1995) argue that belonging can be defined as a need because it is evident to some degree in all cultures. Calhoun (2003a, 2003b) also proposes that belonging to a group is a universal tendency among humans. Just as social relationships are a basic requirement to being an individual, so 'individuals exist only in cultural milieux – even if usually in several at the same time' (Calhoun, 2003a: 535). People are 'necessarily situated in particular webs of belonging' and 'it is impossible not to belong to social groups, relations, or culture' (Calhoun, 2003a: 536). This issue of belonging to culture is explored in more depth in Chapter 7.

It is worth pausing here for a while to consider the concept of 'group' more closely, because we are likely to feel different senses of belonging depending on the type of group. The feminist philosopher Morwenna Griffiths (1995) distinguishes between two kinds of groups: groups defined by social structures, such as gender, social class, ethnicity and age, and 'invisible colleges' that people form on the basis of shared values, tastes or intellectual interests. While our membership in the first type of group is to a large extent determined by whether or not we fall within a particular social category such as 'man' or 'woman', and is thus largely beyond our control, membership of an invisible college can be chosen; although, of course, 'full' membership is reliant on other members of that group accepting one as a member.

How we make connections becomes increasingly complex with age. Early on, we achieve a sense of belonging to groups such as our family or our friendship group on the basis of personal connections, but as we grow older, we are also able to develop a sense of belonging to abstract groupings, such as 'the working class' or 'feminists' (Griffiths, 1995: 87). We also have to make gradually more complex decisions about belonging as our social networks widen and we come into contact with an increasingly diverse set of people. Some groups conflict with each other and we feel we cannot be members of both (Griffiths, 1995: 88). For example, when I was in primary school, and chose woodwork over textiles, the headmaster tried to convince me that woodwork was not really what girls do and that I would feel out of place in a class consisting only of boys. The message that I got loud and clear, despite my young age, was that I could not claim to be a 'real' girl if I showed a preference for sawing blocks of wood and soldering metal rather than sewing and knitting.

On being told that I risked becoming an outcast among my peers if I made the 'wrong' choice, I switched to the textile class. My wish to hold on to my sense of belonging to my classmates and my gender can help explain why I buckled under pressure. Baumeister and Leary (1995) note that people tend to seek approval and intimacy and to resist breaking existing bonds because of this need to belong. In this way, belonging arguably directs much of our behaviour. Similarly, it could be argued that because one of the ways in which a sense belonging can be achieved is in communicating with other people, this explains the need for stimulus and company that humans exhibit (cf. Cooley, 1902; Douglas and Ney, 1998; Miller, 2010: 132). A lack of communication can be experienced as a lack of belonging.

I wish to remind the reader that whenever we speak of 'the self', this should not be understood as a monolithic whole, but rather as 'made up of a number of different, sometimes incompatible, "selves", all of which, taken together, make up the self as a whole' (Griffiths, 1995: 181). Because of this hybridity, we can and do feel a sense of belonging to several groups or communities and make use of a number of languages and discourses to understand and interpret the world, some of which are conflicting. As a consequence, it 'is not unusual for a self to be surprised by itself'.

Knowing the 'rules of the game'

As noted above, a sense of belonging is built not only on our sense of similarity with other people, but also on our sense of ease with our *social and cultural surroundings*. Bourdieu had a lot to say about this aspect of our selves, as discussed in Chapter 4. To recap briefly, Bourdieu argued that we feel at ease in places where our habitus corresponds with the social field we find ourselves in – we feel a 'sense of bodily comfort and ease' because we have a 'feel for the game': we know what to do, how and when (Bourdieu, 1977: 161, 1979: 50–1, 330; see also Fortier, 2000). Conversely, in fields where we do not have this tacit knowledge, where we do not have a feel for the game, we feel ill at ease. Thus, removing ourselves from our familiar context can have a destabilizing effect on our sense of self. As our self is uncoupled from its safe and familiar moorings, we tend to become more consciously reflexive about our self, what we say, what we do and how we are. This sense of mastery of the game (or lack of it) does not emerge 'naturally' but is the result of our habitus, that is, learned habitual ways of thinking and doing.

Habitus can therefore go some way towards explaining belonging, but where the concept of belonging differs from habitus is in its recognition of the intersubjective nature of our self (see Bottero, 2009: 413–14). This is because belonging is created in interaction and the collective understandings on which belonging is built are negotiated accomplishments, as will be discussed below. Bottero (2009) and Murphy (2011) have both criticized Bourdieu for emphasizing structures, without considering the substance of these. They also critique his concept of habitus for not being relational enough. Although habitus is relational in that people are seen to exist in networks of relations, Bourdieu does not focus on the interactional element of relationality or on social relationships. Instead, his account is characterized by an 'abstract emphasis on objective structural relations' that does not explore 'how, in what social interaction contexts, we develop our second "natures"' (Bottero, 2009: 401, 412). Bottero (2009: 413) argues that it is important to understand habitus as the result of intersubjective negotiation and coordination of practices, not merely 'individuals internalizing their shared conditions in the same fashion'. This means emphasizing 'the concrete interpersonal networks of interdependency, obligation and constraint through which intersubjective negotiation and accountability flow' (Bottero, 2009: 413). Think, for example, of the way in which social order is created as people interact with each other in patterned ways, as discussed in Chapter 4.

By using the concept of belonging, I hope to address some of Bottero's concerns. Belonging differs from habitus in that it is a relational concept that necessarily focuses on social interaction and intersubjectivity, and on how belonging is achieved and accomplished, both individually and collectively, as explored in Chapters 7, 8 and 9. The concept of belonging also enables a focus on the emotional content of social interactions and intersubjectivity, such as the emotions that follow from belonging or not belonging. I return to this issue of the emotional impact of belonging below.

Home

One word that has already repeatedly been used in relation to belonging is 'home'. Indeed, some notion of feeling 'at home' seems central in defining belonging. Felski (2000) notes that the home is where we begin and end our day; it is where we head off from and return to. Ideal notions of home depict it as a place of security and comfort. It is a private space that inhabitants are meant to have considerable control over, for example in terms of who is allowed to enter or how things are done there. Home is where we can 'be ourselves'. Goffman (1959), for example, described the home as part of our back region where we can let aspects of our 'front' slip. We can walk around in our underwear (or even naked) and perhaps behave in a slightly less considered manner than we would in public.

But homes are not safe, comfortable havens for everyone. For people on low incomes, homes can be defined by poverty and lack, as well as intrusion and monitoring by outside institutions, for example in the form of social workers, while some women and children are subject to years of violence and abuse at home. And, of course, there are people – such as the homeless and people living permanently in institutions such as jails – who do not necessarily have a home to call their own.

Homes are also depicted as spaces for leisure – it is where we relax and unwind after a hard day's work. This is not necessarily the case for women, however, who even today are tasked with most of the housework and childcare. As Hochschild (1989) noted, many working women routinely carry out two shifts, one at work and one at home. Nevertheless, idealized and romanticized notions of home as a safe refuge from the harsh world outside permeate our understandings of what it means to belong.

Home is also very familiar. Of all the everyday settings in our lives, home is perhaps the one where we can act most 'instinctively'. We know where every-thing is, we know the peculiarities of the front door that does not close unless you push it a certain way, the weird noises that the fridge makes, and how to work the heating system. We have established many routines that we do in our homes – getting showered and dressed, cooking and eating, watching televi-sion or cleaning – that we perform almost without thinking (Harrison, 2000). We also tend to know the people we share our homes with rather intimately, especially if they are family or friends. We know their quirks and habits, what to expect from them, how not to annoy them, and what they are interested in doing and talking about. Home is the everyday environment par excellence.

But the notion of home is not enough in terms of offering an exhaustive picture of what it means to belong. This is because belonging is not a static state as indicated by Heideggerian notions of 'dwelling', nor is it necessarily about fixed roots, but about something more transitory and fluid (Leach, 2002: 286). In other words, belonging is not tied to a specific place, but is a phenomenon that emerges in many situations, contexts and also in the imaginary. Chapters 7, 8 and 9 explore these many sources of belonging, ranging from cultures to people and to the material world.

Belonging and power

It is important to remember that belonging is not just an individual feeling or something that individuals achieve on their own. Belonging also has a collective element: it is a negotiated accomplishment involving other people. In order to *truly* belong, it could be argued, it is not enough for an individual to merely feel that they belong, but this feeling must also be reciprocated by others. If belonging is what connects us to the surrounding world, it stands to reason that the world must allow this connection to take place in order for this sense of belonging to be sustainable. Thus, 'belonging' entails more than identifying with a particular group – it means being accepted by others as an integral part of a community or society (Cohen, 1982b: 21).

This is where issues of power, negotiation and conflict become pertinent to any analysis of belonging. As Yuval-Davis (2011) points out, there is always a politics involved in belonging, that is, groups engage in political projects with the aim of securing their claim to belonging over that of other groups, which, by definition, means excluding another group. In order to belong, we must feel that we can take part in the 'reflexive arguments' of society:

> that is, arguments about what should be argued about, and why ... to be able to feel that in doing so one is contributing to one's own world, one must be able to participate in the argument, interpersonally, in interaction with others, as well as intrapersonally, in one's 'thinking', in one's own 'inner speech'. (Shotter, 1993: 193)

According to Shotter (1993: 195), those who are excluded from this vital argument over what counts in a society are not able to belong, because 'to live within a narrative *order* not one's own is to live in a world not one's own'. Shotter is talking about public participation, the right to have a say in the workings of a society and one's life within it. For example, having the right to vote in elections can offer people a 'sense of empowerment, entitlement and belonging', although this sense may be misleading in cases where power rests elsewhere than in the elected bodies (Yuval-Davis, 2011: 51–2). Women interviewed by Fenster (2005: 227–8) in Jerusalem and London expressed the right to participate in decision-making and the right to choose where to live, how to decorate one's home or how to use public space, as necessary in order to achieve a sense of belonging. South African people who had experienced forced removals during the apartheid era expressed similar sentiments when interviewed by McEachern (1998): not having the right to choose where to live had meant that they had lost part of their identity and their sense of belonging in the city:

> These people were ... forced into a racialised kind of suburbia, a mode of living and an identity which was not of their own choosing. And in doing so they lost a significant element of their identity as South Africans. They lost their right to determine their own identities. (McEachern, 1998: 514)

Thus power relationships, such as those between men and women, working-class and middle-class people, and the dominant ethnic group and minority ethnic groups, come to influence our self (Griffiths, 1995: 67).

If belonging requires that one is able to participate in and contribute to the construction of society, it also requires mutual 'seeing and hearing', which, in turn, 'depends on the recognition of both difference and identity among those involved in the interaction' (Silverstone, 2002: 766). This mutual recognition or acceptance is a precondition for the development of self-confidence, self-respect and self-esteem – conversely, it is difficult not to let rejection impact on one's self-esteem (Honneth, 1995; Griffiths, 1995). A further point that

Honneth makes is that recognition must be institutionalized in the form of legal recognition if people are to be able to exercise their capacities of personhood.

The work of the feminist postcolonial theorist Gayatri Spivak (1999) adds an important layer to this issue of participation and recognition. She has been concerned with the plight of the 'subaltern', that is, people who have been subordinated as passive objects of imperialist knowledge and power, such as poor women in the global South. Spivak argues that the subaltern have been systematically disempowered by being silenced, such that there is no rhetorical space from which they can speak 'in the "European theater of responsibility" where decisions are made that affect the life and environment of the people of the global South' (Morton, 2007: 60). Instead, 'benevolent transnationally illiterate liberals' claim to speak for these groups, although they have not learned their language and culture (Spivak, 1999: 416).

Being included in the reflexive arguments of a society or in collective decision-making is not an automatic right in any society; some people find themselves on the margins or excluded. Shared cultures and values, or understandings of who 'we' are and what 'we' stand for, are the result of struggles over representation and membership. As a consequence, they tend to reflect the existing power structures of that society and to serve the interests of those in power (for example Williams, 1977: 115–17; Shotter, 1993; Probyn, 1996; Miller, 2003; Weedon, 2004). Griffiths (1995) notes how the more powerful in society, such as men or those belonging to a majority ethnic group, seem to have an easier way to self-esteem because their belonging is not under question and they have to make fewer compromises in order to be accepted. She offers the dark underbelly of the English class system as an example. This system operates on the exclusion of working-class people, for example by ridiculing them, as evidenced by recent 'class disgust' against 'chavs' (Tyler, 2008). Those 'insiders' who refuse to collude with such oppressive systems can also find themselves the object of ridicule – such as when men who object to sexist language are called 'poofters' (Griffiths, 1995: 121).

In other words, there are hierarchies of belonging (Wemyss, 2006), and not everyone is allowed to belong. It is not surprising therefore that belonging is a hotly contested political issue (Weedon, 2004). As Yuval-Davis (2011: 10) notes, belonging tends to become politicized when it is under threat. One key aspect of belonging that has frequently been the focus of political debate is that of citizenship. For example, in contemporary Britain, the debate over 'multi-culturalism' and who is allowed to claim a British identity erupts regularly. Nation states play a crucial role in defining who is allowed to belong, using technologies such as birth certificates and passports to bestow citizenship on certain individuals while denying it to others (Yuval-Davis, 2011). Politicians are also key actors in the politics of belonging, setting (or trying to set) the political agenda.

But it is not only the 'official sphere' that determines who is allowed to claim belonging to a citizenry; 'ordinary' citizens also take part in these debates. Studies have found that ethnic minority people may find their claims for British identity rejected in everyday interactions with neighbours, colleagues, strangers and even friends (Eade, 1994; Ifekwunigwe, 1999; Wemyss, 2009). Such racist exclusion and stereotyping can have a negative effect on people's sense of belonging, identity and self-worth (Weedon, 2004: 88). Thus, belonging has both an emotional component of 'feeling at home' or 'yearning for a home', and a political element of claim-making for space and recognition within a society (Bell, 1999; Miller, 2003; Scheibelhofer, 2007: 321).

It is worth noting that technological developments have meant that the means available to people to participate in public debates have, at least on the surface, increased. With the emergence of the internet, people can use media such as blogging and Twitter to voice their opinion, and can easily correspond with politicians, organizations and businesses via email. It seems that many young people, in particular young women, actively use these media to voice their opinion (Harris, 2008), although Esteva and Prakash (1998) sound a warning that these media have not necessarily increased people's ability to participate in a meaningful way. Future research must determine the impact that these new participatory opportunities are having on people's sense of belonging to a public commons. Chapter 7 explores the issue of the politics of belonging in more depth.

Is belonging an ideal state?

For many people, belonging is a concept laden with positive connotations such as feeling at home and a sense of security. If belonging is understood as a sense of ease with one's surroundings, not belonging can arguably be characterized as a sense of unease. In other words, our sense of 'ontological security' (Giddens, 1991), of knowing what to expect of our surroundings, is shaken, as our immediate social context becomes less predictable or comfortable for us, and we no longer feel that we 'fit' with our surroundings. To use Bourdieusian terms, we lack a feel for the game and so are unsure as to how to act. Most people would probably assume this ontological insecurity to be an uncomfortable and undesirable state. Shotter (1993) and Weedon (2004) maintain that *not* having a sense of membership in a community or society has a damaging effect on our sense of self: 'If we *first* have to qualify for membership, *before* we can receive respect, it is corrosive of our confidence in ourselves' (Shotter, 1993: 194).

Casey (1993: ix) argues that failing to identify with a place can have negative consequences such as 'place-panic' or 'place-alienation', where 'we confront the imminent possibility of there being no place to be or to go', feel without place and estranged, and experience symptoms such as homesickness, disorientation, depression, desolation, or 'a sense of unbearable emptiness'. Casey points out that displacement and losing a connection with place is not solely the experience of those in exile, but in some shape or form all of us in today's 'speed-bound era', where things can change very rapidly, are bound to feel it at various times in relation to our locality, city, region, culture or the world.

According to Casey (1993: 307), such place alienation has a profound effect on people's sense of who they are. An alteration in place leads to an alteration in self, and those who are alienated from place may feel 'other than' themselves (Casey, 1993: 308).

A health warning is in order at this point, however, lest we start idealizing belonging and arguing that not belonging is automatically harmful. A feeling of not belonging need not always be experienced negatively. For many of us, there exists a tension between wanting to be similar to and belong with others, and wanting to be unique and different from others (Simmel, 1971a; Elias, 1991). Elias (1991) noted that the irony of modern life is that we have an increased wish to stand out from each other but also a wish to belong. This leads to the somewhat paradoxical situation where 'we both perceive ourselves as similar to others (and are therefore able to recognize ourselves and be recognized at the same time) and also affirm our differences as individuals' (Melucci, 1996: 30).

Cooley (1902: 262) proposes that conformity or endeavouring 'to maintain a standard set by a group' is voluntary and intentional rather than mechanical. For example, we might choose to conform to particular turns of speech. We conform in order to avoid the pain and inconvenience that follows nonconformity; although as discussed in Chapter 4, people must strike a balance between conformity and feeling that they are presenting an authentic self. For example, dressing inappropriately, such as wearing a bikini to a lecture, is likely to lead to one's social self being viewed unfavourably. Consequently, the surrounding world 'constrains us without any definite intention to do so' (Cooley, 1902: 263).

Conformity also aids a sense of ease, while it can be difficult to feel at ease with people who differ considerably from us, for example in dress or behaviour. It is the small and often unnoticed similarities that can offer 'a *prima facie* at-homeness with each other highly favorable to sympathy', one that 'we all wish to have ... with people we care for' (Cooley, 1902: 263–4). Cooley (1902: 264) goes on to note that 'the repression of nonconformity is a native impulse' and any breaks in 'our habitual system of thought' can be annoying, which is why 'our first tendency is to suppress the peculiar, and we learn to endure it only when we must'.

But it would be too easy to say that we simply belong to a group and happily conform to its unwritten rules of behaviour. Even in the midst of belonging we can feel ambivalent – there are perhaps some aspects of the group that do not sit so well with us. Take gender for example. Griffiths (1995: 23) mentions that, in some situations, she has felt more of a sense of belonging with men than with women, and points out that it is possible to derive enjoyment out of both belonging and not belonging. So, for example, because of my feminist ideals, I derive pleasure out of rejecting some feminine conventions such as wearing skirts and high heels or changing my surname upon marriage, but at the same time I do experience a deep sense of belonging to the category 'women' and do embrace some forms of femininity such as wearing makeup.

More importantly, the tension between wishing to conform and wishing to be unique can be productive. Nonconformism is crucial for social change.

Conformity and nonconformity are 'normal and complementary phases of human activity', with conformity offering 'pleasure in social agreement and the easy flow of sympathy', while nonconformity can be an outlet for 'creative impatience' and 'the primal need to act' (Cooley, 1902: 272–3). Indeed, some people seek a sense of not belonging, for example by changing place through travel (Casey, 1993: 308–9), perhaps in order to 'broaden their minds'. It is at the moment when dispositional habitus is disrupted that reflexivity is awakened (Bottero, 2010: 8), which can also be understood as something akin to Lefebvre's ([1961]2002) 'moments' or Benjamin's (1999) 'shock experiences' that interrupt the smooth flow of everyday experience and the taken for granted. Such fractures or joins can make us take note of our surroundings in a new and potentially productive way by allowing us to realize the 'rich and manifold possibilities that are presented to us at given historical conjunctures' (Gardiner, 2004: 243), and to see 'what could be' rather than just 'what is' (McCracken, 2002: 151).

In other words, a sense of not belonging can open up new possibilities of, for example, political action if we become conscious of the fact that the 'way things are done around here' is not the only possible one. Indeed, some identities – such as the Quebecois identity in Canada – may be constructed on the margins or outside dominant belongings (Probyn, 1996; Stychin, 1997). Stychin (1997: 33–5) further argues that when groups such as non-heterosexuals question what is deemed acceptable, this can help develop 'deep diversity', where identities are not predetermined or totalizing but flexible and open to multiple belongings. Such resistance to dominant forms of belonging has also led to the development of new narratives of identity, such as narratives of lesbian identity, which have provided people with 'new material possibilities and social positions' (Duggan, 1993). In other words, not belonging does not have to have purely negative consequences, just as belonging is not necessarily a positive thing or an ideal state. While some people are clearly prevented from belonging, others may resist belonging (Probyn, 1996; Ahmed and Fortier, 2003: 256).

Having said this, the fact remains that belonging is an important aspect of what it means to be a relational self, and even those people who resist dominant forms of belonging tend to seek *some* form of alternative belonging. For the rest of this chapter, I examine the two aspects of belonging that render it particularly useful to a phenomenological study of the relationship between social change and the self: first, belonging is dynamic and takes places in the everyday, and second, belonging is complex.

Dynamic belonging in the everyday

A sense of belonging is based on everyday habits (Jackson, 1983: 334). This brings us within the territory of the everyday, where the 'official' and 'unofficial' spheres intersect, and the phenomenological world of Schutz's (1962) 'natural attitude', of everyday practices that, although constitutive of social order, remain largely in the realm of the taken for granted and the 'seen but unnoticed' (Garfinkel, 1967: 180). Belonging can therefore be understood as an everyday mode of being that is largely unconscious or not the focus of conscious thought (Felski, 2002). In other words, one of the ways in which a sense of belonging can emerge is if we can go about our everyday lives without having to pay much attention to how we do it. Conversely, a disruption in our everyday environment can make us feel uprooted (Jackson, 1983: 328). When our expectations of the everyday are not met, when we cannot go about our mundane tasks as we are accustomed to, and when we become consciously aware of our habitual ways of being and doing, we can awaken to a feeling of not belonging.

As noted in Chapter 4, there is a similarity between belonging and Bourdieu's notion of habitus. According to Bourdieu (1979: 171–2), our habitus fits a specific social field and as long as we remain in this field, we are not necessarily aware of our habitus, rather, it feels 'natural' to us. We only become aware of our habitus when we step outside the field we have a 'feel for the game' in. What the concept of belonging allows us to do that habitus does not is to understand how people can be embedded in a familiar everyday world yet feel that they do *not* belong there. As discussed above, belonging is an intersubjective experience that necessarily involves other people. We make claims for belonging that others either reject or accept, and we might come to resist prescribed forms of belonging. Therefore, mere familiarity with a place, a group of people or a culture is not enough for us to gain a sense of belonging.

Bourdieu's analysis has been further critiqued for being structurally deterministic: because habitus is viewed as the result of structure, it has no movement of its own and can only change as a result of changing structures (de Certeau, 1984: 57–8). As Bottero (2010) notes, this account leaves little room for reflexivity. Although we do act habitually, we also have to be reflexively aware of what we are doing in order to be able to negotiate with others the common meaning of a situation or 'what should happen'. We are accountable to others, and it is in this process of accounting for what we have done that we enter into a negotiation between our own and others' expectations.

In other words, habitus does not happen automatically, although it may feel as though it does, but requires reflexive thought. The concept of belonging allows us to encompass this because belonging is something that is achieved in interaction with other people. So, a sense of belonging does not 'just happen', but must be created through a process of establishing a sense of identification with one's social, relational and material surroundings (Miller, 2003: 223), or 'of recognising – or misrecognising – the self in the other' (Leach, 2002: 287).

Savage et al. (2005) talk of 'elective belonging' as a way of indicating that belonging is not a given. For example, people seek to live in or visit places where they feel comfortable, and avoid places where they do not. As a result, people with a similar habitus tend to end up inhabiting the same spaces (Savage et al., 2005: 101). The concept of elective belonging has been criticized, however, for assuming that a person can choose where they live. Clearly, this is not always the case – some people may be tied to an area through lack of funds (because they cannot afford a house elsewhere), external constraints (this is the only area the local authority will rent them a house), or practicalities (this is the only conceivable area they could live in, for various reasons, such as distance to work). Phillipson and Thompson (2008), for example, argue that working-class people are less likely to express 'elective' belonging because they often have less choice about where they live.

Implicit in the discussion above is the notion that belonging is a trajectory not only through space but also time (de Certeau, 1984). Our sense of belonging changes over time, not only because the surrounding world changes but also in response to changes in our self. For example, becoming a parent can lead to a person developing a stronger sense of belonging to a locality (Savage et al., 2005; Fenster, 2005). Parents find themselves engaging in new routines, such as taking children to the playground, nursery or school, and new interactions with teachers and other parents, which serve to connect them to a locality in a different way from before (Savage et al., 2005: 54). In her study, Fenster (2005: 223) found that after becoming mothers, women started using their local neighbourhood and its services, such as shops, schools and libraries, more intensely, and consequently many felt a stronger sense of belonging to their area.

Thus, belonging is not something we accomplish once and for all. Because the world and the people in it, including ourselves, are constantly undergoing change, belonging is something we have to keep achieving or doing through an active process (Bell, 1999: 3; Miller, 2003: 223; Scheibelhofer, 2007; Bennett, 2012). Belonging offers an apt window into studying the interconnectedness of social change and the self – as the world around us changes, so does our relationship to it.

Multidimensional belongings

The second reason why belonging lends itself to the study of the interlinking of self and social change is that it is a multidimensional experience that interweaves many aspects of our being in the world (Bennett, 2012). Focusing on belonging allows us to study the different dimensions of people's lives where social change becomes apparent. For example, the global restructuring of the economy has meant flows of migration as people have moved in search of work, which, in turn, has meant a depopulation of some localities, while others have seen an influx of migrants (Soja, 2000; Short, 2004; Dürrschmidt and Taylor, 2007). In addition, deindustrialization has left its mark on many urban landscapes, leaving behind derelict buildings and sites – many of which are now being regenerated as residential buildings and sites of consumption (Savage et al., 2003; Tonkiss, 2005; Jayne, 2006; Edensor, 2007). Technological advances mean that how we interact with others, how we travel and how we conduct many of our daily tasks, such as shopping, cooking and cleaning, have changed

(Dennis and Urry, 2009; Silva, 2010). As a result of these and other social changes, people's cultural, relational and material surroundings have undergone both gradual and sudden shifts, which have then had an impact on their sense of belonging.

Not only society but also the self is multifaceted, comprising age, gender, ethnicity, social class, sexuality, religion, education, occupation, hobbies, cultural tastes, and more. This means that a person might feel a sense of belonging on one axis but not another; for example, they may feel a sense of affinity with others who share their religious beliefs, but not necessarily feel they belong with people from the same occupation or social class precisely because of a difference in religious affiliation. Because of this complexity, a person's sense of belonging cannot be predicted.

Chapters 7, 8 and 9 explore three key sources of belonging: cultures, people and material surroundings comprising both place and objects. Calhoun (1999: 222) has criticized social scientists for privileging one form of belonging – that is, belonging to a specific culture – over others, although there are 'different senses of belonging and multiple modes of social solidarity'. Cultural belonging is indeed the aspect of belonging that has been researched most thoroughly within the social sciences. One dominant area of research focuses on issues of nation and citizenship; for example, the extent to which migrants and ethnic minorities can claim belonging to a nation. But the other two dimensions of belonging are no less important. Adopting a relational view of the self means understanding belonging to other people as crucial to wellbeing. Social geographers would argue that belonging to place is also significant in terms of a person's sense of self, while a theorist of material culture would remind us of the importance of things because we use material objects to practise and experience a cultural identity. All these aspects of belonging will be explored in Chapters 7–9.

The emotions of belonging

As mentioned above, emotions are not addressed adequately by Bourdieu's concept of habitus, but the concept of belonging does help us to focus on them. Drawing on Bottero's (2009) arguments, Murphy (2011: 3) critiques Bourdieu's neglect of 'the emotional content of familial and communal relations'. Because Bourdieu defines relationality not in terms of intersubjective ties but of objective relations, he ends up privileging 'relations between social positions at the expense of exploring the substance of these positions', while 'the interactional properties of habitus, field and social space are left unexamined', which, in turn, 'leads to a disengagement with the intersubjective world' and, in sum, 'a one-sided theory of relationality' (Murphy, 2011: 4).

Bourdieu's world of objective structural relations, social fields and habitus is thus devoid of emotional content, yet habitus is not merely embodied but also emotional – when one's habitus fits the social field one is in, this can give rise to a *feeling* of belonging. Indeed, the process of identification is not merely cognitive, but also affective (de la Rúa, 2007: 687). Honneth (1995) points out that conflicts over recognition involve emotions, and not being accorded the recognition one feels one deserves can lead to suffering. Griffiths uses the concepts of love and acceptance to describe the emotional impact of belonging, while she characterizes not belonging in terms of resistance and rejection:

> Thus, love is wanting to belong with an other or others, or with a particular social group. In contrast, resistance is not wanting to belong with an other or others, or with a particular social group. These relationships may not be reciprocal. Thus love is also wanting an other or others to belong with oneself or with one's group. Resistance is the opposite. Acceptance is the result of some degree of love by others: being allowed to belong with an other or others. Rejection is the result of resistance on the part of others: not being allowed to belong with an other or others. Again, feelings may not be reciprocal. Acceptance is also allowing an other or others to belong with oneself or one's group, and rejection is not allowing an other or others to belong with oneself or one's group. (Griffiths, 1995: 86)

As illustrated by a number of studies on social class, people experience their social position and their intersubjective ties as drenched with emotion. Willis's (1977) study of working-class men shows that there is a strong affective dimension to feeling a sense of belonging to a group (what Griffiths would call love), often coupled with a sense of antagonism towards another group (resistance). Conversely, as a result of not meeting the dominant middle-class norms of what a 'respectable' person should be like (rejection), many working-class people can experience a range of feelings from anxiety to resentment. Skeggs (1997) found that any failures to 'pass' as middle class, for example in 'posh' shops, could trigger profound emotions such as shame or anger in the working-class women who took part in her study (see also Sayer, 2005 on how class in general gives rise to feelings of shame and embarrassment). Being rejected by a group on the basis of, for example, gender or ethnicity can lead to anger, but also to politicization, as we have seen through the formation of countless social movements, such as the civil rights movement, the women's liberation movement and the gay liberation movement.

Returning to an issue discussed in Part 1, it is difficult for people to reinvent themselves. This is because some aspects of our selves, such as social class, are written into our bodies and minds and operate at a deep emotional level. Walkerdine et al. (2001) propose that it is important to examine the emotional aspect of experience, including desires and fears. Rogaly and Taylor (2009: 150) found that working-class people who have moved across class boundaries, for example through education or occupation, can express 'ambivalence and unsettlement' over their social mobility. Some who had attended university described their meetings with middle-class culture through a sense of anger or dislocation, especially if they had met with patronizing attitudes towards the working classes (Rogaly and Taylor, 2009: 151). Others who now lived middle-class lives could feel alienated from their own children who were experiencing a middle-class childhood different from the one the respondents had gone through. But people who had undergone 'class travel' also expressed a sense of alienation from their own family or origins or place where they grew up, as well as envy that those who had stayed 'put' need not be self-conscious of their own background or accent in the same way as those respondents who had 'moved' felt they had to (Rogaly and Taylor, 2009: 154). Some with academic potential chose not to move away from their social class and locality and eschewed formal education (Rogaly and Taylor, 2009: 157), perhaps for fear of such a sense of dislocation and the attendant emotions this could give rise to (cf. Walkerdine et al., 2001).

A sense of belonging can lead to experiences of joy, contentment, happiness, or fulfilment. But, as pointed out above, belonging is not always necessarily experienced as positive, and can lead to a sense of being hemmed in, of things being *too* familiar and 'safe', thus lacking any excitement or chance for adventure. In addition, for people who have 'moved on' from or rejected their origins, feeling at home is not always a comfortable feeling. For example, Fortier (2000: 133) says that she experienced the habitual space of a Catholic church, where everything felt intelligible and familiar to her, as unpleasant. She does not elaborate why this was so, but the fact that Fortier has renounced the Catholicism in which she was brought up is perhaps a clue as to why this familiarity did not give rise to positive emotions.

Game (2001) argues that feelings of belonging are often associated with instances that take us back to our childhood and our childlike ability to take wide-eyed pleasure in the world as new. We experience a sense of belonging when we experience something as both familiar ('I know this already, I've felt this before, this feels familiar') and new ('this is exciting, fresh, new'), that is, when we experience a sense of existing in between past, present and future. Such moments of excitement and perhaps even ecstatic joy (when, as it were, a sense of connectedness hits us) are moments when we *notice* belonging. These are not Lefebvre's moments that disrupt our sense of ease, but quite different experiences of heightened connectedness with the world.

What we can take from these examples is that the issue of habitus and 'sense of ease' is much more complex than Bourdieu lets on. Because belonging is by definition affective, it allows a focus on the emotions involved in feeling at home or out of place in particular settings, situations or social positions.

Conclusion

This chapter has aimed to provide a definition of what constitutes belonging. We construct our identity in relation to other people, based on who we feel we belong with and who we do not. In other words, belonging is important, if not fundamental, to our sense of self. It is a feeling that tells us about our connection to the surrounding world. Belonging can be characterized as a sense of ease, often unnoticed until disturbed or under threat. Because we undergo change, for example as the result of ageing, and because the surrounding world never stays static, our sense of belonging undergoes change over time. The concept also allows us to focus on the complexity of people's connection with the world, because belonging can have multiple sources, including people, cultures and the material world. Belonging is a concept that allows for a sociology that is situated 'where we are actually located, embodied in the local historicity and particularities of our lived worlds' and connects this with 'the powers, processes, and relations that organize and determine the everyday context of that seeing' (Smith, 1987: 8, 9).

In Chapters 7–9, I examine three different sources of belonging – culture, relationships and the material world – and their impact on our sense of self. Although they are treated as distinct domains, it is important to remember that they are interlinked and are therefore not experienced as singular, nor can their independent impacts always be determined. These overlaps will be discussed throughout Chapters 7–9.

Cultural Belongings

7

Introduction

In his highly entertaining book *Pies and Prejudice: In Search of the North*, Stuart Maconie (2007: xii), 'a northerner in exile', recounts his 'attempt to rediscover ... my own inner northerner'. Maconie describes how the idea for the book came after a Sunday brunch, during which one of his friends asked 'Where are the sun-dried tomatoes?', to which Maconie had replied 'They're next to the cappuccino maker'. Maconie attributes this as a key moment in realizing that he had become a 'southerner':

> A ghastly, pregnant silence fell. Slowly, we turned to meet each other's gaze. We didn't say anything. We didn't need to. Each read the other's unspoken thought; we had changed. We had become the kind of people who rustle up brunch on Sundays ... the kind of people who had sun-dried tomatoes and cappuccino makers. Southerners, I suppose. (Maconie, 2007: xi)

Whichever country you live in, you will no doubt recognize the sentiment expressed by Maconie regarding the boundary between 'us' and 'them', with 'them' having laughable habits such as drinking cappuccino, whereas 'we' do not bother with such frivolities. From a sociological point of view, this is how cultures operate, by demarcating *our* way of life in contrast to *their* way of life. Another culture can feel alien and uninviting, whereas one's own culture means 'home':

> Good or bad, 'the north' means something to all English people wherever they hail from. To people from London ... it means desolation, arctic temperatures, mushy peas, a cultural wasteland with limited shopping opportunities and populated by aggressive trolls. To northerners it means home, truth, beauty, valour, romance, warm and characterful people, real beer and decent chip shops. (Maconie, 2007: 2)

Chapter 4 discussed relational theories of the self, according to which we develop our sense of self within a system of shared norms that we use to judge

95

our own behaviour, as well as that of others (Melucci, 1996: 31). Furthermore, in order to gain a sense of belonging, a person must understand these (often unwritten) moral and behavioural codes and be able to hold themselves accountable to them (Mead, 1934). We come to understand who we are as individuals by being members of a group, which Calhoun (2003b: 563) argues is a universal tendency among humans: 'In all settings, people find themselves in, and actively work to situate themselves in, groups.'

This chapter explores belonging in relation to culture by focusing on three sources of cultural belonging, namely social class, ethnicity and nationality. I begin by attempting a definition of 'culture' and how it operates as a source of belonging.

The meaning of 'culture'

As discussed in Chapter 6, people are 'necessarily situated in particular webs of belonging' (Calhoun, 2003a: 536). We cannot choose *not* to belong 'to social groups, relations, or culture', and there is no person who can choose all their identifications (Calhoun, 2003a: 536). From these groupings, **cultures** emerge: shared ways of seeing the world, of thought and action, which, in turn, engender collective identities, a shared sense of 'us', of 'who we are and what we do'. Culture helps make us into persons by 'enabling biological humans to be psychological and sociological humans' (Calhoun, 2003b: 559). This is because people create a sense of self partly in relation to these collective histories and traditions that help make up culture, and make claims for belonging by citing these shared understandings of who 'we' are and what 'we' do in terms of, for example, language, religion or cultural habits (Fortier, 2000; Brubaker and Cooper, 2000).

Cohen (1982a: 11) has described culture as 'nebulous threads' that are 'felt, experienced, understood, but rarely explicitly expressed', leaving much of culture at a subconscious level. Members of a culture 'just know' how to behave, or 'just happen to' think alike. As Bourdieu (1977: 80) points out, this is not 'natural' but the result of the 'orchestration of habitus', as a consequence of which there is consensus over what certain behaviours or things mean, and other people's behaviour seems intelligible and foreseeable. As a result, we do not constantly have to ask each other 'What do you mean?', nor explicitly enquire as to each other's intentions. This perhaps helps explain why sharing a common culture is 'inherently productive of groupings', and why groups appear to their members (and sometimes others) as 'natural and necessary rather than arbitrary and optional' (Calhoun, 2003b: 559).

Much of culture is learned and internalized at an early age, and becomes 'second nature' that remains unspoken, which is why a culture can be difficult to access by an outsider. It is, however, these unspoken aspects that are 'the substance of belonging' because they 'bind members to their culture so closely that they take from it the means by which to make the world known to themselves, and to make themselves known to the world' (Cohen, 1982a: 11–12).

Social class helps exemplify how difficult it can be for an 'outsider' to access a culture. Skeggs (1997) notes how middle-class women have been brought up with a habitus of ease, restraint, luxury, dependence and passivity, which is equated with 'respectability'. Working-class women, traditionally defined as hardy, robust, vulgar and tasteless, can find it difficult to achieve 'respectable' femininity. Partly, this is because 'being respectable' requires the ability to behave in a particular classed way, as well as having access to forms of cultural capital – derived from education and being brought up to appreciate certain cultural tastes – all of which is 'not part of their [working-class women's] cultural baggage' (Skeggs, 1997: 100). For the women in Skeggs's study, a middle-class habitus denoting 'respectability' was not 'second nature' and they lacked a certain 'feel for the game'. As a result, they were prone to make 'mistakes' that belied their working-classness, such as saying or wearing the 'wrong' thing, which meant that their claims for belonging within 'respectable' femininity were frequently questioned by others.

So, why don't working-class people just define their own standards and ignore those of middle-class people? To an extent they do, as shown by Willis's (1977) classic study of how working-class men come to reject middle-class values, such as education, and form a counter-culture. Nevertheless, there are some important consequences if one does not have access to a privileged habitus. One possible consequence is that one's habitus is not attuned to 'the dominant sociocultural organization', which, in turn, can limit one's capacity for action within important fields and organizations, such as education, business or politics (Calhoun, 2003b: 560).

Consider, for example, an important state institution such as the education system, which is imbued with many middle-class norms. Those with a privileged habitus are likely to find it easier to act within this field, because they already have some 'feel for the game' from the outset (cf. Walkerdine et al., 2001). As Calhoun (2003b: 560) notes, a mismatch between people's 'embodied capacities to generate action and some of the fields in which they are forced to act' can undermine their ability to act 'on a larger stage' (cf. Shotter, 1993). As Calhoun (2003b: 560) describes, in moments like these, people are like rugby players trying to play football and 'being consistently called for fouls'. It is not surprising therefore that people tend to gravitate towards others 'who play the same game'.

The 'subterranean' nature of culture also means that people are not always conscious of their cultural membership except when 'brought up against its boundaries: that is, when we become aware of *another* culture, of behavior which deviates from the norms of our own' (Cohen, 1982a: 4). People are generally not aware that their behaviour is distinctive until they meet others who behave differently. For example, a person who has learned to eat with a knife and fork only becomes aware of this as a *cultural* habit once they realize that there are other ways of eating food, for example with chopsticks.

There is a tendency to see cultures and cultural identities, for example national identity, as homogeneous; think, for example, of the American pledge of allegiance that talks about a 'nation indivisible'. This means that members of a culture tend to be viewed as similar, based on the assumption that:

> all members of a group might share the same interests and indeed be much more identical to each other than they are – and as though there were much more agreement about both interests and identity than there is. (Calhoun, 2003a: 541)

Such a view does not allow for the complexity that 'a culture' holds *within* it. Cultures are not unified but can contain groups that have different interests, sometimes even opposing viewpoints. At the heart of any negotiation or competition that ensues between such groups is the question of who has the right to make claims over how 'we' do things – that is, who 'really' belongs. Some groups' claims for belonging are successful, while others have theirs rejected. It tends to be those belonging to the majority whose claims for belonging are seen as uncontroversial, while people belonging to various minority groups, such as ethnic minorities, can find that their claims are not accepted by the majority groupings (for example Weedon, 2004; Wemyss, 2009; Skey, 2011). For example, Jamaican immigrants who came to live in postwar Britain, who in many ways had culturally been brought up to think of themselves as 'British', experienced 'a sometimes violent repudiation of what they had seen as their own British identity' (Miller, 2010: 106–7).

Thus, fundamental to 'culture' is people's awareness of a difference between 'us' and 'them' in terms of thought and practice, and constant negotiations over where the boundary between these lies. Cultures are not unified, but consist of internal divisions and tensions as different groups jostle for the right to define 'who we are'. I now explore in more detail this issue of boundaries and how they are drawn.

Drawing boundaries

If a culture only gains meaning in relation to other cultures, then the drawing of boundaries is also inherent to culture. These boundaries distinguish between self and other, both on a personal and a collective level (Lyon, 2007: 212). Drawing on Lamont's (1992) work, Lyon (2007) distinguishes between three types of boundary. When interviewing Dutch and Italian women about immigrant women, Lyon found that they drew *moral boundaries* between themselves and 'the other' by expressing suspicions over immigrant women's respectability and sexuality. They alluded to *cultural boundaries* around perceived differences in intelligence and manners, while *socioeconomic boundaries* were drawn on the basis of wealth and professional success, for example by arguing that immigrant women are dependent on men. Distinctions such as these are one way of patrolling the borders of 'our' group.

Similarly, in their study of 'split' communities, Meinhof and Galasiński (2005) found that people use negative out-grouping devices that revolved around work, status or taste. In a German community that straddled the former border between West and East Germany, 'easterners' were depicted by 'westerners' as greedy because they did not accept differential rewards for work, and as instantly recognizable because of their old-fashioned taste in clothing (Meinhof and Galasiński, 2005: 90).

The boundaries between 'us' and them' are never fixed or given, but are constantly contested, as discussed below. Nor are these boundaries always clear-cut, but exhibit a permeable character. In some instances, a person who is defined as 'one of them' on the basis of nationality, for example, could be counted as 'one of us' on the basis of their religion (Lyon, 2007: 219–21). In other words, the boundaries between 'us' and 'them' are, to an extent, dependent on the situation and context, and are therefore not immovable.

'Ideal types' versus categories in practice

In our everyday lives, we have a general sense of a rather abstract group of people that we may belong to. For example, one may feel British or French – and feel that there is something that unites people of the same nationality – or that one is 'working class'. We may also experience a sense of belonging to an ethnic identity, such as 'African Caribbean' or 'Flemish Belgian'. This sense of identifying with a larger group is not based on knowing everyone in this group personally. Instead, we feel an affinity with a general construct of what we think that group represents in terms of shared values or behaviours. In other words, such groups constitute 'imagined communities' (Anderson, 1983) based on 'ideal types' that emerge not out of our experiences with a particular person, but from a synthesis of our experience of others (Schutz, [1932]1967). People belonging to the same ideal type, for example police officers or postal workers, are expected to behave in particular ways.

Thus, culture offers us 'identity categories' or collective identities, such as 'French' or 'mother'. These can be 'mobilized by some, evaded by others, used, perhaps abused, lacking in clear boundaries and shifting over time and with contexts' (Calhoun, 2003b: 565). We should not make the mistake of assuming that people automatically feel a sense of belonging to the identity categories they seemingly fit or that they feel a sense of affinity with others within the same category. Take the category of lone motherhood, for example, which is used to categorize particular women as 'lone mothers', often with stigmatizing effect. Yet, lone mothers themselves do not necessarily feel a sense of 'groupness', of belonging to the same group, merely on the basis of their family structure (May, 2010).

As discussed in Chapter 4, such external categorization is not something that the categorized person can necessarily ignore, given the 'looking-glass' character of the self. What others think of us is of no little importance because 'we know who we are because others tell us' (Jenkins, 2000: 11). In other words, individuals can never fully choose their own identity, because identities are, to a degree, ascribed to people, for example on the basis of gender, ethnicity or family structure (Calhoun, 2003b).

This does not mean that people do not try to 'escape' negative categorization as best they can. This is something that Bourdieu's theory of habitus fails to account for, namely why a person who is in 'their own' social field can nevertheless experiences a sense of *not* belonging. For example, the working-class women in Skeggs's (1997) study did not feel at home in the social field they had grown up in, but aspired towards a middle-class habitus and tried to distance themselves from what it meant to be 'working class'. As Skeggs (1997: 1) explains, this is the understandable result of the stigmatization of the working classes, who have 'consistently been classified as dangerous, polluting, threatening, revolutionary, pathological and without respect'. It is interesting to note that Paul Willis (1977) encountered a very different attitude towards working-class culture among young men, who expressed pride in their own culture and defiance against middle-class culture and authority (more on this study below). This is a good example of internal divisions within a 'culture', such that being 'working class' can, for example, be experienced differently by women and men.

Melucci (1996: 32) argues that a gap always exists between self-identification and identification by others. The tension this gap produces tends to be kept in check due to 'a certain level of reciprocity of recognition', and it is in situations when this reciprocity fails – for example if someone denies another's claim for belonging – that conflict and competition ensues:

> what people struggle for is always the possibility to recognize themselves and be recognized as subjects of their own action. We enter a conflict to affirm the identity that our opponent has denied us, to reappropriate something which belongs to us because we are able to recognize it as our own. When during a conflict we secure solidarity from others, when we feel ourselves part of a group, identity is reinforced and guaranteed. (Melucci, 1996: 32)

Hopkins (2008: 364) proposes that group cultures should be viewed as 'providing a set of symbolic and argumentative resources with which alternative visions of who we are, and could be, are advanced'. These resources can be used by groups to change or redefine stigmatizing or exclusionary identity categories, such as when ethnic minority groups have challenged exclusionary definitions of what it means to be 'British'. In this way, group identities are constantly being contested, both within and between groups.

The use of shared cultural products

As we have discussed, people construct a sense of belonging to an 'us' as distinct from 'them'. The understanding of 'who we are' is partly based on, and mediated by, cultural products such as language and tradition, which are part of 'the intersubjective world common to us all' (Schutz, [1932]1967: 218). We not only internalize these cultural products as we grow up, but also use them as we build a sense of belonging, and they come to help characterize 'who we are' (Calhoun, 2003b: 559). A person comes to understand themselves as someone who speaks English or Hindi, who celebrates Christmas or Diwali, and who wears jeans or a sari, and these cultural products are symbolic of which culture we belong to.

Language is a key element of any culture, and plays a pivotal role in terms of our sense of belonging. Language is our means of making sense of the surrounding world by attributing names and categories to things and events. The words we have comprise (to a degree) the boundaries of what we can comprehend. We also use language to communicate and build relationships with those around us. For example, one British interviewee in Bagnoli's study (2009: 552) talked about how important learning Italian was for him to start feeling at home in Italy: 'My Italian is getting a bit better, I'm now able to have relationships with my friends properly, I can talk about things ... so I feel I can live in this world a bit easier.'

But we also use language in a more fundamental way in our constructions of self, because language provides us with a way of seeing and interpreting not only the world but ourselves as well. For example, while men tend to view themselves as autonomous individuals, women are more likely to understand themselves as embedded within relationships (Benhabib, 1992; Gilligan, 1993). Learning a language entails not just learning the meaning of words, but also understanding which words are 'fitting' for one to use, given one's age, gender, class and so on, and speaking these in an appropriate manner (cf. Bourdieu, 1979; Burkitt, 1999: 88; Adams, 2007: 146). So, for example, women often speak with a higher pitch than men, and in a more hesitant and uncertain manner (Krøløkke and Sørensen, 2006).

Our culture also provides us with narratives that enable us to make sense of our experiences and to communicate to others who we are. These stories are 'like containers that hold us together' by giving us a 'sense of coherence and continuity' and 'imposing a comforting order on our experiences' (Mason-Schrock, 1996: 176). The key thing to remember in relation to belonging is that the narratives we use to construct and convey a sense of self do not originate from within the individual, but are shared cultural tools: 'We come to be who we are (however ephemeral, multiple, and changing) by being located or locating ourselves (usually unconsciously) in social narratives rarely of our own making' (Somers, 1994: 606).

Cultures share some assumptions about what a life looks like and how it can be told, and these shared narratives or frameworks are part of the cultural package or toolkit we internalize as children. We develop our capacity to tell self-narratives in interaction with other members of our society, and acquire culturally appropriate ways of thinking, remembering, feeling and behaving. Children are taught, in everyday interactions with their parents, for example, to pay attention to particular aspects of their experiences, and to put these experiences together in a culturally shared framework of understanding (Wang and Brockmeier, 2002). This framework lets them make sense of themselves and others, and provides a source of cultural belonging. At a fundamental level, these narratives are not only about 'who I am' but also about 'who we are'.

A good example of how children learn to do this comes from Emily, whom we met in Chapter 4. The recordings of Emily's bedtime monologues reveal that in trying to make sense of her experiences, Emily is figuring out whether she can expect particular experiences to be 'canonical', or whether they are one-offs. She does so by practising the use of words, such as 'again', 'once', 'usually', or 'not supposed to'. Emily is also trying to understand what the people involved in the action intended, her own opinion of what happened, and how her perspective compares with the point of view of others (Bruner and Lucariello, 1989). In these monologues, Emily is constructing herself as part of a community that acts in unison and understands each other's actions. Benhabib (1992: 198) borrows from Hannah Arendt, who has emphasized that from birth we are immersed in a 'web of narratives' that we tell and that others tell about us. The individual with a coherent sense of self-identity is the one who succeeds in integrating these tales and perspectives into a meaningful life story. In other words, we lead storied lives: we understand our lives in narrative form, seeing events as related sequences in an unfolding story (Riessman, 1993).

By the time we reach adulthood, we are equipped with the ability to convey our life events within shared narrative frameworks, such as the tragedy or romantic epic (Gergen and Gergen, 1983: 263). In this sense, we are always working with 'hand-me-downs', with 'derivatives of what has come before' (Freeman, 1993). In order to communicate with each other, the stories we tell must be comprehensible to others:

> Life stories must mesh, so to speak, within a community of life stories; tellers and listeners must share some 'deep structure' about the nature of a 'life', for if the rules of life-telling are altogether arbitrary, tellers and listeners will surely be alienated by a failure to grasp what the other is saying or what he [sic] thinks the other is hearing. (Bruner, 1987: 21)

Thus, life stories, as we come to understand them, are not 'natural' ways of telling the story of a life, but rather one of numerous possible ways of doing so. This becomes apparent when we compare how people from different cultures tell autobiographical stories, as Wang and Brockmeier (2002) did in their study of how children learn what to remember and how to convey these memories in narrative form. Interactions with parents are a key part of this process of acquiring culturally appropriate ways of thinking, remembering, feeling and behaving.

Wang and Brockmeier observed American and Chinese parents interacting with their children, and found that the American children were encouraged by their parents to tell self-focused stories about what they had done and felt at a particular time. In doing so, American children learned to present themselves as the central character of their own story, and to draw a clear distinction between an independent and autonomous 'I' and a 'we'. In contrast, the Chinese children drew a less clear distinction between 'I' and 'we', instead presenting an interdependent and relational self. Chinese parents encouraged their children to tell stories that depicted collective activities and centred on relationships. The end result of such parental coaxing is two very different cultural understandings of the self as either independent or interdependent:

> the promotion of individuality, self-expression and personal sufficiency in Western societies facilitates the development of an *independently oriented* self that is essentially well-bounded, distinct and separate from others and from natural and social contexts. In contrast, the emphasis on social hierarchy, interpersonal harmony and personal humility in many East Asian cultures gives rise to an *interdependently oriented* self that is fluidly defined and inextricably connected within a relational network that localizes the individual in a well-defined social niche. (Wang and Brockmeier, 2002: 50)

Thus, social scientists are interested in the narratives people tell about themselves, not only for what these say about individuals, but also the social contexts they are embedded in. In particular, second wave feminists used women's personal narratives to demonstrate that the 'private troubles' of women were, in fact, collective and therefore political problems (Gluck and Patai, 1991). The Personal Narratives Group (1989) proposed that it is important to study women's life stories because these give us an insight into the power relations between men and women, and the ways in which 'ordinary' women have fought against oppression in their everyday lives. Black feminist theorists have emphasized the importance of findings one's voice, of having the right to define oneself, in the face of racist and sexist oppression (hooks, 1981; Collins, 1990). Thus, the narratives that people tell about themselves matter, and the right to be able to tell one's story and to have that story heard can be said to be a key step in making a claim for belonging in society (cf. Shotter, 1993).

Culture as 'tradition'

I discussed above how culture is not simply 'already there', but is produced and reproduced in a shared process of practical action. Particular ways of thinking and doing, if repeated by enough people for long enough, can become sedimented as 'the way to do things'. These ritualized and formalized practices come to be understood as 'tradition', and participating in them can act to reinforce 'a sense of belonging to, and inheritance of, a particular ethnic [or other] background' (Fortier, 2000: 111). We participate in such practices from childhood onwards, whereby culture becomes an embodied part of who we are. We grow accustomed to wearing particular types of clothing, eating specific foods and performing certain bodily movements, such as kneeling in church. This sedimentation of bodily practices has been termed 'body hexis' by Bourdieu (1977), a concept that is examined in more detail in Chapter 9.

Calhoun (2003a) argues that individuals can exercise choice in relation to their participation in a culture. The most extreme choice is to move to another country and perhaps reject a culture altogether, or a person may 'claim or reject various ostensibly common cultural values, delve into and reproduce historical traditions, or let them fade' (Calhoun, 2003a: 549). Thus, belonging to a culture is not a passive state but rather the product of (some degree of) active choice as well (Calhoun, 2003a: 549).

As discussed in Chapter 4, tradition has been understood by many theorists as relatively fixed, as a 'historicized segment of a social structure: tradition as the surviving past' (Williams, 1977: 115). But it is more than this because tradition is always the result of a process of selection, whereby certain meanings and practices are selected, and hence preserved, while others are neglected, and hence die away. In this way, the creation of a shared collective memory is not only a process of remembering but also of forgetting (Sargin, 2004). Once particular ways of thought and action have been selected, they are 'presented and usually successfully passed off as "the tradition", "*the* significant past"' (Williams, 1977: 115).

This selection does not happen of itself, but is done by particular (powerful) groups and thus tradition is an actively *created* history that reflects not only past but also *contemporary* social and cultural organization, and that serves the interests of the most powerful groups. What becomes selected as tradition tends to be a version of the past that connects with and helps validate the present, such as hierarchies between 'us' and 'them'. What tradition offers is a sense of '*predisposed continuity*' (Williams, 1977: 116), a sense that this was the only way that things *could* have turned out.

Contested belongings

Collective understandings of 'who we are' change over time as the result of continued power struggles during which different groups in society vie for *their* version of history to be included (Williams, 1977: 117). Who belongs or is allowed to claim belonging to a particular collectivity is linked to issues of power and inequality of, for example, gender, ethnicity, class, age or sexuality (Miller, 2003). National histories are based on hegemonic constructions of national identity, which exclude the experiences of certain sections of the population who are deemed not to 'fit'. For example, women and ethnic minority people have learned to exist inside a discourse that is not theirs and that does not reflect their everyday experiences of sexism or racism (Smith, 1987; Shotter, 1993).

I now turn to the East End of London to exemplify the contested nature of belonging. Both Eade (1997) and Wemyss (2006) have found a hierarchy of belonging in terms of who is considered an 'East Ender'. In the postwar period, many traditionally white working-class areas have experienced a significant shift in the ethnic composition of residents, and have seen intermittent racial unrest. At the top of the hierarchy of belonging we find white people, who are 'normalized as being the natural and historically legitimate occupiers of East End spaces in the discourses of the local and national media' (Wemyss, 2006: 228). Ethnic minority people are often aware that their claims to being an East Ender are controversial:

> Of course I would call myself an East Ender ... a number of people, particularly white people would disagree (Saif).

> I sometimes feel a bit pressured, a bit like I shouldn't be calling myself an East Ender because I'm black (Alice).

> White East Enders, to some extent they do see me as one [an East Ender], but I don't have the same rights as they do, in terms of belonging, because they have been here for generations, I don't have the same sort of status as other East Enders. A recent arrival like my [Bengali] parents I suppose (Julekha). (Wemyss, 2006: 230)

So when it comes to discussions about 'us' East Enders, ethnic minority people often feel excluded. As Wemyss points out, such hierarchies of belonging are not necessarily based on 'facts' of how long a particular group has resided in an area. Instead, versions of history are constructed that present whites as having a long history of residence going back several generations, while the residence of other ethnic groups is downplayed. For example, South Asians, who have lived in the East End since the 1600s, are nevertheless 'constructed as having had no relationship with the area prior to the 1970s', and therefore as having little right to claim belonging (Wemyss, 2006: 233). Ethnic minorities have contested such exclusions in the East End and elsewhere. Eade (1997: 140), for example, found that second-generation Bangladeshis challenged dominant definitions of what an 'East Ender' is and claimed belonging to the East End on the basis of having a Cockney accent.

Belonging is thus linked to debates about citizenship (Young, 1990). People develop a feeling of belonging to a citizenry through everyday activities, such as participating in civic life as well as having the right to use and inhabit public spaces (Hodgetts et al., 2008: 934; cf. Fenster, 2004, 2005). It is through taking part in the everyday life of a community that people gain a sense of belonging, but the right to be included is not equally distributed.

Nationhood

One important form of collective identity that has received much attention from researchers examining belonging is nationhood, which acts as 'a salient idiom of belonging' (Fox and Miller-Idriss, 2008: 542). Nations tend to have shared narratives about 'who we are' in relation to other nations. National identity is often built on symbolic myths and sites of commemoration 'because they serve as a strong mechanism to construct belonging and collective identity' (Fenster, 2004: 405). Collective identities are symbolized by national anthems, flags, monuments, buildings and landscapes, such as the Palace of Westminster, Uluru (Ayers Rock) or the Lincoln Memorial (Urry, 2000: 137), which 'help to create and sustain narratives about who we are and where we have come from' (Weedon, 2004: 24). The choice of such symbolic sites is rarely straight-forward, as can be seen in Israel, where opposing Jewish and Palestinian claims for belonging have impacted on the choice of places deemed 'historic sites' that are to be protected from development (Fenster, 2004).

It is through such production of nationhood that governments and other ruling groups define what is worth remembering, that is, what constitutes the 'correct' history for that nation and what its shared memories and values are. This helps to produce a 'national heritage' that is classed, gendered and racial-ized. There are, however, always competing definitions of what constitutes 'national heritage'. As a result of these power struggles, the meaning of national identity never stands still but is 'contingent upon the dynamics of an on-going conversation' (Hopkins, 2008: 364) between different groups in society. For example, in South Africa, the Truth and Reconciliation Commission offered a public, official channel through which people could voice and give testimony to their experiences of apartheid, thus helping to rewrite a nation's history (McEachern, 1998). Such collective acts of remembering can also help recon-stitute understandings of who 'we' are, which can then have a profound impact on people's sense of self.

In Britain, for example, ethnic minorities were, until quite recently, excluded from what it meant to be British, and their role in British history was silenced. As ethnic minorities have gained social, economic and political standing in the country, they have been able to affect a partial rewriting of this history and chal-lenge dominant definitions of 'Britishness' (Eade, 1994; Ifekwunigwe, 1999; Weedon, 2004). Britain's role in the slave trade and the impact this had on millions of slaves and their descendants is now more openly discussed, for example in school textbooks, and commemorated, for example at the International Slavery Museum in Liverpool. Furthermore, books such as Monica Ali's *Brick Lane* and Andrea Levy's *Small Island* and films such as Gurinder Chadha's *Bend It Like Beckham* have brought the lives of migrants from the former colonies into main-stream consciousness. Weedon (2004: 44) argues that this ability to impact on British culture and the writing of British history is important because it can help create 'a space in which non-white Britons can belong'.

Although there is a top-down cultural and political production of meanings of nation, nationhood is not solely produced by states or other powerful insti-tutions such as the media, but is 'simultaneously the practical accomplishment of ordinary people engaging in routine activities' (Fox and Miller-Idriss, 2008: 537). Thus, alongside 'official' histories and monuments, we can find vernacu-lar traditions that produce alternative iconic landscapes and memorials, such as coal mines, docks and mills, thereby offering alternative versions of 'our history'. For example, in Scotland, Gaelic culture has been a strong cultural heritage competing against 'Britishness' (Urry, 2000). Meanings of nation are thus negotiated, understood and expressed at the grassroots level.

This is where local context becomes important. Meinhof and Galasiński (2005: 7) argue that although individual identities draw on shared social resources, such as linguistic resources or 'ready' patterns of speaking, this 'grammar of identity' is nonetheless adapted within a local context of inter-action (Meinhof and Galasiński, 2005: 65). It is not unusual for people to reassess collective narratives if there is a lack of fit between the 'grammar of identity' and the local experience (Meinhof and Galasiński, 2005: 10). This is perhaps particularly the case for those groups who have experienced the redrawing of national boundaries, such as people in Belarus and the Hungar-ians in Romania. The Belarusians have responded to being annexed by several different nations over time by defining 'us' and belonging in terms of locality rather than nationality: those who belong are those who come 'from here' (Pershai, 2008: 88). The Hungarians in Romania, who are technically of Romanian nationality but who feel they belong to a 'greater cultural nation of Hungarians', affirm this sense of belonging with (formerly forbidden) public displays of Hungarian national symbols, such as the Hungarian flag and national anthem (Fox, 2006: 223).

But it is not only what happens within (or to) national borders that has an impact on people's sense of national belongings. These can also be strengthened as a result of globalization, that is, the global movement of people, culture, information and money. Eriksen (2007) notes, for example, that Norwegians have become increasingly keen on celebrating Constitution Day on 17 May, which for many includes wearing traditional dress. Emphasizing national iden-tities in this way can aid the maintenance of 'a predictable and secure group identity' in the face of social change (Eriksen, 2007: 104).

Migration and local belongings

As discussed above, belonging to a culture remains largely invisible except at the boundaries when two different cultures interact with each other. It makes sense therefore that belonging becomes particularly visible in the case of transnational migration. Indeed, migration is another key area of interest for researchers studying belonging. As a result of transnational mobility, self-understandings of identity and belonging come under stress, not only for those who migrate but also for those who are already established residents in the receiving countries. There is a consequent need for adaptation, reconfiguration and reconceptual-ization of cultural identity, which is 'keenly experienced at the everyday level of ordinary identity and human relations' (Meinhof and Galasiński, 2005: 1).

One such reconfiguration comes about as migrants create *local* belongings in their new home country. When migrants settle, they engage with 'locals' in a politics of belonging over what it means to be 'from here' (Bönisch-Brednich and Trundle, 2010: 3; Benson; 2010). For example, people of European descent living in New Zealand, whose families settled there several generations ago, define 'localness' through a connection to the land (Trundle, 2010). When talking about who does and does not belong in New Zealand, the 'locals' draw moral boundaries between 'foreigners' (especially Americans), who are seen to view land merely as a commodity, and 'locals', who have a right to claim belonging because they see land as embodying history and representing a 'community'. The reader will probably know that this claim is somewhat controversial to say the least, given the history of the colonization of New Zealand and the impact this had on the existing Māori population, who themselves had originally migrated from Polynesia.

As mentioned above, there is a politics of belonging involved, where both migrants and 'locals' negotiate claims for local belonging. So, it is important to look at how 'locals' view incomers and their willingness to engage with incomers (Benson, 2010). This is a collective process of claims-making and acceptance or rejection of another group's claims. It is also in connection with this process that individuals must decide how much they are willing to adjust aspects of their self in order to 'fit in' (see Chapters 4 and 6). Ifekwunigwe (1999) points out that in Britain, the 'majority' group (white British) tend to 'accept' a non-white person if they feel this person is 'like them' rather than fundamentally 'other'. It is therefore not surprising that some migrants wish to highlight their similarity with 'locals', such as the Americans living in New Zealand and the British living in France who wished to distinguish themselves from stereotypical expats who fail to integrate (Trundle, 2010; Benson, 2010). They did so by aligning with 'local' values as a way of claiming 'legitimate' belonging, as if to say 'I am one of *you*, not one of *them*'. In effect, this requires that one dilutes one's 'otherness', as remarked by one of Ifekwunigwe's respondents:

> Gradually, I realized just how racist this culture is, and how many people it excludes – how I found I was excluded from very many areas. Which isn't really so because, if you want to, *you can actually claim to be, you can sort of assimilate yourself* into this culture on sort of fairly decent terms if you are willing to. You can do it if only you are willing to take on its prejudices. How can I be more specific? You can get into there on the terms of you're the one 'good nigger'. Right? You can actually do it. I think. So, I have come to the realization that sometimes actually sussing it out that when someone is being friendly to you, they're doing it because they are so relieved that they have found a Black person that they can relate to. (Ifekwunigwe, 1999: 144, emphasis added)

Having one's claims for belonging rejected can be a powerful negative experience with profound consequences for the person. For example, some of the second-generation Bangladeshi Muslims living in Britain who Eade (1994) interviewed expressed a wish to leave Britain because of the rejection they had experienced from the majority white population.

Multiple belongings and hybrid cultures

As discussed in Chapter 6, we generally do not have a single source of belonging but many. Cohen (1982a: 16) notes that 'much of social life is involved with the consequences of "plural membership": of the imperatives, strains and strategies which follow from it'. Thus, all of us will experience belonging to different types of 'entities', as Cohen calls them. Family, neighbourhood, friendship and nationality are but a few examples. These sources of belonging do not exist in isolation from each other, but are interlocking. For example, our experience of nationality is mediated by where we live and who we interact with. This means that belonging 'is the almost inexpressibly complex experience of culture' (Cohen, 1982a: 16). Melucci (1996: 43) proposes that such multiplicity is characteristic of contemporary societies, where 'we find ourselves enmeshed in multiple bonds of belonging created by the proliferation of social positions, associative networks, and reference groups'. Each of these worlds we participate in has 'a culture, a language, and a set of roles and rules to which we must adapt whenever we migrate from one of them to another' (Melucci, 1996: 43), creating a pressure on us to change.

In a similar vein, Calhoun (2003a: 547) suggests that ethnicity and nationality are never expressions of 'one basic identity common to all members of a group', but within any ethnic or national group, we can find internal differentiations on the basis of, for example, social class. It is not therefore a given that people of the same ethnic background will experience a sense of solidarity with each other, because at times these other identities can provide the basis for solidarity *across* ethnic boundaries (Calhoun, 2003a: 547). Members of a culture will be familiar with, and can even enjoy, these internal differences:

> We are ... comfortable with particular ways of expressing ourselves and with particular sorts of differences from others, as well as with sameness or identification with 'people like us'. We even enjoy, I would posit, particular ways of feeling different from others, and one of the unsettling things about entering new cultural contexts is that we lose some of those familiar differentiations, not just familiar identifications. (Calhoun, 1999: 222–3)

In other words, knowing what the internal differences are, for example being able to distinguish between people from different class backgrounds, can offer a sense of belonging to a culture.

When they move, migrants have various ways in which they can set up a life in their new home country. They can self-consciously mix cultural forms into hybrid cultures; they can take on new cultural forms and, to an extent, 'assimilate' with the local culture; they can maintain a sense of belonging in their country of origin; or they can form transnational attachments to several places (or none) (Eriksen, 2007: 113). It is likely that most migrants adopt elements of a few if not all of these strategies.

Some strategies that emphasize belonging to a country of origin – such as seeking a spouse there, or retaining a distinct ethnic identity – can be seen as a 'rational' response to the lack of citizenship or acceptance in one's new home country (Eriksen, 2007: 93, 95; Kennedy, 2010: 93).

Hall (1992) notes that the meeting of cultures – for example as a result of transnational migration – can go one of two ways: tradition or translation. Whereas tradition involves each culture holding on to their own cultural traditions, perhaps even emphasizing the differences between them, translation means that when a local and an 'imported' culture meet, both interact and undergo a process of translation, forming a new hybrid culture. For example, Bhangra music mixes traditional South Asian music with London garage and hip hop, while the Chinatowns in many Western cities, such as Manchester, London and San Francisco, are a mixture of Chinese and Western culture (Urry, 2000).

Not only hybrid cultures but also hybrid identities can be produced in this process of translation. In her study of an Italian émigré community in London, Fortier (2000: 107) found that the émigrés had established familiar cultural practices and institutions as a way of creating a sense of belonging in their new country of residence. Fortier (2000: 2) uses the phrase 'migrant belongings' in order to capture 'the productive tension that results from the articulation of movement and attachment, suture and departure, outside and inside, in identity formation'. She argues that migrant populations vacillate between 'national identity' and 'émigré identity', producing a 'cultural citizenship that is grounded in multilocality' (Fortier, 2000: 97). Younger, British-born generations have a sense of belonging to Britain, but because they grow up embedded in Italian language and cultural practices, they also develop a sense of belonging with Italy.

Another term that has been used to describe such migrant belongings is 'diasporic identity'. Diaspora is used to describe people who share a geographical or cultural origin, but have migrated to different countries, such as the 'Irish diaspora', 'Kurdish diaspora' or 'South Asian diaspora'. Nash (2002: 32) argues that the identities of such diasporic people challenge notions of identity as based on one nationality or as linked to a specific geographical location, 'because they are based on multiple identifications and multiple belongings that are always in motion between the place of residence and other places'. Take, for example, the Italian Americans and the Irish Americans, who hold on to an American identity and a sense of being Italian or Irish. Even fourth-generation descendants of Irish migrants, who have perhaps never even been to Ireland, can consider themselves as 'Irish' (Eriksen, 2007: 101–2).

People of mixed heritage or migrants may experience manifold, and at times contradictory, senses of belonging (Ifekwunigwe, 1999). Eade (1994: 386) found that second-generation Bangladeshi Muslims living in Britain can formulate complex national, regional and religious belongings. Many saw their different forms of belonging as competing, and reconciled this by constructing 'composite, hierarchically ordered identities' (Eade, 1994: 391), where some aspects of their identity were seen as more important. As one respondent explained:

If you had to go on one to ten scale of who you are, what you are, it [goes] Muslim, then Bengali and then British and then whatever the things that make me up. If you take the top two away that wouldn't be me. If you take the British bit away, I think that would still be me. (Eade, 1994: 386)

Hybridity of this kind can also create conflicts and tensions with the 'host' population (Kennedy, 2010), as can be seen in the ongoing debates over the current hot topic in Europe and the USA, namely Muslim identity. For example, the British Prime Minister David Cameron announced in a speech in 2010 that multiculturalism had 'failed' because 'too many' Muslim youths did not integrate into British society. Leaving aside the complex reasons why Muslims have become a source of concern for many (especially rightwing) politicians and laypeople alike, what is interesting to note about Cameron's speech is that he used the level of 'integration' (that is, adopting British culture) as a measure of the success of migration, as well as his lack of focus on the role that the 'host' population play in achieving such integration.

Yet the testimonies of people with hybrid or diasporic identities belie any such simplistic pronouncements. In *Scattered Belongings*, Ifekwunigwe (1999) focuses on the lives of people who have multiple sources of belonging, who belong 'nowhere and everywhere'. Although her particular focus is people of 'mixed race', many of the issues that she identifies are perhaps common to all people with some form of 'mixed parentage': belonging on the margins, uncertain of one's identity, being questioned by others over one's claims for identity and belonging ('You're not *really/fully/authentically* x'). Ifekwunigwe (1999: 40) describes her own experiences of having a mixed heritage:

'Where are you from?' On an empowered day, I describe myself as a diaspora(s) daughter with multiple migratory and ancestral reference points in Nigeria, Ireland, England, Guyana and the United States. On a disempowered day, I am a nationless nomad who wanders from destination to destination in search of a singular site to name as home.

For people with mixed heritage, the unanswerable question can sometimes be 'Where is home?', because 'home' seems to evoke an image of a singular hearth, the one place of origin we can call our own. Bisi, one of Ifekwunigwe's respondents who has a white British mother and black Nigerian father, and who has lived in both England and Nigeria, sums up this dilemma:

Where I would call home is very difficult, because now I have been here. Well, I came [to England] when I was 17, and then I went back for a year, so I'm, right at the middle. I'm 36 now, so, I've lived as many years here as I did there. I know I grew up there [in Nigeria] and yet, how can I call that home? It's a very fond experience to grow up, you know. But I had my children here, and I changed a great deal through that. So, I don't know where I would call home. (Ifekwunigwe, 1999: 145)

It would seem that despite the existence of hybrid identities, cultural belongings are still mainly understood in the singular. When it comes to people with hybrid identities in terms of, for example, nationality, ethnicity or social class, they are regularly asked to pick which identity category they 'really' belong in.

Conclusion

This chapter has provided a discussion of what 'culture' means and how it operates as a source of belonging. By 'culture', I mean a group's way of thinking and doing, which is often sedimented in 'tradition'. This culture is not a given, but the result of remembering and forgetting, of doing things one way rather than another. It is the product of ongoing power struggles within and between social groups, and often reflects the interests of the most powerful groups. Therefore, it is important to focus on who gets to define not only what a culture is but also who is allowed to claim belonging to it. Claiming cultural belonging is thus always a political act that takes place within broader systems of power.

This chapter has also explored the complexity of culture at the level of everyday life. Cultures are internally complex, and always in motion. In addition, many people come to form multiple belongings, for example on the basis of their different social affiliations, such as ethnicity and social class, or on the basis of a hybrid cultural identity as a result of transnational mobility. I have discussed the ways in which these multiple or hybrid belongings are constructed, but also the ways in which they can lead to political contestation, as in the current debates over 'multiculturalism'.

Of course, these definitions of who 'we' are and how 'we' are expected to behave are, to a large degree, learned and negotiated in concrete relationships and interactions with other people. But we create a somewhat different sense of belonging to specific people as compared to cultures. In the latter, belonging entails a fairly anonymous, indirect or abstract way of relating to other people. When it comes to our interactions with specific people, 'you and I can grasp each other's living stream of consciousness simultaneously' (Schutz, [1932]1967: 219). It is the sense of relational belonging that will be explored in Chapter 8.

Relational Belongings

8

Introduction

This chapter explores relationships as a source of belonging. Chapter 4 intro-
duced the notion that people's sense of self is relational, that is, created in
interaction with others and partly constructed in terms of similarities with
or differences from other people. In other words, we understand who we are
partly on the basis of whom we feel we belong (or do not belong) with. But
our social and personal relationships matter at another fundamental level as
well. As discussed in Chapter 6, it could be argued that humans have a need
for stimulus and company (Cooley, 1902: 49–50). Empirical research shows
us, for example, that people who are integrated in a social network are likely
to experience a higher sense of meaning in life compared to those whose links
with others are weak (Krause and Wulff, 2005: 82).

Our experience of others ranges from intimate face-to-face contact through
to more remote ways of connecting with, or being aware of, others. Schutz
([1932]1967: 180–1) distinguishes the following six types of 'others' that we
can be aware of: people whom we interact with face-to-face such as friends;
those whom a person I know knows personally (for example 'your friend');
those whom I am just about to meet; contemporaries who I know exist,
but who I am not aware of as individuals but through their organizational
or social function, such as a postal employee; collective entities that I know
exist, but whose members I cannot name individually (for example, parlia-
ment); and anonymous entities of which I can never have direct experience such
as 'state' or 'nation'. The further along this list we go, 'the more anonymous
its inhabitants become' (Schutz, [1932]1967: 181). These anonymous entities
have already been explored in Chapter 7 under national belongings and imagined communities. This chapter explores the earlier parts of this continuum,
each offering qualitatively different sources of relational belonging: family
and friends, acquaintances and strangers, and neighbourhood and community.
Although the sources of belonging do become more anonymous as this chapter
progresses, I will argue that this does not necessarily mean that they are any less
important for achieving a sense of belonging.

Family

Chapter 4 examined theories of how people's sense of self emerges in inter-actions with other people in the process of socialization, which begins the moment a person is born. The key people in this process are parents or carers, who not only teach their children how to behave, but also act as important 'mirrors' in terms of a child's sense of self. It is no wonder, then, that families tend to be considered a key source of relational belonging: 'Irrespective of who his (or her) parents are, a child born into a family is part of that family, so he (or she) naturally belongs' (Braithwaite, 1962: 101). We can question whether or not people 'naturally' belong within their families of origin, but what can be said is that a person's family is *expected* to provide a key source of belonging:

> A person 'belongs' to their kin group in a way which is not true of other social groups of which they might be a member. Especially in relation to the family of origin, a kin group is the group into which a person is born, in which the membership is in no sense chosen, and where relationships still exist throughout life even if they are left dormant. (Finch and Mason, 1993: 169)

This widespread belief that family should offer our primary source of rela-tional belonging is expressed in sayings such as 'blood is thicker than water'. It is specifically being genetically linked that is thought to offer a 'natural' sense of belonging (Mason, 2011b). And, for many, family does constitute an important set of relationships. One way in which this becomes apparent is in the special sense of connection that people have with their kin, both living and dead, which can offer them the feeling of being a part of a chain or network, and of 'belonging to a line' (Kramer, 2011: 306). It is a fairly common notion in Western cultures to think of a person's identity as bound up with family history, which is seen to explain 'where I come from' (Lawler, 2008; Nash, 2008; Kramer, 2011).

The importance of having this (genetic) link to the past is perhaps under-lined for people who do not have access to it, such as adoptees, many of whom consequently experience their sense of self as fractured or partial (Edwards, 2000; Lawler, 2008). Indeed, one reason that adoptees give for tracing their biological kin is so that they can 'know where I came from', to be 'complete' and to 'find out who I am' (Carsten, 2000: 689). This is not surprising, given that the prevailing sense is that everyone 'needs' to know 'their roots', not least in order to understand which personality traits or physical attributes they have inherited from whom (cf. Mason, 2008). Carsten (2000) notes that another important reason for adopted people to search for their biological 'roots' is in order to be able to repair ruptures in their 'kinship time' so as to construct a biography that links past, present and future.

Although blood kin are generally assumed to matter most, there are many people for whom biological relatedness does not, in a straightforward manner, offer a sense of belonging. Family relationships can be violent and oppressive, or otherwise a source of pain. It is understandable, therefore, that some people come to define non-kin as 'the people who matter most to me' (see Mason, 2011b). For example, non-heterosexual people who have been shunned or cut off by their biological kin can construct 'families of choice' that comprise a mixture of friends, ex-lovers and biological kin (Weston, 1991; Weeks et al., 2001). The important point to take from this in relation to belonging is that, even though families of origin do not always offer a source of belonging, there seems to be a tendency among people to seek 'alternative' groups of intimate belonging that are 'family-like'. This is testament to the continuing cultural significance of the concept of 'family' as an important source of belonging (Morgan, 2011b).

Not only are the people who matter most to us an important source of belonging, but they can also influence our other forms of belonging. Take, for example, migrants, whose belonging to culture was explored in Chapter 7. Migration also has an impact on relationships, which are often disrupted (Miller, 2010: 125). Migrants then have to reconstruct their relational belongings not only 'here' but also 'there', with those left behind. And it is this (geographical) disruption in significant relationships, rather than more abstract notions of nationality or cultural belonging, that can be the key defining aspect of how they experience migration:

> if one actually asked the migrants themselves what mattered most to them in terms of the impact of becoming a migrant, they are more likely to respond with a very different topic [than identity or citizenship]: their core relationships of love and obligation, exemplified by mothers separated from children. People tend to care rather more about the people they love than the definition of who exactly they are. (Miller, 2010: 125)

Relationships with the 'people left behind' – such as children and grandchildren – can have an impact on how well migrants are able to settle in their new home country, as Banks (2009) found in his study of American and Canadian retirees living in Mexico. Many of Banks's (2009) interviewees used the 'swinging gate metaphor' to indicate that they might return to the USA in order to be more closely involved with their grandchildren's lives. Thus, family relationships offer not only an important source of belonging, but can also influence other dimensions of our lives, for example the extent to which we can form a sense of belonging to where we live.

Friends

Friends are also a significant source of belonging, and perhaps for some people in specific life stages, such as students who have left home and experience independent living for the first time, they can be the most important relationships

(Pahl and Pevalin, 2005). Spencer and Pahl (2006) remind us, however, that there is not always a clear-cut distinction between 'family' and 'friends'. They speak of a suffusion of these relationships, where family can take on friend-like qualities, and vice versa, and argue that the term 'personal communities' is a better way of capturing the complex and varied networks of belonging that people are a part of (Pahl and Spencer, 2004). Some people's personal communities comprise relationships with friends, others are based on family relationships, with a range of types of personal community in between.

It is important to remember that these personal communities are socially patterned according to, for example, class and ethnicity (McPherson et al., 2001). This means that it is not entirely down to chance or personality who our partners and friends are, but it is possible to see underlying social patterns, such that, on average, people tend to be friends with others who are of the same class, ethnic background and the same age as they are. Of course, this only describes what happens *on average*, and there are many individual friendships that are forged across such cultural boundaries.

Chapters 4, 6 and 7 discussed Bourdieu's theories of how we tend to feel an affinity with people who resemble us in terms of, for example, nationality, ethnicity, class, lifestyle and interests. In other words, 'similarity breeds connection' (McPherson et al., 2001: 415). This has also been called the 'homophily principle', which, in effect, translates as 'birds of a feather flock together'. Homophily is the result of similar people being more likely to come into contact with each other, because they move about in similar social fields. Social sorting also takes place because when they meet, similar people are more likely to develop ties that last (Granovetter, 1973: 1361), while ties between people who are dissimilar are more likely to dissolve (McPherson et al., 2001: 436). Thus, married couples, for example, tend to come from rather similar ethnic, racial or social class backgrounds, as do, to a lesser degree, friends (McPherson et al., 2001). The closer the relationship, for example partner or confidant, the more likely it is to be between people of a similar age (McPherson et al., 2001: 424–5). This homophily principle has been borne out by many empirical studies. For example, Baerveldt et al. (2007) found that Flemish and Dutch school children tended to have friendships with others in the same ethnic group, while Li et al. (2003) found that friendships are structured by class.

Once again, Bourdieu's theories are helpful in understanding what happens in practice that leads to homophily. When we meet a new person, we (to an extent unconsciously) 'decode' them on the basis of, for example, the clothes they wear, the food they like or the accent they speak with. A person who shares my habitus is one I am more likely to feel an instant affinity with, according to Bourdieu. Conversely, we may view those who do not share our habitus in a negative light as 'other' (de Castro, 2004). But rather than viewing any similarity as derived from a shared social position, people tend to believe that such affinities are based merely on things like 'personality', which are seen as inherent 'essential characteristics' of a person rather than socially produced (Bourdieu, 1979: 243).

Acquaintances

A common assumption seems to be that our sense of belonging to those people we know personally is of more importance than our (weak) ties to acquaintances and strangers. Schutz ([1932]1967: 219) notes that the more anonymous and less personal a relationship is, the more 'conceptualized' are our dealings. In other words, how we interact with another person depends on how much we know about them. For example, if we have gained some personal knowledge about a person by bumping into them on a daily basis at the local supermarket, we can use this knowledge to interpret their actions and predict how they might behave.

Compared to our friends and family, our knowledge of acquaintances and strangers is either less detailed or indirect. This means that we cannot fall back on personal knowledge to interpret their actions but must instead make use of stereotypes of how 'people like them' are expected to behave (Blokland, 2003: 90). Consequently, our connections with them probably feel 'thinner' than our bonds with friends whom we know as unique individuals rather than as 'types'. But the argument I wish to put forward here is that acquaintances and strangers are significant people in our lives.

As Granovetter (1973: 1361) points out, it makes sense to think of ties along a continuum of strong, weak and absent, with ties becoming stronger the more time people spend together, the more emotionally intense and intimate their relationship is, and the more the parties reciprocate favours. Strong ties have been called 'bonding ties', which help bind a group together by promoting common goals and outlooks (Putnam, 2000). 'Common sense' would seem to dictate that the stronger the tie, the more important it is. This is where common sense would be wrong, according to Granovetter, who proposed that weak ties play a crucial role in 'bridging' different groups. This is because if everyone merely interacted with the people they share a strong tie with, groups would soon become isolated. It is through weak ties, for example by talking to a person who works at a different company, that important pieces of information are transmitted from one group to another: 'those to whom we are weakly tied are more likely to move in circles different from our own and will thus have access to information different from that which we receive' (Granovetter, 1973: 1371). Thus, Granovetter (1973: 1378) warns us against focusing merely on the strength of ties, without also taking into consideration their *content*.

Morgan (2009: 115) points out that when Granovetter is talking about weak ties, he is talking about acquaintances. Morgan notes that acquaintance relationships, especially those we encounter on a daily basis, can also act in a bonding fashion. I can feel a (weak) bond towards the people I see at the swimming pool several mornings a week for example. By contributing to the bonding of people, relationships between acquaintances are of fundamental importance, because they offer not only a sense of security, but are also an important aspect of 'social ordering' (Morgan, 2009: 116). In other words, if we examine loosely acquainted groups, such as local communities, we can see that they are formed with the help of 'weak' ties built on a sense of familiarity and affinity (Granovetter, 1973: 1373; Blokland, 2003: 85–6).

It is these 'fleeting encounters' that help turn an anonymous urban setting into one characterized by some degree of familiarity and predictability (Morgan, 2009). Lofland (1998) points out that strangers and acquaintances are significant because they play a part in determining the character of a place. The encounters I have with acquaintances and strangers can impact whether I view a particular place as 'friendly' or 'unfriendly', as well as whether or not I feel at home there (Morgan, 2009). In other words, acquaintances can help render a location 'safe' (or 'unsafe'), and so, I would argue, play an important part in a person's sense of belonging (May, 2011c).

Strangers

As we move along the continuum of relationships, we find strangers, of whom we have no personal knowledge. Sociologists have been particularly interested in the nature of stranger relationships in the context of cities, which are characterized by anonymous forms of sociality and where we are said to live as strangers to each other (Simmel, 1950; Radley et al., 2005: 275). For example, Simmel (1971b), in his essay 'The metropolis and mental life', argued that as a way of defending themselves against the relentless pace and excess of stimuli in cities, urban inhabitants develop a blasé and 'matter-of-fact' attitude to each other. Accounts such as Simmel's chime with the well-known sociological narrative explored in Chapter 2 about the shift from small-scale and cohesive *Gemeinschaft*, where people know each other personally, to a large-scale and functionally fragmented *Gesellschaft*, characterized by anonymous relationships.

But it can be argued that such romanticized notions of community are based on idealizing small group relations and face-to-face interactions. Although there is a qualitative difference between small group relations and other relations, Young (1990: 233) denies 'a unique value to such face-to-face groups' and argues that they should not be privileged or posited as a model for how society should be organized. As Young points out, having a society in small scale does not automatically prevent domination and oppression. Think, for example, of the small feudal societies where feudal lords wielded practically unlimited power over their serfs. Or, to take the example of even smaller 'societies', think of oppressive friendships that people can find it difficult to break free from (Davies, 2011; Smart et al., 2012), or abusive and violent family relationships.

There is an alternative take on modern city life, one that recognizes its positive characteristics, such as the values of privacy, solitude and an acceptance of difference. Both Young (1990) and Lofland (1973) point out that utopian visions about a retreat into some form of earlier *Gemeinschaft* are unrealistic because of the large number of inhabitants on the planet (over half of whom live in cities) and because contemporary societies require highly developed divisions of labour in order to function. They urge that it is better to work towards envisioning ways in which social justice and wellbeing can be increased in cities rather than harking back to a mythical past. This is why I now examine what enables a person to feel as though they belong in urban settings, which are characterized by stranger relationships.

City inhabitants develop a range of skills in order to cope in this world of strangers. They learn how to quickly 'code' people, locations and behaviour (Lofland, 1973). Elijah Anderson (1990), in his ethnography of an inner-city area in the USA, noted how people made rapid appraisals of passersby on the street as to whether they posed a potential threat. As discussed above, the less we know about a person, the more likely we are to appraise them according to some stereotype of how we expect people in certain categories (such as 'woman' or 'old') to behave (Schutz, [1932]1967). Anderson (1990) talks of the fear that the 'anonymous black male' gives rise to because of the stereotypical and prejudiced view that all black men pose a potential threat because a high proportion of crime in inner-city areas is committed by blacks.

Anderson (1990) says that when people make such appraisals that are based on broad categories, they are making use of 'street etiquette'. He contrasts this with the more refined 'street wisdom', which allows others to be evaluated as individuals, for example by drawing nuanced distinctions between those black males who might pose a threat and those who do not. Anderson notes that people who have developed 'street wisdom' are more likely to go about their daily business with less fear than those who rely on the rather rough 'street etiquette'. Anderson (1990) proposed that people's understanding of a particular area is partly based on the nature of their interactions with strangers. If we live in an area where we consider most anonymous people to be threatening, this is likely to have a negative impact on our sense of belonging to that area.

Another skill developed by city inhabitants is the ability to navigate their way through throngs of strangers while nonverbally communicating that they do not wish to interact with others, thus being able to sustain a sense of being 'in private', as it were, even in busy public spaces (Lofland, 1973). You probably know many of these tactics, such as keeping one's facial expression impassive, minimizing body and eye contact, seating oneself apart from others, and not paying attention to and actively avoiding people who behave in an 'odd' manner. By developing such skills of public interaction, we can minimize our contact with strangers even when we are in a public space full of them.

Many of these strategies have been recorded by Goffman (1963), who coined the term 'civil inattention', which, he argued, comprised one of the cornerstones of urban sociality. Think of when you board a bus that is already full of people for example. What most people do in this situation is quickly scan the people on the bus, thus indicating an awareness of their presence. This forms the 'civil' part of civil inattention. Then, once we have found a suitable spot on the bus to sit or stand, we do not stare at other people and we act as though we cannot hear their conversations, nor do we engage them in lengthy conversation. This is the 'inattention' part of civil inattention.

Some rules of public interaction are important because they allow these interactions to take place in a fairly routine fashion, thus rendering them, and the public spaces in which they take place, predictable and 'safe'. And this, I argue, is one element of allowing us to form a sense of belonging in urban environments. We can feel simultaneously 'private' and part of a totality of people who follow the same unwritten rules of interaction. There is a pleasure to be derived from the 'lonely liberty' that derives from the 'exquisite solitude' and privacy of cities, if it means that people can be left alone and *not* be looked at (Tonkiss, 2003: 298, 300, 302; Lofland, 1998). This is a sense of privacy that women, for example, many of whom are used to being verbally or physically harassed on the streets, may value. Tonkiss (2003: 301, 300) goes a step further by saying that learning to 'look past a face' is an expression of an ethic of indifference, whereby 'differences go unremarked because unremarkable'. Instead of seeing anonymity as something that fragments social ties, Tonkiss proposes that anonymity can be interpreted as the result of mutual respect that can help weaken antagonisms.

But we also engage in practices that help transform an anonymous public space into a semi-private one, thus lessening the sense that we are living in a world of strangers. Lofland (1973) has identified three strategies urban inhabitants adopt to make city spaces feel less public and thus safer. First, we can create home territories that we have an intimate knowledge of, such as a local café we frequent. These can act as a 'home away from home', where we can try to minimize the number of encounters we have with strangers and maximize the number of encounters we have with those we know personally (Lofland, 1973: 119). Manzo (2005) offers the example of a group of men who regularly meet up at a café and spread their things across several tables and hold loud conversations with each other, thus signalling to other patrons that 'this is our space, stay away'. Second, we can create urban villages where we know many of our neighbours, as can be found in ethnic neighbourhoods such as Little Italy in New York. Today, the urban village can be more geographically dispersed, because of the ease of transport offered by the private car.

While the two first strategies for semi-privatizing public space are, to an extent, geographically bound, the third strategy, travelling together with people we know personally, allows us to create temporary mobile 'homes' (Lofland, 1973: 118). Consider a family on an outing to the zoo – DeVault (2000) has noted how family groups usually walk through the zoo in close proximity, maintaining 'groupness' through eye contact and talk. While doing so, family groups tend to be aware of other groups and respect their boundaries – collisions rarely happen. So, for example, parents will place themselves in 'open areas' and instruct their children to keep to these, and admonish children who 'trespass' on the territory of another group.

In summary, although on the face of it contemporary (city) life is more anonymous than life in past societies, we should not assume that people's sense of belonging has been diminished as a result. As illustrated above, people adopt a variety of strategies through which they make urban life feel 'safe' and transform anonymous public spaces and situations into something more 'private', even akin to 'home'.

Belonging in neighbourhoods

As has been established, our interactions with strangers and acquaintances can help determine the extent to which we feel 'at home' or 'out of place' in a particular place. Here, I explore more closely the role that 'weak' ties, such as those between acquaintances, play in creating a sense of belonging. According to Granovetter (1973: 1378), these weak ties can fundamentally influence the degree to which people feel integrated in their local community.

In their study of belonging in Greater Manchester, Savage et al. (2005) found that a person's sense of belonging depended to a large extent on the kinds of people who lived in the same area. Those who felt they lived among 'people like us', in terms of occupation, wealth or values, expressed a greater sense of connectedness with their area. As discussed in Chapter 4, whether or not a person feels a sense of affinity to another person is partly dependent on habitus. People who share habitus are likely to feel a sense of ease with each other. Conversely, living among people with a different habitus from oneself can lead to a sense of being surrounded by 'others' whose outlook on life seems so distant from one's own that little ground for mutual understanding exists.

One potential dividing factor that has been frequently researched in relation to neighbourhood relations is ethnicity. The 'multiculturalism' of many countries means that different ethnicities live, if not always side by side, in adjacent areas or streets. The focus of much attention in both public and academic debates has been the ethnic and racial tensions that can spring up as a result (for example Anderson, 1990; Skifter Andersen, 2003; Wacquant, 2008). I argue that in order to understand such tensions, which sometimes flare up into open conflict, it is important to focus on how residents create a sense of belonging.

Bonilla-Silva et al. (2006: 247) found that people living in predominantly white areas tend to have a 'white habitus', which leads them to view non-whites negatively, while considering their own white lifestyle as the 'correct' and 'normal way of doing things'. So, it is not surprising that when the ethnic composition of a neighbourhood changes, this can have an impact on how inhabitants feel about their area. In the USA and the UK, in many places, white residents have responded to such shifts by moving to a different (whiter) neighbourhood (Anderson, 1990; Tonkiss, 2005; Short, 2006). This is the so-called 'white flight' that many inner-city areas have witnessed in the past few decades.

Garland and Chakraborti (2006) found that non-white people who move to predominantly white rural English villages experience a process of 'othering'. They may, for example, come across explicit reactions to their skin colour, some hostile and others seemingly more benign, such as comments along the lines of 'Oh isn't it great that our village is not only for whites'. But even such positive reactions, because they serve to point out another person's different ethnicity, are part of a process of othering. Ethnic minorities can also face cultural boundaries that are difficult to cross; for example, Muslims are, in effect, excluded from many 'traditional' rural community activities because these often take place either in the village church or pub.

Community

One concept that has already appeared several times in the discussion above and that seems to embody a sense of local belonging is that of community. As Jenkins (2008: 133) notes, 'community' is 'a powerful everyday notion in terms of which people organize their lives and understand the places and settlements in which they live and the quality of their relationships' and it is 'among the most important sources of collective identification'. Indeed, as discussed above, community can provide people with important support networks and access to resources (Calhoun, 2003a: 537).

In daily usage, 'community' equals a group one belongs to, made up of both intimates and strangers (Blokland, 2003: 209). Yet, as Tonkiss observes, 'community' is not an easily defined concept, and is used in many different guises and for a variety of political ends:

> 'Community' is one of the shiftier concepts in contemporary social and political theory. Difficult to define, harder to observe and unvirtuous to reject, it opens itself to conservative or progressive uses even as it confuses the distinction between them. Depending on how you put it, the language of community can provide an idiom for the gathering together of identity, for fantasies of collective personality or for the marking of difference. (Tonkiss, 2003: 298)

Tonkiss (2003: 298) also notes that community can be defined 'in terms of shared spaces, in terms of social ties or networks and in terms of identities of interest', further adding to the conceptual confusion. Blokland (2003: 61–2), for example, found that the residents of Hillesluis, a neighbourhood of Rotterdam, the Netherlands, used the word 'community' to denote a variety of things, including the pleasant and warm togetherness of the past, an ethnic category of members responsible for each others' actions, and religious groups sharing moral values.

As Tonkiss (2003) remarked above, community is 'unvirtuous to reject'. In other words, 'community' is generally seen as a 'good thing' that all should strive for. The term evokes images of a (romanticized) family writ large, held together by positive affect and the absence of conflict – which Ahmed and Fortier (2003) argue amounts to a form of fetishizing community. More critical takes on 'community' define it as an effect of power that will take different shapes in different contexts depending on *who* has the power to define it (Ahmed and Fortier, 2003: 256).

Community tends to be conceived as a community of similars – we are expected to belong with those who in crucial ways resemble us, for example in terms of gender, ethnicity, religion, age, occupation or interests. Such definitions of community equate it with a group 'that shares a specific heritage, a common self-identification, a common culture and set of norms' (Young, 1990: 234). Thus, at first glance the word 'community' might seem innocuously positive as well as straightforward. However, while some communities can be based on acceptance of difference, in many cases 'community' is produced through a rhetoric of similarity that, to an extent, denies or masks difference (Cohen, 1982b: 21; Ahmed and Fortier, 2003: 251; Tonkiss, 2003: 299):

> In many towns, suburbs, and neighborhoods people do have an image of their locale as one in which people all know one another, have the same values and life style, and relate with feelings of mutuality and love. In modern American society such an image is almost always false; while there may be a dominant group with a distinct set of values and life style, within any locale one can usually find deviant individuals and groups. (Young, 1990: 235)

The darker side of community becomes apparent in 'defensive exclusionary behavior', such as pressuring minority ethnic families into moving away from a 'white' neighbourhood or lobbying against the building of underground links or council housing for fear of attracting 'the wrong kind' (read 'poor') of residents (Young, 1990: 235). As a result, some academics are critical of the term 'community' because 'the language and politics of community are too often tainted by a suspicion of otherness', either by 'promoting conformity as a condition of belonging' or by 'marking boundaries against outsiders or incomers' (Tonkiss, 2003: 303).

Community 'often operates to exclude or oppress those experienced as different' and 'tends to value and enforce homogeneity' (Young, 1990: 234). This is evident, for example, in people's tendency to define communities in opposition to 'other groups, who are feared, despised, or at best devalued' (Young, 1990: 234–5). In other words, there is a tendency to view 'our community' as somehow 'better' than 'their community'. Below, I explore two aspects of community in more detail: whether there has been a 'loss of community', and the exclusionary effects of community.

From given to chosen communities

As noted above, there is some concern over 'communities lost', echoed in public debates such as the British Prime Minister David Cameron's speeches detailing what he sees is a 'broken Britain' characterized by a weakening of responsibility and community spirit. There is, however, empirical evidence, especially of working-class communities, that counters these fears (for example O'Byrne, 1997; Rogaly and Taylor, 2009).

In her study of Hillesluis, Blokland (2003) notes that although we can see shifts in people's relationships with neighbours and their use of the neighbourhood, these should not automatically be read as a 'loss of community'. Up until the mid-1950s, most residents regularly interacted with each other as they worked and shopped locally, and attended the local church and leisure amenities such as the pub. This high neighbourhood use promoted familiarity between residents, which was further facilitated by the fact that residents shopped and visited the public baths on the same days and at the same time of day. But, Blokland points out that this familiarity did not lead to uniform solidarity, as social distinctions were drawn within the community. Neighbours would, for example, monitor each others' cleanliness and hygiene, on the basis of which they would distinguish between 'respectable' and 'less respectable' people. Distinctions were also made on the basis of social class, the receipt of clothing vouchers, or unemployment.

Since the 1950s, neighbourhood use has reduced considerably in Hillesluis as in many other urban neighbourhoods. Deindustrialization meant that local factories and dockyards closed and people had to travel further to find employment, while technological innovations such as the telephone and the private car have meant that relationships can more easily be conducted across geographical distances (Blokland, 2003: 109–13). The professionalization of the welfare state has also contributed to people's decreasing dependence on those around them as they now prefer to turn to professionals for help with births, childcare, illnesses and deaths. Consequently, local residents no longer interact with each other as regularly as they did, and neighbourhood relations have changed from public-familiar to anonymous.

But Blokland (2003: 122–4) argues that the residents of Hillesluis have not become less social or helpful, merely that the structure of neighbourly relations has changed. There is no longer one 'automatic' community that people belong to by default; rather, communities have become private affairs based on individual choice and bonds rather than attachments. These bonds can inspire a stronger sense of belonging, because they can give rise to affection in a way that neighbourly attachments did not.

Blokland (2003: 154) also found that the residents of Hillesluis experience a diminished pressure to conform because it matters less what 'the neighbours say or what the vicar thinks'. For example, women have stopped scrubbing door frames, which in the past was done 'for the neighbourhood'. This does not mean that people no longer care what others think, or do not conform to any shared mores, because the views of friends and family remain important. There is no longer one morality, however; the abundance of roles that people have in different networks, for example family, work and leisure, means that people encounter several moralities. 'We' and 'they' are consequently plural and less fixed than in the past, and judgements of others are based less on universally recognizable categories such as class. Who is counted as 'one of us' depends on how a person is viewed as an *individual* (Blokland, 2003: 156).

Blokland warns us of jumping to the conclusion that lower neighbourhood use and diminished familiarity among community members is to be interpreted as a 'loss of community' or a disintegration of 'morality'. What has happened instead is that a general familiarity with many neighbours has shifted into a more intimate familiarity with fewer neighbours. Affinity and affection between neighbours has not disappeared, it has merely changed in content and intensity.

In-groups and out-groups: creating a community

As noted above, a sense of community is constructed in relation to 'other' communities that are seen to be 'different' in some way. Central to the creation of a community is a process known as 'out-grouping', which consists of constructing a group boundary between 'we', the in-group, and 'them', the out-group. Young (1990: 235) argues that by idealizing community, we also validate the 'fear and aversion some social groups exhibit towards others':

> If community is a positive norm, that is, if existing together with others in relations of mutual understanding and reciprocity is the goal, then it is understandable that we exclude and avoid those with whom we do not or cannot identify. (Young, 1990: 235)

Various empirical studies have shed light on how this out-grouping operates. In her ethnography of Elmdon, Essex, Marilyn Strathern (1982: 258–9) found that villagers made distinctions between those who did and did not belong there, based on lineage, birth and political interests. Those who were defined as being 'real Elmdon' could claim belonging, and were seen to have a superior right to claim, for example, housing and employment, both of which were seen to be threatened by prosperous 'outsiders' buying up village property. For others, it could be a question of the right to express their interest in how village events should be run.

These processes of out-grouping play an important role in helping cement a sense of community. In their study of a working-class estate in England, Rogaly and Taylor (2009) found that residents' sense of belonging could be strengthened by a sense of 'us' versus 'them'; 'us' being estate residents who looked out for each other, as described by one of Rogaly and Taylor's respondents (2009: 62):

> I was brought up on there, lovely place to live ... soon as you walked on the road, in my day when I was a kid, it was like going into someone's house you, kind of go through the door and the doors shut, you felt secure all the way along the road you knew all the neighbours, by 'auntie' and 'uncle' and they were all looking out, they're all snugging out the window ... [laughs] we used to think they were nosey but they were all looking after you all.

This picture of close-knit community is in direct contrast to the hostility these people experienced outside the estate, where they were met with the negative attitudes of others ('them') towards estate residents. But not all residents felt the same sense of belonging to the estate. 'Others' within the estate, such as migrants, were excluded because they were seen to be in the 'wrong place' (Rogaly and Taylor, 2009: 62). And some excluded themselves, expressing a sense of belonging to a subculture. They had a limited sense of belonging to the place, and described their support networks as existing outside the estate (Rogaly and Taylor, 2009: 63).

Approaching community from the perspective of belonging means that 'community' does not become a question of self-evident boundaries. Instead, community is interrogated from the point of view of the person: which settings or groups do they feel a need or a wish to belong to (their sense of 'groupness' as it were) and to what extent does this belonging come 'naturally', without thinking, or does it have to be worked at and strived for? In other words, a focus on belonging means that we have to take into account the social and structural barriers that may obstruct a person's ability to feel they belong or, indeed, prevent them from even wanting to belong.

Relational belongings in an age of mobile technologies

As mentioned above in relation to Blokland's (2003) study, technological advancements such as the car and the telephone have had an impact on how people conduct their relationships. But developments within transport and communication technologies have also had a profound ontological impact on how we view the world, shifting our understandings of time and space. The world has undergone a 'time-space compression' due to the ever-increasing speed at which things (production, delivery, communication, travel and so on) happen, while modern transport and communication technologies allow us to feel (instantly) connected to faraway places, thus making the globe feel accessible in an unprecedented manner (Short, 2004). We are now said to live in a culture of speed and immediacy (Tomlinson, 2007).

Here, I explore the impact that information and communication technologies (ICTs) such as mobile phones and the internet have had on relational belongings. Giddens (1991) saw ICT as one of the mechanisms that helps 'disembed' individuals from the local. Because we are able to communicate instantly and in real time with people on the other side of the world, we are globally connected and no longer as reliant on local relationships as before. We can now be in two places at once, and a new type of 'being present' has emerged in addition to physical 'co-presence', namely 'telepresence'. Elliott and Urry (2010) argue that although we are able to stay connected with friends and family across vast distances, 'meetings' on the internet or over Skype are not the same as embodied face-to-face meetings where we can touch a person, feel their breath, smell their perfume and share food and drink with them. This is one of the reasons why so many people do travel, sometimes at great expense, to meet up with family and friends. I explore the significance of our embodied connections in more depth in Chapter 9.

Researchers are also talking about 'mediated intimacy' and 'mobile intimacy', meaning that we can perform intimacy on the move through increasingly portable technological media such as mobile phones and computers (Sawchuk and Crow, 2012; Hjorth and Lim, 2012). We can keep in touch with people even on the go, thus rendering our social lives flexible. One consequence of this is 'flexible punctuality', as we can now coordinate our life with the lives of others down to the last moment, for example by texting someone that we are running 15 minutes late or to rearrange the location of our meeting (Elliott and Urry, 2010).

As with any new developments, mediated or mobile intimacy brings with it both positive and negative impacts on relationships. On the one hand, telepresence can be a way of staying connected with friends and family across long distances in a way that previous generations could not, and to do so relatively cheaply and in many cases in real time, for example through email, Skype or instant messaging (Miller, 2011; Davies, 2011; Frizzo-Barker and Chow-White, 2012). On the other hand, technology can be seen to disconnect people. For example, the grandmothers interviewed by Sawchuk and Crow (2012) commented on how their grandchildren's penchant for staying in touch with their friends via their mobile phones acted as a barrier to face-to-face communication within families. They felt it was difficult to feel connected to a person who is clearly 'present but absent' – physically in the same space but mentally engaged in conversations elsewhere. This example also points towards the generational differences that are emerging in relation to how ICTs are used in relationships.

The internet has brought with it new forms of social networking such as blogs, internet forums and social networking sites (SNSs), which have been met with some degree of concern and 'puzzled dismay regarding a generation that, supposedly, has many friends but little sense of privacy and a narcissistic fascination with self-display' (Livingstone, 2008: 393). Such panics over the introduction of new media are nothing new (Gershon, 2011) and represent a long line of theories that present people as cultural dopes who foolishly follow any fashionable fad with disastrous consequences (cf. Gardiner, 2000; Felski, 2002).

I think we can give people more credit than that – people are not naive in their use of ICTs, as has been borne out by numerous studies that show that people's use of ICT is intelligent and discerning, and that they have an understanding of issues of privacy and safety (Livingstone, 2008; Agosto et al., 2012). Indeed, sites such as Facebook have taken the lead from their users by creating more nuanced ways in which users can delineate what remains private and what becomes public, such as who gets to see which status update or photograph. (It is worth noting that most of the research on the use of SNSs, particularly Facebook, is based on college/university samples; as yet, we know little about how people of different ages and from different educational backgrounds use SNSs.)

ICT has also brought with it a new range of sophisticated and nuanced 'unwritten rules', such as netiquette and Facebook etiquette. While some of these are similar to existing 'offline' social norms of behaviour and interaction, others have developed out of the particularities of these media, such as what kind of posts are 'appropriate' and how to deal with 'norm violations', such as tagging a photo of a clearly drunk and dishevelled friend (McLaughlin and Vitak, 2011). Thus, ICT is connected to the issue of cultural belonging; being able to use these technologies appropriately, having a 'feel for the game', can engender a sense of belonging.

While some highlight the novelty of these technologies, and also decry the loss of old forms of relating, such as face-to-face interaction, saying that this is eroding the bonds between people, others argue against such apocalyptic notions by pointing out that these methods of communication are an extension of earlier practices and are not necessarily replacing 'old-fashioned' ways of conducting friendships. People still see their friends in person, but they also keep in touch by text and online, in addition to which they might interact with a wider network of more distant friends via SNSs.

So, for example, sharing photos on Facebook can be seen as a new form of the holiday postcard, while emails and texts share similarities with the traditional practice of writing letters or an even older practice of leaving visiting cards (Hjorth and Lim, 2012: 478). These changes are complex: new forms of communication do displace some old ones – we might now be more likely to communicate via Facebook than send a letter – incorporate others, for example SNSs include instant messaging, while others are supplemented, such as the way in which people are now communicating with close friends on SNSs as well as continuing to see them face to face (Livingstone, 2008: 395–6). In addition, although the media through which we communicate might change, some of the basic fundamental aspects do not – namely, we are continuing to keep in touch and to keep others informed of what we are up to.

What is being implied in the fearful pronouncements over the perceived loss of face-to-face interaction is that this will lead to a loss of 'community'. What such comments do not take into account is that online communities can also offer important sources of belonging and support. Indeed, one of the main reasons for using SNSs is the need to belong, alongside the need to present a self (Nadkarni and Hofmann, 2012). SNSs offer a way of connecting with a wide range of like-minded people – such as the 'get the British National Party off Facebook' campaign (Enli and Thumim, 2012). The internet can be especially useful in this respect to those who are housebound because of illness or disability. Psychologists have found that among teens, the use of mobile phones and SNSs is likely to increase a sense of belonging and decrease a sense of loneliness (Agosto et al., 2012). As Miller (2011) notes, virtual communities can be experienced as less intrusive and vicious than 'real' communities, and can offer a welcome break from the intensity of close-knit communities. Indeed, SNSs can become 'meta-friends' in themselves; someone we can always turn to no matter what time of day or night.

One issue that has gained attention from social scientists is whether or not our conception of friendship is changing thanks to SNSs. People still make nuanced distinctions between different types of friend, just as they have done in the past (cf. Spencer and Pahl, 2006), although these are being revised somewhat. Thus, we now have the distinction between an offline friend and someone who is 'just' a Facebook friend, while people seem to be communicating with different types of friend through different technological means. For example, Agosto et al. (2012) found that their research participants used texting with close friends, stayed connected with more distant friends via Facebook, and used email for more formal communication such as with teachers or employers. The closer the relationship, the more frequent these interactions were – just as with face-to-face interactions.

Although it would seem that, for many people, their online social networks overlap significantly with their offline networks, the two are also somewhat different. There are indications, for example, that more distant Facebook 'friends' are only called 'friends' online – offline, they are termed 'acquaintances' (Agosto et al., 2012). What we can be sure of is that as our ways of communicating with each other change, so do our understandings of our relationships – the meaning of 'friendship' is a socially constructed one, which means it has changed and will continue to change over time (Emli and Thumim, 2012). Children of today growing up in this world of ICTs will no doubt develop a slightly different attitude towards friendship, socializing and connectedness than the generation for whom the internet only became an everyday reality in their twenties; but important continuities will also remain.

Conclusion

Other people play a significant part in our sense of self because it is important that our claims for identity are accepted by others, and that we are acknowledged as part of a group, community or culture. This chapter has explored the significance of social networks of family, friends, acquaintances and strangers for a sense of belonging. There is a continuum of relationships, from intimate to stranger relationships, based on the level of personal knowledge we have of others. The argument I have put forward is that these are equally important in creating a sense of belonging, but in different ways. Whereas close relationships can be the source of individual support and acknowledgement, acquaintances and strangers help determine the feel of a place and our sense of attachment to it. It is also important to remember that not all our relationships are positive in character, but can be oppressive and even violent, and thereby act to hinder a sense of belonging.

Our sense of relational belonging is at least partly based on similarity. We experience a sense of affinity with some people, and a sense of being different from others. In our interactions with others, we (consciously and unconsciously) present ourselves as members of particular categories, others categorize us, and we categorize them, as either 'one of us' or 'one of them'. As a result of these in-grouping and out-grouping processes, a sense of 'community' emerges.

Adopting a sociological perspective means paying attention to the ways in which relations of power are implicated in such relational belongings.

Of course, our relational networks never remain static. People move away or die, we fall out with some, and make new friends. Particularly as we age, we may find that the death of friends leads to a lack of like-minded people in our lives. It is not just the surrounding world that changes, we also undergo personal change across the life course. This can mean that we come to view our friends, family, neighbours, as well as acquaintances and strangers, differently over time (as they us), which may, in turn, lead to changes in our relationships and interactions with others. In other words, our sense of connection with those around us undergoes constant shifts.

Furthermore, relational belonging encompasses aspects of belonging that are not merely individual, but are the result of the interconnected nature of our lives and intersubjectivity. Thus, we can have collective or shared experiences of belonging, and our sense of belonging can be affected by the sense of belonging experienced by those close to us. Social relations also play an important role in our broader sense of belonging because they are the interface between the individual and the 'broader imagined territorial communities' (de la Rúa, 2007: 690), such as nationality, that were discussed in Chapter 7.

As already mentioned, our relationships with people take place in a broader context: for example, shifts in the labour market brought on by globalization can have an impact on who we interact with on a daily basis and where. The people in Blokland's study found that deindustrialization meant the loss of local jobs, and people had to travel outside the neighbourhood for work. This decreased the number of local interactions people had in their daily lives, and changed the feel of the neighbourhood. Thus, change on the individual level is always linked to social change, and social shifts have a complex impact on individuals' sense of relational belonging. Conversely, these changes in how people conduct their everyday relationships are also contributing to broader social change: what we mean by terms such as 'globalization' and 'deindustrialization' encompasses these shifts in relational behaviour.

The topics covered so far, culture and relationships, although significant, are not our only source of belonging. Chapter 9 examines a third source of belonging that is easily forgotten by sociologists, although I argue it is as important as the first two, namely our material environment.

Sensory Belongings

9

Introduction

Chapters 7 and 8 explored culture and other people as sources of belonging. A third source of belonging, namely the material world, is examined in this chapter. Because we experience the world through our bodies, the link between self and society is always embodied. As a result, our sensory experiences of the sights, sounds, smells and feel of our surroundings constitute an important dimension of belonging.

It could be argued that humans have a 'need for physical proximity and intimacy with concrete others' (Gardiner, 2000: 16), meaning that humans also strive for belonging on an embodied level. Belonging is not only a cognitive phenomenon, but can also entail physical closeness. Touch is an important element of intimate relationships, for example, involving a range of tactile behaviours such as kissing, hugging and sex. Similarly, cultural belongings are experienced in an embodied manner, for example when singing a national anthem, wearing a familiar piece of clothing or eating a national dish.

Cartesian dualism, discussed in Chapter 5, which makes a clear distinction between the rational mind and the mechanical body, has greatly influenced the way Westerners see the world. Westerners tend to distinguish between the 'rational' and the 'irrational', that is, emotions. Such distinctions can also help explain why sociology largely ignored the body for so long. As noted by Dorothy Smith, 'embodied, active subjects' were 'deleted from the sociological gaze, and replaced by a system of abstract concepts and logical relationships' (Gardiner, 2000: 184).

This mind–body distinction has also commonly been viewed in gendered terms, with men seen to represent the virtues of rationality, while women have been stereotyped as irrational and emotional (Griffiths, 1995: 95; Skeggs, 1997). Women are seen as 'in thrall' to and 'in tune' with their bodies, whereas men are thought to be in control of theirs, as exemplified by their sexual prowess. Similarly, non-white and working-class people have been depicted as more 'primitive' than middle-class white people (Griffiths, 1995: 97). Gardiner (2000: 193) argues that there is a link between viewing bodies as of marginal interest and the marginalization of women in sociology – bodies usually only entered into focus in relation to reproduction, specifically, women's reproductive bodies.

Perhaps it is not surprising that embodiment has been a particular focus for many feminists, including Judith Butler (1993) and Iris Young (2005). What unites these theorists is their argument that the gendered ways in which we use our bodies are not the result of some innate characteristics, but the outcome of being taught a particular way to be in the world. This chapter begins by discussing Bourdieu's concept of 'body hexis', which provides an account of how we learn our embodied ways of being. I then examine the ways in which our sense of belonging is rooted in our sensory engagement with our surroundings. Two aspects of the material world that are significant for our sense of belonging, place and material objects, are explored in more depth.

Body hexis and habitual spaces

Previous chapters have explored how Bourdieu's notion of habitus can be used to understand the link between self and society. According to Bourdieu, people's dispositions are embodied, thereby necessarily located *somewhere*. This means we experience feelings of comfort in certain places and discomfort in others (Savage et al., 2005: 8). There is also another, linked concept he developed that is relevant to belonging, namely 'body hexis'.

Bourdieu (1977: 82, 87) defined **body hexis** as a pattern of postures we learn as part of our habitus. As noted in Chapter 4, habitus is a structured way of thought *and practice*. In other words, we not only learn to think in certain ways, but also how to walk, sit and use implements. In addition, our facial expressions and style of speech are similarly learned. Think back to the times when your parents admonished you for sitting or eating in a particular way. Through this process of being told to 'stand up straight' or to 'hold your knife in your right hand', we learn (unconsciously) to embody our culture through our dress, comportment, speech and manners (Bourdieu, 1977: 94; Young, 2005: 17).

This body hexis is also gendered. In her essay 'Throwing like a girl', Young (2005) explains how women are not born with the innate ability to move 'like a girl'. Instead, girls learn a body hexis that involves not taking up 'too much' space, such as not sitting with their legs sprawled like men do. Women throw 'like a girl' not because the structure of their arms is somehow different from men's, but because they have been taught that it is more ladylike to throw a ball by flicking their wrists than it is to swing their arm behind them and throw using their whole torso (Young, 2005).

Just as with habitus, there is a corresponding fit between body hexis and social field, which can lead to a sense of belonging. For example, in her study of Italian immigrants discussed in Chapter 7, Anne-Marie Fortier (2000), a French Canadian, found that there are 'habitual spaces' that feel familiar to us because we know instinctively what to do and how to behave the minute we step into them:

Even though the ceremonies were not performed in the French vernacular I was brought up with, my first visit to St Peter's [church] struck me because it was a 'habitual space'. A space where I need not try to make sense of what was going on: all was familiar, intelligible (Fortier, 2000: 133)

These habitual spaces are created through an 'architecture of reassurance', that is, by organizing a space in such a manner that people feel at home there. For example, the main church in the area of London that Fortier studied had been refurbished so that its spatial layout resembled that of Catholic churches in Italy, evoking a sense of familiarity and belonging in the Italian émigrés who attended the church. In addition, the familiar rituals of kneeling and making the sign of the cross, and lighting votive candles offered a sense of belonging to churchgoers. Habitual spaces that look and feel familiar, where we know the 'rules of the game' in terms of how to move our bodies, can offer us comfort zones. Our body hexis, which we take for granted as 'a part of us', is the result of countless repetitions of the same movements over time:

As I sat there in the pews [of the church], it seemed as if I was watching a rerun of part of my identity *in the making*: the 'stylized repetition of acts' (Butler, 1990: 140) reached into some deep seated sense of selfhood that had sedimented into my body. The rituals cultivated a sense of belonging. This short episode made me realize the extent to which cultural identity is embodied, and memories are incorporated, both as a result of iterated actions. And how these, in turn, are *lived* as *expressions* of a deeply felt sense of identity and belonging. (Fortier, 2000: 133)

Neither habitus nor body hexis, however, explain the role *the senses* play in our connection with the world (Friedmann, 2002). As discussed in Chapter 5, we come to know the world through our sensuous embodied experiences of touch, sound, smell and taste, which help us achieve 'a holistic way of understanding three-dimensional space', otherwise also known as 'haptic perception' (O'Neill, 2001: 3). Our senses are thus tangled with each other (Mason and Davies, 2009: 600). From a phenomenological point of view, it can be argued that our knowledge of the world 'is not just a matter of thought about the world, but stems from bodily presence and bodily orientation in relation to it, bodily *awareness*' (Tilley, 1994: 14). In other words, our body is mindful. I now examine in more detail the role this bodily awareness plays in belonging.

The senses and belonging

It is by moving through and engaging with our surroundings through touch, sound, smell and taste that we come to know, give meaning to, and form an attachment with place (O'Neill, 2001: 3; Leach, 2002: 286). We can also develop a sense of connection or attachment to material things and objects, both natural and manufactured, such as buildings, photographs, mementoes, or features of the landscape. Although we cannot necessarily put this sensory understanding into words and it remains unconscious, it does play an important part in enabling us to feel a sense of ease in the world (O'Neill, 2001).

Vision is a key sense: people use vision to appreciate the forms, colours and textures of their environment, and to differentiate objects from each other (Degen, 2008: 47). Sight alone only gives access to surfaces, but together with the other senses and our memories and speculations, we can gain a more multi-dimensional understanding. As Gibson (1979) points out, what we 'see' is based on our experiential knowledge of the world. For example, because we have experienced walking round corners, we can implicitly understand that there is a 'round the corner' even though we cannot see it in terms of visual stimuli. In other words, seeing is a creative interpretation of the surfaces we perceive visually (Rodaway, 1994: 117). The visual tends to be *the* central sense for those with sight, who can immediately identify a familiar person, place or cultural artefact by sight. Thus, vision plays an important part in our sense of belonging (Degen, 2008).

Sound is a constant backdrop in our world. Those with hearing can hear their own heartbeat and breathing, as well as a range of external sounds. While writing this sentence, I can hear the traffic outside my city centre flat and the clank of the keyboard as I write. If I pay closer attention, I can make out the sound of a distant church bell ringing, and the whirr of my freezer. These sounds are everyday sounds for me and are part of my soundscape, which makes up the (often unnoticed) backdrop of my experience (Schafer, 1985). Although I could probably not describe them fully, partly because I have, to an extent, become 'deaf' to them, when I go to other places I am aware that these have a different soundscape. Our familiar soundscapes or 'auditory geographies' (Rodaway, 1994) offer us a feeling of 'home', of everything being 'as it should be'.

Our auditory geography is perhaps more complex than most of us realize. The experiences of blind people remind us that humans can 'hear' material objects as well as see them. This 'facial vision' is the result of echolocation, or a 'blending' of different awarenesses, such as sensing changes in air pressure and vibrations through the body (Hill, 1985; Rodaway, 1994: 94). Blind people use sounds such as their own footsteps bouncing off buildings and other physical elements in order to hear postboxes, traffic signs and trees, or to 'feel' the dimensions of a room such as where a doorway is located (Gibson, 1966: 2; Hill, 1985: 102). Familiar places have a familiar acoustic profile:

> To be at home in a place, especially in the dark, means knowing how it sounds and resounds. Thus listening is just as much a means of active inquiry and of orienting oneself in the world as is looking. (Ingold, 2000: 274)

Sighted people pay little attention to this form of perception because they can usually glean information about the layout of their surroundings in a split second just by looking around them, but it is nevertheless a part of everybody's perception (Hill, 1985).

Music is also an important part of many human cultures. In her study of how people use music in the everyday, Tia DeNora (2000: 48) found that it can be used as a 'technology of self', that is, as a resource in the 'active production of self-identity over time'. The women she interviewed used music as a way of creating, maintaining or changing moods, in order to calm down or energize themselves. We can also see our favourite piece of music as an expression or mirror of our self (DeNora, 2000: 70). Music is often evocative of emotions and memories. Hearing a familiar tune can make us feel happy or sad, and remind us of people, places or situations. It is in this capacity that music can offer us a sense of embodied (in)security. Musical experiences have also been known to play an important part in relational and cultural belongings. Music can be used to create a sense of closeness in intimate relationships and many couples come to identify their relationship with 'our song'. Music can also form part of collective experience and identity, as evidenced whenever Liverpool Football Club fans sing 'You'll never walk alone'.

There are also varying rules for touch, for example when we are to kiss, hug or shake hands, and where we can do these activities, for example on the street or in the bedroom. Western public spaces are designed to offer plenty of space so that we are not squeezed together (compared to Arab souks and markets, which appear overcrowded from a Western point of view), while homes are more compact (Rodaway, 1994: 149).

We also use smell and taste, which are closely linked, to engage with the world. But because our sense of smell adapts to smells, we are often unaware of the everyday smells of our environment, and are more likely to notice 'unusual' or 'new' smells (Rodaway, 1994: 64; Degen, 2008: 44–5). Our taste/smell system plays an important role in helping us to locate ourselves in space and identifying ourselves with a home space (Rodaway, 1994: 61).

There is cultural variation in olfactory sensitivity and practices. A generally accepted claim is that in the West, smell plays a less important role than, say, in Arab cultures (Rodaway, 1994: 81). Rodaway (1994: 151) argues that olfactory geographies have been 'domesticated' in the West, meaning that the natural smells of animals and trees remain 'outside', while indoor olfactory experiences are controlled through deodorization, that is, masking unwanted smells and adding synthetic 'bottled' smells with desired properties. For many Westerners, therefore, a *lack* of smells perhaps indicates 'home'. Similarly, it is no longer acceptable for people to smell of sweat or other bodily odours, only of manufactured deodorants and perfumes. Consequently, people in Western cultures now use sight and sound more than smell or touch to gather information about each other (Burkitt, 1999).

When societies undergo transitions, for example the transition to a post-socialist state that occurred in Poland after 1989, this includes important changes in sensory geographies. The people interviewed by Śliwa and Riach (2011) distinguished between pre- and post-1989 smells, with the former described as strong, distinctive and intrusive compared to the deodorized smell-scapes of contemporary Poland. Polish people also speak of a 'smell of capital-ism' that is characterized by manufactured smells such as perfumes, which were scarce in socialist Poland.

Smell is, of course, closely linked to taste. We taste and smell the air we breathe, and the food and drink we consume. Just as with smells, tastes can also evoke strong memories and emotions, and are an important way in which we experience belonging. Take, for example, food, the smell and taste of which can evoke strong memories (Miller, 2008: 53; Andrews, 2010), as explored below.

The senses also blend with relational belongings, such as when we hear the sound of a loved person's voice, or the feel of their touch. How children define who counts as 'kin' has such sensory elements to them, for example, and Mason (2008) speaks of 'interphysicality' and 'sensory relationality' to capture this aspect of relationships. People make sense of their family relation-ships through sensory experience, as Wilson et al. (2012) found in their study of young people whose parents misuse substances. While the parents might try to 'hide' their substance use, their children reported that they could still smell the alcohol on their parents' breath or hear loud noises such as music or argu-ments 'seeping through interior walls' (Wilson et al., 2012: 100). One strategy used by these young people in trying to create a sense of belonging under such disruptive circumstances was to seal off unwanted noises by listening to music. Music could also be used to vent anger or blank out uncomfortable emotions (see also DeNora, 2000).

As Mason and Davies (2009) note, sociological categories such as cultural heritage, gender and ethnicity are experienced as sensory in everyday life. For example, a person speaking of being mixed race is likely to do so, not through abstract identity categories, but in terms of how their hair feels and how it has to be treated. In addition, what and how we sense is likely to be 'classed' and 'gendered'. The sensory is not a separate realm of experience, which is why sociologists 'need better understandings of the ways in which class, gender and the like are themselves sensory' and to remain attuned to 'the complex ways in which the sensory is tangled with other forms of experience and ways of knowing' (Mason and Davies, 2009: 599, 601). Below, I examine how these different domains of experience come together in our consumption of food.

The comfort of food

The foods we grow up with look, smell and taste familiar and are an important source of cultural belonging. There are also often particular cultural practices associated with eating and preparing food that can afford a certain sense of comfort. For example, the various vegetable casseroles prepared on Christmas Eve in Finland evoke a sense of 'home' for me. Indeed, meals are an important part of ritual celebrations in just about every culture. People regularly come together with friends and family to celebrate birthdays, weddings or holidays such as Diwali, Eid or Christmas, and as part of these celebrations, they eat together. This ritual ethnic food consumption, where specific foods are prepared and consumed on particular days, can help construct a sense of belonging.

The foods we like say something about the culture we belong to. However, there are also internal distinctions within a culture. Bourdieu (1979) found that different social classes develop different tastes when it comes to food. While the upper classes develop a taste for haute cuisine, the lower classes exhibit 'a taste for necessity', that is, food that is more immediately nourishing and higher in fat content. Bennett et al. (2009) have found similar cultural distinctions in taste in contemporary Britain, where, for example, the elite are more likely to like and listen to classical music than working-class people. More broadly speaking, our tastes are linked to the broader social and political context, as exemplified by the importation of 'new' foods through trade or colonization, such as the 'Indian curry' that is so popular in the UK.

There are particular cultures around not only *what* is eaten, but also how, when and with whom: at home or in a restaurant, with family or friends, or only with people of the same gender (Appadurai, 1981; Warde and Martens, 2000; Petö, 2007). Eating is an important part of many of our close relationships and can be a way of establishing and maintaining social bonds (Scott, 2009: 93). The archetypical Western 'date', for example, often entails some sort of meal out. There is also the common saying 'the family that eats together stays together', indicating that sharing family meals is an important part of family together-ness, and that it promotes a sense of belonging among family members (James and Curtis, 2010). In other words, food consumption is a cultural and rela-tional practice, and offers an example of how the different sources of belonging (culture, people and the material world) can merge into one.

As discussed in Chapter 7, cultures exist in relation to each other. This means that 'our culture' is defined as different from 'their culture'. Food is an impor-tant way in which these distinctions between self and other are made:

> Food and what counts as food is a signifier of belonging, cultural identity, and home. Food as culture is a site of dwelling. The materiality of food, styles of cooking, and ways of eating are symbolic ways of drawing a boundary between *us* and *them* (Gibson, 2007: 15)

For example, Kate Fox (2004) has noted that English people from different class backgrounds use culturally coded understandings of table manners such as the 'proper' use of a knife and fork to draw distinctions between themselves and 'unmannered' or 'pretentious' people.

Foods are also important in creating a local, regional or national identity, and a way of connecting with this imagined community (Petö, 2007: 159). Examples of regional or national dishes are tripe in the north of England, haggis in Scotland and herring in the Netherlands. Eating a dish that carries with it such collective symbolism can be a reaffirmation of one's cultural identity and one's sense of belonging somewhere. When interviewing migrant women, Petö (2007: 156) found that most of their first impressions about their new country related to food. While some found comfort in adapting to a new culture by learning to cook the foods of their new home country, others talked about an (imagined) culinary link with their homeland that they maintained by preparing 'our' food. The women also talked about the joys of returning to their home country and eating the food there. In other words, these women were negotiating their national and cultural identity through food (Petö, 2007: 157).

Place as embodied experience

Perhaps the most frequently studied aspect of our embodied connection to the world is belonging to place. Within geography, the concept of place is understood to encompass not only the space in question, but also the social interactions that help give meaning to that space and thereby transform it from a space into a place with meaning. Places are not bounded but porous, meaning that the characteristics of a place are not all determined locally, but are also influenced by processes that happen elsewhere (Massey, 1994). Think of the changes that many ordinary streets have gone through in the past few decades, for example, as wooden window frames have been replaced by UPVC windows and as the number of cars and satellite dishes has increased. These local changes have an impact on the meaning that a place holds for residents, while also speaking, 'albeit subtly, of deeper structural processes', such as the rise of consumer culture (Rogaly and Taylor, 2009: 51–2).

Place is experienced as a sensuous, embodied and emotional geography that we come to know through our senses (Davidson and Milligan, 2004: 523; Degen, 2008: 49; Bhatti et al., 2009). As discussed above, a place is made up of 'keynote' sights, sounds and smells. We encounter our everyday material landscapes 'as inconspicuously familiar background' and, as such, they 'retreat from attention' to 'stay as unobtrusive backgrounds to other more important concerns' (Relph, 1985: 24). They are generally brought to our awareness when they change, for example when a familiar landmark is removed or a new one is constructed. Landscapes can also be brought to our attention when we experience a jarring sense of not belonging: 'In such moments, we are reflectively aware of landscapes as integral aspects of our being-in-the-world' (Relph, 1985: 24). For example, when we travel to a foreign country, we are likely to become aware of our surroundings in an intensified manner because the sensescapes they offer us are unfamiliar. And when we return 'home', we may become aware in a heightened fashion of the smells, sounds, tastes and images we used to take for granted, which had remained 'seen but unnoticed'.

The identity of a place and the meaning it has for us is based on our unconscious embodied knowledge that allows us to develop a deep understanding of that place (O'Neill, 2001: 4). This understanding is gained through the performance of daily tasks and movement (O'Neill, 2001: 5). For example, by regularly walking through a place, we develop a sense of the slope and texture of the ground, which become 'familiar identifying features, giving specific identity to every part of the ... landscape' (O'Neill, 2001: 8). Other phenomenological experiences of land, such as planting a vegetable garden, also help shape people's sense of belonging to place (Benson, 2010). In her study of ranchers in rural Montana, O'Neill (2001: 8) found that ranchers spoke of their connection to their ranches in terms of their physical habits and movements: 'ranchers focused on highly tactile, kinesthetic, and somasthetic qualities of how the buildings were constructed, how much effort it took, how it felt to do that work, and who got hurt'.

Having built or repaired many of the structures on their farms, such as buildings and fences, the ranchers had developed 'an intimate tactile knowledge of materials, form, construction details, and structural soundness' of these (O'Neill, 2001: 8). These sensory experiences, which accumulated over time, helped ranchers to 'formulate deep-rooted comprehension' that, in turn, enabled them to make sense of place (O'Neill, 2001: 10). In other words, we build a sense of belonging in the world by moving through and engaging with our environment with all our senses and by giving meanings to these experiences (Leach, 2002: 286).

It is through such habitual uses of space that we create bodily behaviours that Seamon (1980) has called 'place-ballet'. Place-ballets are time-space routines that can become relatively constant and stable, changing little across generations, as O'Neill (2001) found. The ranchers in her study described uses and organization of land and space that had remained similar from generation to generation, so that members of different generations had similar cognitive maps of a place. Our sensory experiences of place are therefore to a degree collective: groups develop shared understandings of the meaning of place (Degen, 2008: 175; Benson, 2010: 76). Our sensuous reality is thus not only determined by raw sensations, such as visual or auditory input, but also by cultural systems of belief. We approach the world with particular expectations in terms of what we can expect to see, hear and smell.

Ingold (2000) has noted that humans grow up in environments shaped by previous generations and carry these earlier forms of dwelling in their bodies, for example in how they use particular spaces and the meanings they attach to them. Learning about the local history of a place – how the land has been used and how specific aspects of the landscape have come about – can be an important way of establishing a link between self and place (Benson, 2010: 76). Different groups can give competing and conflicting meanings to a place. This is the case in Israel, for example, where Jewish and Palestinian citizens wish to commemorate different events and memorialize different places (Fenster, 2004).

Although we are born into a world of ready-made structures, which inform how we interact with our environment as well as the meanings we give it, there is room for individual creativity in everyday life (de Certeau, 1984). People can subvert expectations by using space for their own means, for example, performing different ways of being in a space – 'ways of walking, reading, producing, speaking etc.' (de Certeau, 1984: 30) – that transform that space. People who have moved countries and find themselves in spaces that are structured in unfamiliar ways can bring their own ways of dwelling that are peculiar to their own native country and superimpose them on the existing structures:

> Thus a North African living in Paris or Roubaix (France) insinuates *into* the system imposed on him [sic] by the construction of a low-income housing development or of the French language the ways of 'dwelling' (in a house or a language) peculiar to his native Kabylia. He superimposes them and, by that combination, creates for himself a space in which he can find *ways of using* the constraining order of the place or of the language. Without leaving the place where he has no choice but to live and which lays down its law for him, he establishes within it a degree of *plurality* and creativity. By an art of being in between, he draws unexpected results from his situation. (de Certeau, 1984: 30)

It is through our embodied experiences that we also develop an emotional engagement with a place, be it positive, negative or neutral (Downing, 2003; Bendiner-Viani, 2005). Thus, our sense of belonging is always emotionally laden, whether it is experienced as offering us 'a positive sensation of security' or as 'oppressive and restrictive' (Relph, 1985: 27). When examining belonging to place, therefore, the emotional realm must also be taken into consideration. Much of what we do with our bodies is linked to feelings:

> the most basic bodily tasks of resting, eating, working out or just getting around, can be 'fraught' with fear, guilt and shame, or infused with adrenaline thrills, cravings or dreamt-up desires. Recognition of the inherently emotional nature of embodiment has, thus, led many to the conclusion that we need to explore how we feel – as well as think – through 'the body'. (Davidson and Milligan, 2004: 523)

Consequently, our senses and sensory experiences as well as emotions are central to our experience of place. We live in 'emotional environs' and 'place must be felt to make sense' (Davidson and Milligan, 2004: 524).

Just as with the senses, our emotional reactions also follow common cultural forms (Ortner, 2005: 38). Williams (1977) speaks of a 'structure of feeling', which means that people's emotional reactions are not inherent, but are the product of learning to think and feel within certain parameters. Thus, people in the same culture tend to respond similarly to a death or a romance (Elias, [1939]1978). These 'everyday feelings, sensations, and modes of experiencing' may feel very personal to us, but are in fact a product of 'the social, of styles of life, and so of subjectification in the webs of "quiet agreement"' (Harrison, 2000: 514).

Emplaced selves

Above, I explored our sensory connection to the surrounding world that allows us to make sense of our environment and form an attachment to it. All activity takes place somewhere and everything we do is rooted in place. As a consequence:

> 'Where' is never a there, a region over against us, isolated and objective. 'Where' is always part of us and we part of it. It mingles with our being, so much so that place and human being are enmeshed, forming a fabric that is particular, concrete and dense. (Grange, 1985: 71)

Place is thus fundamental to our sense of self (Leach, 2002: 286). Tilley (1994: 15) proposes that our individual and cultural identities are 'bound up with place' and we create a sense of self 'through place'. Hence, having a feeling of belonging to a place hinges on whether people feel that a place adequately reflects who they are (Fortier, 2000; Savage et al., 2005). We include these places we identify with in our narrative of who we are (Bruner, 1987; Savage et al., 2005). When identifying with a place, we mirror ourselves with our surroundings: we 'introject' the external environment into us, while also 'projecting' ourselves onto the external world (Leach, 2002: 288).

By identifying with a place or region, such as Sussex or New England, a person is not merely saying that they are *from* that place. They are also saying something about their personality and cultural affiliations, and the personality of the other residents – they are all people *of* that region (Relph, 1985: 22). Place, therefore, is often seen to reflect the identity of the people living there and vice versa. Residents of particular areas, such as slums and council estates, can become stigmatized as 'deprived', 'criminals' or 'racist' (Rogaly and Taylor, 2009). In her ethnography of Bacup, Lancashire, Jeanette Edwards (2000) found that by saying they were 'Bacup born and bred', residents were claiming that they shared traits and characteristics with the place. Both Bacup and the people living there were seen as idiosyncratic, blunt and moulded by the harsh climate, industry and poverty. 'Bacup born and bred' people were seen to have skills for survival that 'soft' incomers lacked and were therefore expected to 'not last'.

In sum, we go through a process of 'making sense of place, developing a feeling of belonging and eventually identifying with that place' (Leach, 2002: 292), and in this process we come to understand who we are, both as individuals and as a group of people:

> The place acts dialectically so as to create the people who are out of that place. These qualities of locales and landscapes give rise to a feeling of belonging and rootedness and a familiarity, which is not born just out of knowledge, but of *concern* that provides ontological security. They give rise to a power to act and a power to relate that is both liberating and productive. (Tilley, 1994: 26)

Tilley's argument about the link between belonging and the ability to act echoes that of Shotter (1993). Belonging is not merely a state of mind but is bound up with being able to act in a socially significant manner that is recognized by others.

Belonging to place

Places are not inherently meaningful; rather, they are perceived as meaningful by the people who inhabit them. We develop different attachments to different places depending on what we do in a place and the people we know there. Place encompasses not only the physical characteristics of that place but also the relationships we have with the people we share those places with and the activities we undertake there (Downing, 2003: 213). These personal experiences meld with shared imaginaries to produce an emotional response as to whether or not we feel at home in a place:

> Everyone retains in memory sites of significance: places that surround us with a sense of well-being or from which we recoil in distress or fear; places of vulnerability or power; of dependence or independence (Downing, 2003: 215–16)

Lofland (1998: 65–70) distinguishes between three types of person-to-place connections. First, memorialized locales are those places where significant events such as battles have taken place, or where such events are remembered with the help of a memorial such as a statue (Urry, 2000). These places come to symbolize community and are used by people to distinguish between 'us' and 'them'.

The second type of connection is formed with familiarized locales through which our routine, often daily, paths traverse. These places become familiar to us and we can develop a deep attachment to them, to the point that their loss is experienced as significant. One such place for me was Urbis, a museum of urban life and culture in Manchester that closed its doors in 2010. Although I would only visit Urbis two or three times a year, I often walked past it and enjoyed the beauty of its architecture, remembering the various exhibitions I had been to. In this way, Urbis represented for me very much what Lofland's favourite restaurant did for her:

> an important element in the fabric of my city's 'downtown' – an area that is very much a part of my 'home range'. It gave me pleasure to know the restaurant was where it was, I liked glancing in its windows and smelling the aromas that came out its door. I feel sad, and a bit angry, that it is gone. A small loss, perhaps. Nothing earthshaking. Nothing tragic. But a loss nonetheless. (Lofland, 1998: 67)

Hang-outs and home territories comprise the third type of place to which people form a connection (Lofland, 1998). These are places, such as a clubhouse or a student union bar, that feel like 'home,' where we deem it safe to behave in a slightly less guarded fashion than we would 'out in public', despite the fact that they are technically open to people who are strangers to us.

The extent to which people feel at home in a particular place is partly tied in with how it is designed, built and resourced. As Urry (2000) puts it, the composition and layout of the environment 'affords' certain types of behaviour. We become aware of these affordances by moving through and sensing our surroundings through active 'sensemaking' (Degen, 2008: 48). For example, a comfortable bench can be used to stretch out on for a nap, while singular seats do not afford such comfort. Similarly, blocks of flats with balconies afford a form of sociality as residents can stand or sit on their balconies and chat to passersby (Degen, 2008). Thus, changes in architectural design change our everyday practices, such as how we cook food or wash ourselves, which then impact on our social relationships (Datta, 2008).

Power and inequalities

Different people will perceive the affordances of a place differently. The typical example is that of the long and unlit underpass that many women find too daunting to use at night. Women are known to limit their use of public spaces for fear of physical or sexual attacks (Day, 2001; Fenster, 2005; Green and Singleton, 2006). Other groups, such as the disabled, are denied access to some public spaces on account of how they are designed and built. Riessman (2003), for example, comments on how making public spaces wheelchair accessible has reduced the social isolation of wheelchair-bound people. These issues are important in relation to belonging – if a person feels unsafe or otherwise unable to access a space, they are likely to avoid it. If too many public spaces are like this, this reduces not only people's sense of belonging, but also their sense of a 'right to the city' or citizenship (Young, 1990).

There is a link between the material condition and the resourcing of a place and belonging (Skifter Andersen, 2003; Brownlow, 2006). Wacquant (2008) and Anderson (1990) note that living in extreme poverty in a dilapidated area that has been abandoned by public services and offers little in the way of opportunities for mobility (social or geographic) will inevitably have an impact on people's sense of 'community' and belonging. Public interactions in such spaces can be fraught, to the extent that the slightest incident such as bumping into someone may lead to deadly gunfire. Consequently, many residents avoid these spaces.

But deprivation alone is not enough to explain residents' lack of belonging. Jørgensen (2010) proposes that the nature of social relations in a neighbourhood also plays a part. In her study of two deprived neighbourhoods in Copenhagen, she found that residents living in the area that experienced higher levels of population mobility were less likely to express a sense of belonging compared to people living in an area where 'social relations are intimate' (Jørgensen, 2010: 18).

Because our perception of our material environment is socially shaped, and because the places we live in are differently resourced and given different meanings, it is important to examine the politics of belonging in relation to the material world. We can ask questions such as who decides how public spaces are designed and, as a result, who is 'afforded' a sense of belonging in them?

Material objects

It is not only in relation to place that we come to understand who we are, but material objects also help constitute our sense of self. Daniel Miller (2008, 2010) has argued that material objects and our possessions are not superficial but profound. How a person interacts with or relates to things is often analogous to how they relate to people. According to Miller (2008: 25), the way in which Mr Clarke, one of his study participants, handled all the things in his house with great care constitutes care work saturated with moral principles, which he also adopts in his relationships with people. Objects can store and possess emotions, and can, for example, represent deceased people and allow the bereaved to continue a relationship with them even after death. Clothes, for instance, are able to be 'embroidered with the ghosts of the departed, who can embrace you as easily as you can embrace them' (Miller, 2008: 45). Mason (2008) also highlights the importance of the sensory in our relationships. She speaks of sensory and material affinities that exist between people, such as when a woman wears her dead mother's wedding ring as a way of feeling her presence.

Bourdieu (1977) notes that everyday objects are ordered systematically. Things 'in their right place' reflect a deeper underlying organizational principle of a society. Bourdieu gives the example of Muslim Berbers in North Africa who learn to become a 'typical' Berber through their everyday interactions with material objects such as furniture, implements and tools. Think, for example, of a 'typical' Westerner who sits on chairs, eats at a table, sleeps in a bed, takes the train to work and watches television in the evening. As Miller (2008: 294) puts it, 'the order of things – how to sit, be polite, play and dress – is their education, socialising them to become typical of their people'.

Thus, objects 'hail' us in particular ways. A postbox means something to a letter-writing human, and a person walking with a letter in their hand will feel a pull towards the postbox (Gibson, 1979: 139). We are who we are, not simply because of the people we interact with, but also because of the material objects we learn to use in particular ways, which then guide us in terms of how we 'should' lead our lives:

> In short, material culture matters because objects create subjects much more than the other way around. It is the order of relationship to objects and between objects that creates people through socialisation whom we then take to exemplify social categories, such as Catalan or Bengali, but also working class, male, or young. (Miller, 2008: 287)

Miller (2010) argues that how a culture approaches 'stuff' says a lot about how that culture views the self. Miller compares the Western view of clothing as 'superficial' with Trinidadians' concern with style. While Westerners tend to see clothing or any other attempt to modify one's appearance as an attempt to (mis)represent the 'true' self that lies within – and therefore view people who are interested in clothing as superficial – Trinidadians believe that lies are hidden deep inside, while the truth is to be found on the surface. So, Trinidadians believe that what clothes a person wears and how are an expression of who they are.

Miller (2010) is not concerned with determining which of these metaphors is 'right' or 'wrong'. Instead, he wishes to 'make the familiar strange' by asking why Westerners see the Trinidadians' relationship to clothing as a sign of superficiality. He wonders whether the answer could partly lie in the fact that in the West, identities are understood as accumulated and relatively constant, as reflected in fixed identities and hierarchies such as 'working class'. In contrast, the Trinidadian self is not given by social status or formal occupation. Instead, identities are seen as transient, and people are judged by what they are today, not what they were before. This means that the self can be 'discovered' through clothing – how one looks is who one is. Thus, these different notions of whether or not clothing is superficial reflect different views of the self. In this way, 'stuff' plays 'a considerable and active part in constituting the particular experience of the self, in determining what the self is' (Miller, 2010: 40).

Making a 'home' with objects

Material objects also help constitute 'home' and signify 'who we are'. Skey (2011) found in his study of national belonging that everyday objects such as particular brands of marmalade held a significance beyond their everyday use, as markers of what it means to be 'English'. They are, to an extent, 'portable property', that is, we can re-create 'home' in a new setting with the help of familiar objects we bring with us. In his study of the material objects that British colonizers took with them when they emigrated to India, Plotz (2008: xiii) notes that these 'trinkets and ornaments became the metonymic placeholders for geographically disaggregated social networks'. For example, strands of hair and tokens were sent to people as a sign of 'enduring attachment' and objects became 'extensions of the home and family Victorians on the move had left behind', symbols of community and national identity (Plotz, 2008: xiii–xiv). These objects were important because they were associated with English culture and customs:

> Victorian Greater Britons evidently valued objects (a trinket), locales (an 'English' garden), and even practices (midday walks) that could in some way serve as a direct conduit back to a place nostalgically construed as an alma mater (Plotz, 2008: 18)

What was at stake was 'remaining English' while living in the colonies, and Plotz (2008: 2, 50) interprets the construction of national portable property that symbolized national identity as an effort to establish 'psychic distance from one's actual site of residence'. English migrants could thus feel detached from India and still connected to England.

Ways of staying connected with one's country of origin have changed somewhat since the Victorian era, thanks to technological advancements. Contemporary migrants, as long as they have not fled their country of origin due to political persecution, can often return to visit relatively easily and cheaply thanks to modern modes of transport (Alexandrova and Lyon, 2007). In addition, technology such as phones and computers can enable frequent (live) contact with friends and family who have remained. Migrants can also experience a sense of continued cultural proximity and belonging to their country of origin by reading the same books and watching the same television programmes as people in their home country (Alexandrova and Lyon, 2007: 105).

But we have also seen the emergence of a new kind of 'portable property' in the guise of mobile technologies such as smartphones, which have changed not only how we communicate with others (see Chapter 7), but have also changed our relationship to public spaces (May, 2011c). We can speculate whether public spaces now feel more 'private' to people as the opportunities to create 'quasi-private' spaces while out in public expand. Whereas in my father's youth, if he wanted to speak to someone, he had either to see them face to face or telephone them, which meant making use of landline telephones that remained rooted in place, I can now contact people in a variety of ways while sitting on the bus. Using my smartphone, I can phone, Skype or email someone or go on Facebook, not to mention 'tweeting' about the inconsiderate person sitting at the back of the bus who has created her own quasi-private space by having her music tinnily blaring out of her mobile phone.

We can now 'escape' our physical location by virtually travelling with the help of handheld devices and create a personal bubble by listening to music through headphones while walking down a busy city street (Elliott and Urry, 2010). Portable ICT devices can also make public space feel safer, as Cuminskey and Brewster (2012) found when they surveyed women college students in the USA. The women who took part in the survey tended to think of the mobile phone as a weapon of self-defence that allows them to contact help if attacked, and a more effective one than pepper spray at that. In sum, the material objects in our lives play a central role in how we connect with people, cultures and places, and new technologies that offer new ways of doing this can change our relationship to the world.

Changing material worlds

Our sense of belonging to a place never remains static but shifts as we gain new experiences that make us re-evaluate our relationship to place. We may, for example, use and view a playground differently as toddlers, young children, adolescents and parents (Bendiner-Viani, 2005: 468). The world around us also changes. Material transformations are an important part of social change, as witnessed in any major city; for example, hundreds of years of industrial and social developments have left their mark on the physical contours of Manchester (Edensor, 2007). At the same time, processes of (hyper)urbanization and (de)industrialization have led to the movement of large numbers of people from one region or country to another, affecting who we come into face-to-face contact with in particular places (Short, 2004; Dürrschimdt and Taylor, 2007; Edensor, 2007). New transport links, industrial estates and housing estates have been built, while others have been abandoned or torn down. Technological developments also change the nature of the objects we live among and use, such as vehicles, household objects or self-service tills at supermarkets. All this requires us to re-create our sensory belongings lest we end up feeling out of place (Casey, 1993; Savage et al., 2005; Edensor, 2007; Adams et al., 2007), while also impacting on our everyday habits, such as how we get from A to B.

It is important to explore the impact that such material change has on how people make sense of and form a relationship with their environment. Blokland (2003) found that changes in the built environment affected residents' ability to maintain collective memories about the area and thus belonging. Places are constructed 'in our memories and affections through repeated encounters and complex associations' (Relph, 1985: 26). Landscapes and buildings are full of memories, offering points of recognition that help recall the past. These experiences are no longer brought to mind if a building is demolished or an area rebuilt, and people can easily lose their 'roots' when familiar landscapes disappear (Blokland, 2003: 203, 205).

Sensuous markers and sensescapes

I focused above on changes in the material environment without explicitly engaging with the idea of haptic perception, that is, that the sense we make of the world is based on multisensory perception. I end this chapter by exploring in more detail how social change impacts the **sensescapes** in which people live, and the sociological significance of this.

Each historical period has its own particular form of sensuous experience. The emergence of urban-industrial societies led to major changes in the sensuous experience of people (Schafer, 1977). People were densely packed into the rapidly growing cities which were filled with the sounds of people and horse-drawn carts, as well as with smells of rotting food, faeces and other smells that most Westerners would now consider unpalatable. Towns and cities sprang up around significant industry, and few could escape from the noise and pollution from the factories. Later on, the invention and gradual ubiquity of cars, lorries, trains and aeroplanes, as well as the attendant infrastructure such as roads and railways that are required for these modes of transport, have changed the soundscapes, smellscapes and visionscapes of modern life.

To explore the impact that shifts in sensescapes have on people's sense of belonging, I turn to Degen's (2008) study of two regeneration areas, Castle-field in Manchester and El Raval in Barcelona. Degen (2008: 40) draws on the phenomenological tradition to see the body and the world in a reciprocal relationship. Degen (2008: 199) argues that sensuous markers, such as familiar sounds, smells or sights, can provide a sense of continuity people appreciate and form an emotional attachment to. Changes in the sensory landscape of a place are significant because embodied emotional ties and points of attachment with the physical environment disappear (Degen, 2008: 157).

Degen found that each area had its own 'sensuous landscape' that had been significantly altered through regeneration. Castlefield has become an airbrushed and 'neutral' space of bland colours and a lack of smells (Degen, 2008: 137). Long-term residents of Castlefield resisted this sensuous change by 'attaching positive memories to the sensuous decay of the industrial city', for example the smell of burning rubber tyres or the sound of cement mixers from the various workshops that used to populate the area. These were presented as 'honest' sounds and smells, reflecting the working patterns of the area, in contrast with the bland and sanitized sensescapes of regenerated Castlefield (Degen, 2008: 146).

In El Raval, established residents remarked on the 'multiculturalism' of the area, but rather than using directly racist language, they disguised cultural difference as an aesthetic problem. For example, they talked of the 'ugly' fluorescent lighting that Pakistani families used in their flats (visible to passersby on the street) compared to the more 'pleasant' ambient lighting used in other flats. Established Catalan Spanish residents in El Raval felt that their sense of belonging was threatened, which they experienced through the disappearance of reference points in their everyday sensuous landscapes (Degen, 2008: 190). What is at stake in such situations is a sense of ownership of a neighbourhood. Long-term residents identify strongly with the material landscape and their spatial identity is under threat when this landscape changes. One possible defensive reaction is to use sensuous experiences of 'foreign' versus 'familiar' smells or sounds to draw boundaries between 'us' and 'them' who are seen to defile the area (Degen, 2008: 191).

Conclusion

This final substantive chapter has focused on the third key source of belonging, namely the material world, comprising place and material objects. People's embodied relationships with these have so far been a fairly neglected aspect within sociological studies on belonging, which have tended to focus on cultural and relational dimensions. But as has been shown in this chapter, our embodied and sensory connection to the material world of places and objects is of crucial importance to our sense of self. In addition, social changes are acutely experienced on the material level. Changes in the material landscape have a profound effect on the self and our connection to the world because belonging is partly based on the familiarity of our sensescapes or sensory geographies.

Global processes, such as economic restructuring and the movement of populations, lie behind many of these sensory changes. At the local level, such macro-processes are experienced as a shift in a person's sense of safety in the world. Degen refers to Bauman's (1999) concept of *Unsicherheit* (uncertainty, insecurity), the inner aspect of which cannot be directly addressed. It is easier to tackle the external 'unsafety', which is transformed into a physical problem that can be more easily addressed, for example through 'othering' certain groups and their use of, for example, fluorescent lighting. In the long run, however, such processes are unsatisfactory, because they do not resolve the underlying ontological *Unsicherheit* (Degen, 2008: 191).

The sense of insecurity brought about by changes in our material environment requires us to rebuild our sensory connection with the surrounding world, to find new ways of interacting with our environment and to attach new meanings to these. This, in turn, is productive of further social changes.

We have now ended our tour of the three main sources of belonging: culture, people and the material world. In Chapter 10, I provide some concluding thoughts on the significance of belonging for understanding the relationship between self and social change.

Conclusion: Self and Belonging in a Changing World

10

Introduction

This concluding chapter synthesizes the arguments presented in *Connecting Self to Society* regarding the role that belonging plays in how people live with, respond to and contribute to social change. During the course of this book, I have discussed a range of sociological approaches, including symbolic interactionism, Bourdieu's theory of habitus and capital, ethnomethodology, phenomenology, sociology of everyday life, sociology of personal life, sociology of the body, and theories of material culture, as well as borrowing from other disciplines such as human geography. The aim has not been to provide an exhaustive overview of all the theoretical approaches on the self, but to argue for a novel way of studying the self.

What unites the theories that have contributed to my argument is that they take the point of view of the person as their starting point. Sociologists have a habit of seeing people as inhabiting social categories or roles rather than seeing the 'whole' person (Cohen, 1982a: 10). This is reflected, for example, in identity theories that explore the social identities, categories or roles that people inhabit. Such outside-in approaches risk fragmenting and dissecting people into their constituent parts. This book has argued that it is necessary to adopt a phenomenological approach that takes the experiencing subject as the starting point and therefore allows us to see the 'whole' person.

Furthermore, I have proposed that if we are to understand the relationship between society and the self, as well as social change, we must understand people's relationships to their selves, to other people, to their cultural context and to their material environments. One important way in which the relationship between self and society manifests itself is in a sense of belonging (or not belonging), which is sensitive to any changes. Studying people's sense of belonging can thus tell us something about how changes that occur on the social and the personal level are interrelated.

I begin my concluding discussion by exploring the piecemeal manner in which social change becomes apparent in our everyday lives. The effects of social change on the self are complex and uneven, and at times contradictory.

Belonging offers an apt window into studying this complexity because it is a multifaceted experience, encompassing our relationships to people, cultures and the material world. In practice, however, it cannot easily be dissected into its constituent parts, which is why, in order to understand belonging, we must adopt a holistic view that sees the person as embedded in a complex field of enmeshed cultural, relational and material worlds (Smart, 2007). This means that the person is understood not as an isolated individual, but as a member of a variety of settings and groups, within and between which claims for belonging are negotiated. In other words, belonging is not merely an individual matter, but a collective one. This brings me to my final point, namely that a focus on belonging inevitably leads us to examine power relations and ethical questions such as who is allowed to belong and where.

The fragmentary experience of social change

Many sociologists, such as Marx, Durkheim and Giddens, attribute a certain directionality and coherence to social change. But if you were asked to talk about social change from the perspective of your own personal life, perhaps the first things that would come to mind would be somewhat fragmentary examples. In other words, social change probably becomes apparent in your life in an uneven, incremental and piecemeal manner in the form of, for example, novel technologies, new institutional practices, emerging forms of culture and the changing requirements of the workplace. You are likely to be involved in many different groups and to move through different planes and spheres of life, therefore your life is shaped not by one single force but by many. As they are taking place, the changes in our lives rarely appear to embody an overarching logic. Consequently, we do not tend to experience the wholeness of our lives but see our existence in a fragmentary way (Levine, 1971: xxxviii).

It is usually only with hindsight that we can identify a 'grand narrative' that allows us to understand different developments as constituent parts of a broader thing called 'social change', such as deindustrialization or globalization, that has transformed our society in a particular direction. For example, the advent of the internet has had an impact on our sensory engagement with the world, as computers have become everyday objects and we have gained an understanding of a new dimension, namely 'virtual reality'. How we conduct our personal relationships has also been affected, as we can now stay in touch with friends and family on the go and across vast distances. Furthermore, new collective traditions and cultures have emerged within the new cyberworld, such as netiquette. We adapt to these shifts, often in creative ways, by modifying our daily habits and routines, and these adaptations then engender further social change (de Certeau, 1984). So it is important for any investigation of social change to begin in the material and local world as experienced by people (Smith, 1987: 84).

It is here that I return to Simmel's and Elias's arguments that self and society cannot be regarded as two separate entities. As Simmel (1950: 7–9) points out, if we view the world up close, we see individual people and their characteristics, but as we move further away our perspective changes; the individuals disappear and what we see instead is society. We interpret this as seeing two separate entities, but in fact both are views of the same thing seen differently depending on our distance from it. While structural accounts of social change posit a distinction between self and society, Elias (1991) could be interpreted as saying that inasmuch as society consists of people, we are all 'out there' in society. To paraphrase Merleau-Ponty ([1945]2002), according to whom perception is a mode of being in the world rather than a question of spectating an external world, the self is a mode of being in society rather than something separate from society (May, 2011a). We do not merely spectate a society nor does society direct our lives from the outside. We are *in* it, we *are* it.

The argument that has been put forward in this book is that one of the ways in which people experience this being in society is through a sense of belonging or lack thereof. By focusing on belonging, it is possible to keep in focus the different aspects and modes of being, such as the cultural, the relational and the embodied, and to see how these come together in the lifeworld of a person. To borrow a concept from Jennifer Mason (2010), these different modes of being make a complex whole, or an 'enmeshment'. This enmeshment is located in actual concrete settings, but has intangible aspects that can be difficult to verbalize, yet hugely significant (Smith, 1987: 84–5; May and Muir, 2011).

Belonging as a multimodal enmeshment

I wish to illustrate this multimodal enmeshment with the help of a photograph I have of three people sitting round a dining table: my sister-in-law Minni, my partner Mark and my friend Andrew. An ordinary photo in many respects, not unlike those you are likely to have in your album or among your computer files. But if we inspect the photograph more closely, it opens up a snapshot of how the different modes of belonging (cultural, relational and sensory) blend into each other in complex ways at any moment in our everyday lives. The three people sitting at the table come from different countries – Finland, England and Australia – and thus represent different cultural belongings, some of which I share; for example, I speak different languages with them: English with Mark and Andrew, Swedish with Minni.

My sense of relational belonging to them differs as well, partly due to the length of time I have known each person and the closeness of our relationship. I have known Minni the longest, coming up to 23 years, and she has become a key member of my extended family, while Mark, whom I have only known for 5 years, represents my closest relationship. Andrew, on the other hand, is a friend I have known for over 16 years, and his ex-partner is an even older friend, someone I have known since I was 14 years old. Thus, my biography intertwines with theirs in complex ways and each relationship brings up its own memories and emotions for me.

The photograph was taken during a dinner in Hove, England, which is an important place in my biography. It was here that my grandmother lived from before my birth until her death in 1988. Throughout my childhood we visited her once or twice a year, and I have many significant childhood memories attached to Hove and am rather overcome by nostalgia whenever I visit. These memories are, to a degree, sensory and can easily be triggered by sounds or smells. All I need to do is smell seaside air and hear the sound of seagulls, and I am transported back to my childhood, lying in bed in my grandmother's flat, enjoying the orange glow of the street lights seeping through the cracks in the curtains. I might also remember a Christmas Day walk along the promenade marvelling at the lack of cold and snow (compared to my home country of Finland) or the smell of the restaurant kitchen where I worked as a 'washer-upper' during my first summer of independence in 1989.

The photograph also speaks to other sensory and cultural belongings of mine. When the photograph was taken by me, we were eating salad and drinking wine. My father had previously made his legendary Pimm's cocktail potent enough to bring anyone to their knees. To any English reader, this last sentence in particular probably signals my social class background, while to a Finnish reader it might say nothing. And so, we are back within the realm of cultural belongings.

I could go on at some length about the various forms of belonging that are present in the photograph for me, but I think I have said enough to make my point, namely that it is well nigh impossible to disaggregate the different sources of belonging. They interact with each other, presenting combinations that together form a sort of multidimensional landscape of belonging that exists not only in the present, but also evokes past memories. This landscape often recedes into the background and offers an overall mood or tonality to our experiences. As Julia Bennett (2010) has put it, belonging is like the bass line of a tune that offers it structure and dynamism, a rhythm. We rarely pay much attention to it, unless something significant changes in that landscape that subsequently jolts us into a sense of not belonging. In other words, belonging is not straightforwardly quantifiable: it is complex and ephemeral, and easily eludes the researcher (May and Muir, 2011).

The politics and ethics of belonging

But our exploration does not end here, with the person. Sociologists are always interested in people as part of a bigger whole, such as society. Society is organized in particular ways, and each person has a place somewhere within this organization, which in turn influences their experiences. Not only that, but people are also members of groups, both 'real' and 'imagined', such as family, neighbourhood, social class or nationhood, to which they claim belonging.

Such claims for belonging are therefore always collectively negotiated, with some groups having more power to define the boundaries of who belongs (Yuval-Davis, 2011). In other words, who can achieve belonging and where is always tied to issues of power and inequalities. Thus, to be able successfully to claim belonging is important, because it signifies the ability to act in a meaningful way within society.

If we take it that belonging is a prerequisite for citizenship, or indeed a need, it follows that we should also be considering the ethics of belonging. There are human rights discourses around other basic needs, such as a person's fundamental right to food, water, shelter, privacy and equality. Is it perhaps time to start examining belonging from a similar ethical perspective, that is, to consider a person's moral right to belong, and to ask, what could be done to ensure such belonging? This, I argue, is not merely an issue for moral philosophers, but also for sociologists.

Glossary

Alienation is a concept developed by Marx to describe the effects that the organization of industrial production had on workers, who did not own the means of production nor their own labour. This meant that work ceased to be the basis for self-definition or self-affirmation and became something external to the worker, while the product that the worker produced was an alien object. Indeed, society itself stood as an alien external force and workers' lives became shaped by forces beyond their control.

Anomie is a concept developed by Durkheim to describe what happens to selves if social differentiation goes too far. A state of anomie means that individuals no longer feel they are part of society because they have no shared social values. In other words, they are isolated from each other. At its most extreme, anomie can lead to a sense of despair and, ultimately, suicide. (See *organic solidarity*)

Body hexis is a term developed by Bourdieu to signify that our bodily behaviour, such as how we walk, talk and eat, is not something innate, but is learned. People from different backgrounds, who inhabit different social fields and who end up with different habitus, will also differ in terms of body hexis. For example, people from different social class backgrounds might have different accents when they speak, while men and women might walk or sit differently.

Cartesian dualism refers to the theory of French philosopher René Descartes, according to whom the mind and the body are two separate entities. He argued that the thinking mind is the basis for our self and that we know our selves through our minds, therefore his famous dictum 'I think, therefore I am'. Cartesian dualism states that without a mind, there can be no self, whereas the mind can exist after the body has died.

Culture is a term used to refer to the collection of shared practices and beliefs that come to define a group of people. Culture comprises shared social norms, such as norms around sex and family life, and cultural practices, such as eating certain foods, listening to specific types of music or building houses in a particular way.

Deindustrialization refers to developments in the West from the 1960s onwards, which saw much of the manufacturing production move to countries that offered cheaper labour and less restrictive employment laws. Deindustrialization had a profound impact, leading to mass unemployment and a restructuring from an industrial to a service sector economy.

Determinism denotes a way of thinking, according to which people's lives are predetermined, either because of their biology, such as sexuality, or because of social forces, such as social class.

The Enlightenment refers to a period from the mid-seventeenth to the eighteenth century during which rational thought was promoted as an alternative to tradition and a belief in the progressiveness of modern society became widespread. Strands of Enlightenment thinking are still visible today.

Epistemology means a theory of knowledge, that is, a theory about how we can know reality, and how we can gather information about it. Epistemology is often paired with ontology, because it is generally believed that a particular view of reality leads to a particular epistemological approach. (See *ontology*)

Ethnomethodology is a school of thought within sociology that is interested in studying how people produce social life, for example how social order is created on the streets, where most people can be seen to behave as if according to some unwritten and taken-for-granted rules.

Feminism is both a social movement and a theoretical tradition. Second-wave feminism began in the 1960s in the USA and the UK, and has had a significant impact on women's lives by campaigning for equal rights in working life and in families. The theoretical strand of feminism has been closely linked to the social movement side, and many feminist theorists have also been political activists. There are many different schools of thought within feminism, but one of the key foci has been to critically analyse inequalities between men and women, and the impact these have had on women's lives.

Frankfurt School refers to a neo-Marxist school of thought that originated in the 1920s at the Institut für Sozialforschung in Frankfurt, Germany, which aimed to develop a critical analysis of the homogenizing impact of the highly commercialized mass media and mass culture.

Generalized other is a term developed by Mead when describing the process by which children come to internalize the attitudes of their social group. In the first stages of development, children rely on the instruction of significant others, such as parents, to guide their behaviour. With age, children come to develop an understanding of abstract principles according to which people in their social group behave, and to adopt these to regulate their own behaviour.

Globalization is a term used to denote the increasing international influence that certain organizations and businesses have gained over the past few decades. Whereas before, economic, social and political systems were thought of as national, many now have a global reach. There is even talk of the emergence of a single global market, as exemplified by the increasing power of multinational conglomerates.

Habitus refers to patterned ways of thinking and behaving. This concept was developed by Bourdieu, who argued that we are all born into a particular social field, which partly determines which set of embodied habits we internalize. Depending on our social position, we internalize particular dispositions, which then generate certain practices and ways of perceiving the world. Although our habitus feels 'natural', Bourdieu reminds us that it is, in fact, produced by social structures.

Haptic perception is a concept used to denote the way in which our whole body, including all our senses (sight, sound, smell, taste and touch), is involved in perceiving the world, and how these different modes of perception intermingle. For example, people see not only the objects around them, but also sense and hear the auditory waves bouncing off them; although sighted people are rarely consciously aware of this latter part of their haptic perception. To take another example, we can both smell and taste the air.

Identity category is a term used to describe the shared aspects of our identities. Thus, everyone within a particular category has at least one characteristic in common. For example, people who are defined as 'woman' share the same gender, while identity categories based on sexuality distinguish between 'heterosexual', 'homosexual', 'bisexual' and 'asexual' people.

The individualization thesis has become a central focus of debate within the social sciences. The main thrust of the argument is that as a result of the weakening of traditions in contemporary societies, individuals are freer to make their own life choices.

Industrialization is a process that began in the eighteenth century in Britain, which transformed preindustrial societies into industrialized ones. Central to this process was the development of machine-based forms of production, which took place in large factories that produced hitherto unseen volumes of goods. Industrialization also led to significant social change, as increasing numbers of people moved to towns and cities to become wage labourers and living standards eventually improved.

Intersectionality refers to a theoretical approach developed in response to traditional theories of identity, which tended to examine identity categories, such as gender and ethnicity, separately. According to intersectional theories, it is important to understand the variability within identity categories. For example, the category 'woman' is not homogeneous because the opportunities and lives of women from different ethnic or social class backgrounds differ. Intersectionality also aims to understand how these different identity categories interact with each other, such that white middle-class men are likely to benefit from the fact that their ethnicity, social class and gender come together to reinforce their dominant position in society.

Late modernity is used to describe contemporary Western societies, which are said to have moved to a new stage of modernity that can be characterized as late modern. Theorists of late modernity argue that while there have been some fundamental changes, such as the weakening importance of social class and an increase in people's ability to 'experiment' with their lives, some aspects of modernity have continued. For example, some institutions, such as capitalism, continue to be key within late modern societies.

Mechanical solidarity is a concept developed by Durkheim in his work on the division of labour in society. Durkheim argued that primitive societies were characterized by a form of social solidarity that he called 'mechanical' because it resembled the cohesion that holds together the elements of raw materials. Mechanical solidarity is based on similarity: all members of a group share the same common beliefs. In such societies, individuality is weak. (See *organic solidarity*)

Modernity is used to describe societies that emerged after industrialization. In contrast to traditional agrarian and feudal societies, the hallmarks of modern societies were industrial production, capitalism and flexible social structures based on class.

Neoliberalism refers to an ideology that is said to dominate the West, and to be increasingly powerful globally, to the extent that we are said to live in 'an age of neoliberalism'. The effects of neoliberalism are manifold, perhaps most clearly visible in economic policy that aims to reduce state regulation that is seen to hinder free trade. Neoliberalism is also visible in the belief that individuals are able to make their own way and have control over their destinies. It has been strongly criticized as a dehumanizing logic, where the economic interests of the market are placed above those of solidarity and common responsibility for the wellbeing of citizens.

Ontology means a theory of reality, that is, a theory of what constitutes reality and of what kinds of things can and do exist. (See *epistemology*)

Organic solidarity is a concept Durkehim developed as a pair to mechanical solidarity. Organic solidarity is found in more advanced societies characterized by a complex and highly developed division of labour. In such a society, each group performs a specific role on which the whole society depends, rather like the organs of the body perform a crucial function without which the body would not survive, hence the term 'organic'. Such societies require that individuals are different from each other. If this differentiation goes too far, a state of anomie ensues. (See *mechanical solidarity*)

Phenomenology is an approach that understands social reality as something that is created through thought and action, rather than as something that is given. The focus is on the taken-for-granted knowledge that humans have of the world, how this commonsense knowledge comes about, and how it shapes our view of the world. The starting point for a phenomenological investigation is thus the experience of the person. The influence of phenomenology can be seen in ethnomethodology.

Psychosocial fragmentation thesis is a term used to describe a set of theoretical approaches that claim that social changes, such as industrialization, deindustrialization and globalization, have led to weak, vulnerable and fragmented selves and have eroded social cohesion and solidarity.

Reflexivity refers to thought and action that is done reflectively. A reflexive self is able to hold themselves as the object of their own thought, to think about their own actions, and to regulate themselves.

Relational self is a term that denotes the self not as separate or autonomous from others, but as inherently connected to other people. The relational self gains a sense of self in relationships with and in relation to other people.

Sensescape can be defined as the simultaneous presence of several sensuous experiences. Thus, the sights, sounds, smells, tastes and textures of a particular space constitute the sensescape that this space offers.

Social change is a broad term that is used in sociology to denote not only significant shifts in how people think and act, that is, in social norms and practices, but also in social institutions, such as religion or industry, and systems of governance, for example the shift from feudal states to democratic republics.

Social constructionism is an approach within the social sciences that takes a particular view of the nature of reality (see *ontology*). Rather than accepting social reality at face value, social constructionists argue that much of the social reality we take for granted is socially constructed, that is, it is the product of human thought and activity. For example, 'adolescence' is a stage in the life course that many would take to 'just exist' as a universal given. However, the concept of adolescence is not a universal concept; rather, it emerged at a particular time and in a particular place, and the meanings attached to it are context bound.

Social field is a term developed by Bourdieu to refer to a combination of space and interaction that comprises the boundaries of our experiential context. There can be different kinds of interactions going on in the same space that form different fields. For example, a room at a university can be used for lectures (academic field) or for a concert (cultural field). Conversely, a social field can exist in more than one place. For example, the academic field can take place in a university library, or in a student's bedroom as they revise for an exam. People in the same social position such as social class tend to move through similar social fields, although each individual moves through their own combination of fields.

Socialization refers to a process that children go through as they learn the 'correct' manner of behaviour for their particular society. In other words, children become socialized, in the first instance by their parents, to become acceptable members of their social group who can act 'appropriately' in social situations. (See *social norm*)

Social norm is a term used to describe how, in every society, there are certain socially shared expectations as to how people should behave. For example, the expectation that people do not laugh at a funeral, or that people only have sex with the person they are married to.

Social order comprises the patterns according to which society and social life are ordered, which is of great interest to sociologists. Social life is patterned both at the macro-level, for example men and women's employment patterns, and at the micro-level – people tend to interact with each other in patterned ways, for example in public spaces.

Social structure is a concept used within sociology to describe (semi-) permanent patterns of social life. An example of a social structure is gender: our societies are, to an extent, organized around gender. Men and women, for example, are seen to have different roles within families and at work. Although gender as a social structure influences how men and women behave in their everyday lives, it becomes most clearly visible through social statistics. These show that women look after children more than men, while a higher proportion of men work outside the home and command bigger salaries at work than women.

Sociology of everyday life is a sociological approach that argues that the mundane activities people engage in are significant because they help constitute society, but also because they allow us to view how social structures operate at an individual level.

Sociology of personal life is a sociological approach developed by Carol Smart, who argued that rather than viewing people as autonomous individuals, sociologists would do better to focus on the inherently connected and relational nature of people's lives, which are embedded within networks of relationships as well as culturally embedded. For example, the way we feel and think emerges out of our sociocultural context such that we are likely to think and feel in similar ways to others within that context.

Structuralism denotes an approach to the study of society that highlights the importance of social structures over that of individuals. At its extreme, structuralism presents social structures as 'things' that exist independently of individual thought and action.

Symbolic interactionism is a sociological tradition that investigates how meaning is not inherent in things or in action, but is created in interaction. In other words, meaning is a collective accomplishment. Symbolic interactionists tend to be interested in studying face-to-face interactions between individuals, focusing, for example, on how those individuals come to define a situation.

Bibliography

Adam, Barbara (1996) 'Detraditionalization and the certainty of uncertain futures', in P. Heelas (ed.) *Detraditionalization: Critical Reflections on Authority and Identity*, Oxford: Blackwell.

Adams, Mags, Moore, Gemma, Cox, Trevor et al. (2007) 'The 24-hour city: Residents' sensorial experiences', *Senses & Society*, 2(2): 201–16.

Adams, Matthew (2003) 'The reflexive self and culture: A critique', *British Journal of Sociology*, 54(2): 221–38.

Adams, Matthew (2007) *Self and Social Change*, London: Sage.

Adkins, Lisa (2004) 'Reflexivity: Freedom or habit of gender?', in L. Adkins and B. Skeggs (eds) *Feminism After Bourdieu*, Oxford: Blackwell.

Adorno, Max and Horkheimer, Theodor W. ([1944]1997) *The Dialectic of Enlightenment: Philosophical Fragments*, London: Verso.

Agosto, Denise, Abbas, June and Naughton, Robin (2012) 'Relationships and social rules: Teens' social network and other ICT selection practices', *Journal of the American Society for Information Science and Technology*, 63(6): 1108–24.

Ahmed, Sara and Fortier, Anne-Marie (2003) 'Re-imagining communities', *International Journal of Cultural Studies*, 6(3): 251–9.

Alexandrova, Nadejda and Lyon, Dawn (2007) 'Imaginary geographies: Border-places and "home" in the narratives of migrant women', in L. Passerini, D. Lyon, E. Capussotti and I. Laliotou (eds) *Women Migrants from East to West: Gender, Mobility and Belonging in Contemporary Europe*, New York: Berghan Books.

Anderson, Benedict (1983) *Imagined Communities: Reflections on the Origin and Spread of Nationalism*, London: Verso.

Anderson, Elijah (1990) *Streetwise: Race, Class and Change in an Urban Community*, Chicago, IL: University of Chicago Press.

Andrews, Robyn (2010) 'Little Anglo-India: Making Australia "local" at St Joseph's Hostel', in B. Bönisch-Brednich and C. Trundle (eds) *Local Lives: Migration and the Politics of Place*, Farnham: Ashgate.

Antonsich, Marco (2010) 'Searching for belonging: An analytical framework', *Geography Compass*, 4(6): 644–59.

Appadurai, Arjun (1981) 'Gastro-politics in Hindu South Asia', *American Ethnologist*, 8(3): 494–511.

Baerveldt, Chris, Zijlstra, Bonne, de Wolf, Muriel et al. (2007) 'Ethnic boundaries in high school students' networks in Flanders and the Netherlands', *International Sociology*, 22(6): 701–20.

Bagnoli, Anna (2009) 'Beyond the standard interview: The use of graphic elicitation and arts-based methods', *Qualitative Research*, 9(5): 547–70.

Banks, Stephen P. (2009) 'Intergenerational ties across borders: Grandparenting narratives by expatriate retirees in Mexico', *Journal of Aging Studies*, 23(3): 178–87.

Bauman, Zygmunt (1999) *In Search of Politics*, Cambridge: Polity.

Baumeister, Roy F. and Leary, Mark R. (1995) 'The need to belong: Desire for interpersonal attachments as a fundamental human motivation', *Psychological Bulletin*, 117(3): 497–529.

Beck, Ulrich (1992) *Risk Society: Towards a New Modernity* (trans. M. Ritter), London: Sage.

Beck, Ulrich (1994) 'The reinvention of politics: Towards a theory of reflexive modernization', in U. Beck, A. Giddens and S. Lash (eds) *Reflexive Modernization: Politics, Tradition and Aesthetics in the Modern Social Order*, Cambridge: Polity.

Beck, Ulrich and Beck-Gernsheim, Elisabeth (1995) *The Normal Chaos of Love* (trans. M. Ritter and J. Wiebel), Cambridge: Polity.

Beck, Ulrich and Beck-Gernsheim, Elizabeth (2002) *Individualization: Institutionalized Individualism and its Social and Political Consequences* (trans. P. Camiller), London: Sage.

Bell, Vikki (1999) 'Performativity and belonging: An introduction', *Theory, Culture & Society*, 16(2): 1–10.

Bellah, Robert N. (2010) 'Durkheim and history', in I. Strenski (ed.) *Emile Durkheim*, Farnham: Ashgate.

Bendiner-Viani, Gabrielle (2005) 'Walking, emotion, and dwelling: Guided tours in Prospect Heights, Brooklyn', *Space and Culture*, 8(4): 459–71.

Benhabib, Seyla (1992) *Situating the Self: Gender, Community and Postmodernism in Contemporary Ethics*, Cambridge: Polity.

Benjamin, Walter (1999) *The Arcades Project* (trans. H. Eiland and K. McLaughlin), Cambridge, MA: Belknap Press.

Bennett, Julia (2010) 'Belonging, history and memory', paper presented at Vital Signs 2, University of Manchester, 7–9 September.

Bennett, Julia (2012) 'Doing belonging: A sociological study of belonging in place as the outcome of social practices', unpublished PhD thesis, University of Manchester.

Bennett, Tony, Savage, Mike, Silva, Elizabeth et al. (2009) *Culture, Class, Distinction*, London: Routledge.

Benson, Michaela (2010) '"We are not expats; we are not migrants; we are Sauliacoise": Laying claim to belonging in rural France', in B. Bönisch-Brednich and C. Trundle (eds) *Local Lives: Migration and the Politics of Place*, Farnham: Ashgate.

Bernard, Philippe (2010) 'The true nature of anomie', in I. Strenski (ed.) *Emile Durkheim*, Farnham: Ashgate.

Bhatti, Mark, Church, Andrew, Claremont, Amanda and Stenner, Paul (2009) '"I love being in the garden": Enchanting encounters in everyday life', *Social & Cultural Geography*, 10(1): 61–76.

Blokland, Talja (2003) *Urban Bonds: Social Relationships in an Inner City Neighbourhood* (trans. L.K. Mitzman), Cambridge: Polity.

Bonilla-Silva, Eduardo, Goar, Carla and Embrick, David (2006) 'When whites flock together: The social psychology of white habitus', *Critical Sociology*, 32(2/3): 229–53.

Bottero, Wendy (2009) 'Relationality and social interaction', *British Journal of Sociology*, 60(2): 399–420.

Bottero, Wendy (2010) 'Intersubjectivity and Bourdieusian approaches to "identity"', *Cultural Sociology*, 4(1): 3–22.

Bourdieu, Pierre (1977) *Outline of a Theory of Practice* (trans. R. Nice), Cambridge: Cambridge University Press.

Bourdieu, Pierre (1979) *Distinction: A Social Critique of the Judgement of Taste* (trans. R. Nice), London: Routledge.

Bourdieu, Pierre (2000) *Pascalian Meditations* (trans. R. Nice), Cambridge: Polity.

Braithwaite, Edward R. (1962) *Paid Civil Servant*, London: Bodley Head.

Brownlow, Alec (2006) 'An archaeology of fear and environmental change in Philadelphia', *Geoforum*, 37(2): 227–45.

Brubaker, Rogers and Cooper, Frederick (2000) 'Beyond "identity"', *Theory and Society*, 29(1): 1–47.

Bruner, Jerome (1987) 'Life as narrative', *Social Research*, 54(1): 11–32.

Bruner, Jerome and Lucariello, Joan (1989) 'Monologue as narrative recreation of the world', in K. Nelson (ed.) *Narratives from the Crib*, Cambridge, MA: Harvard University Press.

Bruno, Giuliana (2002) *Atlas of Emotion: Journeys in Art, Architecture, and Film*, New York: Verso.

Budgeon, Shelley (2011) *Third Wave Feminism and the Politics of Gender in Late Modernity*, Basingstoke: Palgrave Macmillan.

Burkitt, Ian (1991) 'Society and the individual', *Current Sociology*, 39(3): 1–27.

Burkitt, Ian (1999) *Bodies of Thought: Embodiment, Identity and Modernity*, London: Sage.

Burkitt, Ian (2004) 'The time and space of everyday life', *Cultural Studies*, 18(2): 211–27.

Burkitt, Ian (2008) *Social Selves: Theories of Self and Society* (2nd edn), London: Sage.

Butler, Judith (1990) *Gender Trouble: Feminism and the Subversion of Identity*, New York: Routledge.

Butler, Judith (1993) *Bodies that Matter: On the Discursive Limits of Sex*, New York: Routledge.

Bönisch-Brednich, Brigitte and Trundle, Catherine (2010) 'Introduction: Local migrants and the politics of being in place', in B. Bönisch-Brednich and C. Trundle (eds) *Local Lives: Migration and the Politics of Place*, Farnham: Ashgate.

Calhoun, Craig (1999) 'Nationalism, political community and the representation of society: Or, why feeling at home is not a substitute for public space', *European Journal of Social Theory*, 2(2): 217–31.

Calhoun, Craig (2003a) '"Belonging" in the cosmopolitan imaginary', *Ethnicities*, 3(4): 531–53.

Calhoun, Craig (2003b) 'The variability of belonging: A reply to Rogers Brubaker', *Ethnicities*, 3(4): 558–68.

Carr, Edward Hallett (1961) *What is History?*, London: Macmillan.

Carsten, J. (2000) '"Knowing where you've come from": Ruptures and continuities of time and kinship in narratives of adoption', *Journal of the Royal Anthropological Institute*, 6(4): 687–703.

Casey, Edward (1993) *Getting Back Into Place: Toward a Renewed Understanding of the Place-World*, Bloomington, IN: Indiana University Press.

Chamberlain, Mary (2006) *Family Love in the Diaspora: Migration and the Anglo-Caribbean Experience*, New Brunswick, NJ: Transaction.

Chase, Malcolm and Shaw, Christopher (1989) 'The dimensions of nostalgia', in C. Shaw and M. Chase (eds) *The Imagined Past: History and Nostalgia*, Manchester: Manchester University Press.

Cohen, Anthony P. (1982a) 'Belonging: The experience of culture', in A.P. Cohen (ed.) *Belonging: Identity and Social Organisation in British Rural Communities*, Manchester: Manchester University Press.

Cohen, Anthony P. (1982b) 'A sense of time, a sense of place: The meaning of close social association in Whalsay, Shetland', in A.P. Cohen (ed.) *Belonging: Identity and Social Organisation in British Rural Communities*, Manchester: Manchester University Press.

Collins, Patricia Hill (1990) *Black Feminist Thought: Knowledge, Consciousness, and the Politics of Empowerment*, New York: Routledge.

Cooley, Charles Horton (1902) *Human Nature and the Social Order*, New York: Charles Scribner's Sons.

Crenshaw, Kimberle (1991) 'Mapping the margins: Intersectionality, identity politics, and violence against women of colour', *Stanford Law Review*, 43: 1241–99.

Crossley, Nick (1995) 'Merleau-Ponty, the elusive body and carnal sociology', *Body & Society*, 1(1): 43–63.

Crossley, Nick (2006) 'The networked body and the question of reflexivity', in D. Waskul and P. Vannini (eds) *Body/Embodiment: Symbolic Interaction and the Sociology of the Body*, Aldershot: Ashgate.

Cumiskey, Kathleen and Brewster, Kendra (2012) 'Mobile phones or pepper spray?', *Feminist Media Studies*, 12(4): 590–9.

Datta, Ayona (2006) 'From tenements to flats: Gender, class and "modernization" in Bethnal Green Estate', *Social & Cultural Geography*, 7(5): 789–805.

Davidson, Joyce and Milligan, Christine (2004) 'Embodying emotion sensing space: Introducing emotional geographies', *Social & Cultural Geography*, 5(4): 523–32.

Davies, Katherine (2011) 'Friendship and personal life', in V. May (ed.) *Sociology of Personal Life*, Basingstoke: Palgrave Macmillan.

Davies, Katherine (2012) '"Turning out": Young people, being and becoming', unpublished PhD thesis, University of Manchester.

Day, Kristen (2001) 'Constructing masculinity and women's fear in public space in Irvine, California', *Gender, Place & Culture*, 8(2): 109–27.

de Castro, Lucia Rabello (2004) 'Otherness in me, otherness in others: Children's and youth's constructions of self and other', *Childhood*, 11(4): 469–93.

de Certeau, Michel (1984) *The Practice of Everyday Life* (trans. S. Rendall), Berkeley, CA: University of California Press.

Degen, Mónica Montserrat (2008) *Sensing Cities: Regenerating Public Life in Barcelona and Manchester*, Abingdon: Routledge.

de la Rúa, Ainhoa de Federico (2007) 'Networks and identifications: A relational approach to social identities', *International Sociology*, 22(6): 683–99.

Dennis, Kinsgley and Urry, John (2009) *After the Car*, Cambridge: Polity.

DeNora, Tia (2000) *Music in Everyday Life*, Cambridge: Cambridge University Press.

de Quieroz, Jean Manuel (1989) 'The sociology of everyday life as a perspective', *Current Sociology*, 37(1): 31–9.

Desjarlais, Robert (2003) *Sensory Biographies: Lives and Deaths among Nepal's Yolmo Buddhists*, Berkeley, CA: University of California Press.

DeVault, Marjorie (2000) 'Producing family time: Practices of leisure activity beyond the home', *Qualitative Sociology*, 23(4): 485–503.

Douglas, Mary and Ney, Steven (1998) *Missing Persons: A Critique of the Social Sciences*, Berkeley, CA: University of California Press.

Downing, Frances (2003) 'Transcending memory: Remembrance and the design of place', *Design Studies*, 24(3): 213–35.

Duggan, Lisa (1993) 'The trials of Alice Mitchell: Sensationalism, sexology, and the lesbian subject in turn-of-the-century America', *Signs*, 18(4): 791–814.

Durkheim, Emile ([1912]1965) *The Elementary Forms of Religious Life* (trans. J.W. Swain), New York: Free Press.

Durkheim, Emile ([1887]1972) 'A review of Ferdinand Tönnies's *Gemeinschaft und Gesellschaft: Abhandlung des Communismus und des Socialismus als Empirischer Culturformen*', *American Journal of Sociology*, 77(6): 1193–9.

Durkheim, Emile ([1893]1984) *The Division of Labour in Society* (trans. W.D. Halls), New York: Free Press.

Durkheim, Emile ([1897]1989) *Suicide: A Study in Sociology* (trans. J.A. Spaulding and G. Simpson), London: Routledge.

Dürrschmidt, Jörg and Taylor, Graham (2007) *Globalization, Modernity & Social Change: Hotspots of Transition*, Basingstoke: Palgrave Macmillan.

Eade, John (1994) 'Identity, nation and religion: Educated young Bangladeshi muslims in London's "East End"', *International Sociology*, 9(3): 377–94.

Eade, John (1997) 'Reconstructing places: Changing images of locality in Docklands and Spitalfields', in J. Eade (ed.) *Living the Global City: Globalization as Local Process*, London: Routledge.

Edensor, Tim (2007) 'Sensing the ruin', *Senses & Society*, 2(2): 217–32.

Edwards, Gemma (2011) 'Personal life and politics', in V. May (ed.) *Sociology of Personal Life*, Basingstoke: Palgrave Macmillan.

Edwards, Jeanette (2000) *Born and Bred*, Oxford: Oxford University Press.

Edwards, Rosalind, Hadfield, Lucy, Lucey, Helen and Mauthner, Melanie (2006) *Sibling Identity and Relationships: Sisters and Brothers*, London: Routledge.

Elias, Norbert (1991) *The Society of Individuals* (trans. E. Jephcott), Oxford: Blackwell.

Elias, Norbert ([1939]1978) *The Civilizing Process*, vol. 1: *The History of Manners* (trans. E. Jephcott), Oxford: Blackwell.

Ellison, Nicole, Heino, Rebecca and Gibbs, Jennifer (2006) 'Managing impressions online: Self-presentation processes in the online dating environment', *Journal of Computer-Mediated Communication*, 11(2): 415–41.

Elliott, Anthony and Urry, John (2010) *Mobile Lives*, London: Routledge.

Enli, Gunn Sara and Thumim, Nancy (2012) 'Socializing and self-representation online: Exploring Facebook', *Observatorio Journal*, 6(1): 87–105.

Eriksen, Thomas Hylland (2007) *Globalization: The Key Concepts*, Oxford: Berg.

Esteva, Gustavo and Prakash, Madhu Suri (1998) *Grassroots Postmodernism: Remaking the Soil of Cultures*, New York: Zed Books.

Felski, Rita (2000) *Doing Time: Feminist Theory and Postmodern Culture*, New York: New York University Press.

Felski, Rita (2002) 'Introduction', *New Literary History*, 33(4): 607–22.

Fenster, Tovi (2004) 'Belonging, memory and the politics of planning in Israel', *Social & Cultural Geography*, 5(3): 403–17.

Fenster, Tovi (2005) 'The right to the gendered city: Different formations of belonging in everyday life', *Journal of Gender Studies*, 14(3): 217–31.

Finch, Janet and Mason, Jennifer (1993) *Negotiating Family Responsibilities*, London: Routledge.

Fortier, Anne-Marie (2000) *Migrant Belongings: Memory, Space, Identity*, Oxford: Berg.

Foucault, Michel (1977) *Discipline and Punish: The Birth of the Prison* (trans. A. Sheridan), New York: Vintage Books.

Fox, John (2006) 'Consuming the nation: Holidays, sports, and the production of collective belonging', *Ethnic and Racial Studies*, 29(2): 217–36.

Fox, John and Miller-Idriss, Cynthia (2008) 'Everyday nationhood', *Ethnicities*, 8(4): 536–76.

Fox, Kate (2004) *Watching the English: The Hidden Rules of English Behaviour*, London: Hodder.

Freeman, Mark (1993) *Rewriting the Self: History, Memory, Narrative*, London: Routledge.

Friedmann, John (2002) 'Placemaking as project? Habitus and migration in transnational cities', in J. Hillier and E. Rooksby (eds) *Habitus: A Sense of Place*, Aldershot: Ashgate.

Frizzo-Barker, Julie and Chow-White, Peter (2012) '"There's an app for that": Mediating mobile moms and connected careerists through smartphones and networked individualism', *Feminist Media Studies*, 12(4): 580–9.

Frow, John (2002) '"Never draw to an inside straight": On everyday knowledge', *New Literary History*, 33(4): 623–37.

Furedi, Frank (2004) *Therapy Culture: Cultivating Vulnerability in an Uncertain Age*, London: Routledge.

Game, Ann (2001) 'Belonging: Experience in sacred time and space', in J. May and N. Thrift (eds) *Timespace: Geographies of Temporality*, London: Routledge.

Gardiner, Michael (2000) *Critiques of Everyday Life*, London: Routledge.

Gardiner, Michael (2004) 'Everyday utopianism', *Cultural Studies*, 18(2): 228–54.

Garfinkel, Harold (1967) *Studies in Ethnomethodology*, Englewood Cliffs, NJ: Prentice Hall.

Garland, Jon and Chakraborti, Neil (2006) '"Race", space and place: Examining identity and cultures of exclusion in rural England', *Ethnicities*, 6(2): 159–77.

Gergen, Kenneth J. (1999) *An Invitation to Social Construction*, London: Sage.

Gergen, Kenneth J. and Gergen, Mary (1983) 'Narratives of the self', in T.R. Sarbin and K.E. Scheibe (eds) *Studies in Social Identity*, New York: Praeger.

Gershon, Ilana (2011) 'Un-friend my heart: Facebook, promiscuity, and heartbreak in a neoliberal age', *Anthropological Quarterly*, 84(4): 865–94.

Gibson, James J. (1966) *The Senses Considered as Perceptual Systems*, Boston, MA: Houghton Mifflin.

Gibson, James J. (1979) *The Ecological Approach to Visual Perception*, Boston, MA: Houghton Mifflin.

Gibson, Sarah (2007) 'Food mobilities: Traveling, dwelling, and eating cultures', *Space and Culture*, 10(1): 4–21.

Giddens, Anthony (1991) *Modernity and Self-identity: Self and Society in the Late Modern Age*, Cambridge: Polity.

Giddens, Anthony (1992) *The Transformation of Intimacy: Love, Sexuality and Eroticism in Modern Societies*, Cambridge: Polity.

Gilligan, Carol (1993) *In A Different Voice: Psychological Theory and Women's Development* (rev. edn), Cambridge, MA: Harvard University Press.

Gluck, Sherna Berger and Patai, Daphne (eds) (1991) *Women's Words: The Feminist Practice of Oral History*, New York: Routledge.

Goffman, Erving (1959) *The Presentation of Self in Everyday Life*, Harmondsworth: Penguin Books.

Goffman, Erving (1963) *Behavior in Public Places: Notes on the Social Organization of Gatherings*, New York: Free Press.

Goodstein, Elizabeth (2002) 'Style as substance: Georg Simmel's phenomenology of culture', *Cultural Critique*, 52: 209–34.

Grange, Joseph (1985) 'Place, body and situation', in D. Seamon, and R. Mugerauer (eds) *Dwelling, Place and Environment: Towards a Phenomenology of Person and World*, Malabar, FL: Krieger.

Granovetter, Mark (1973) 'The strength of weak ties', *American Journal of Sociology*, 78(6): 1360–80.

Green, Eileen and Singleton, Carrie (2006) 'Risky bodies at leisure: Young women negotiating space and place', *Sociology*, 40(5): 853–71.

Green, Gill, South, Nigel and Smith, Rose (2006) '"They say that you are a danger but you are not": Representations and construction of the moral self in narratives of "dangerous individuals"', *Deviant Behavior*, 27(3): 299–328.

Green, Lorraine (2004) 'Gender', in G. Taylor and S. Spencer (eds) *Social Identities: Multidisciplinary Approaches*, London: Routledge.

Griffiths, Morwenna (1995) *Feminism and the Self: The Web of Identity*, London: Routledge.

Hall, Stuart (1992) 'The question of cultural identity', in S. Hall, D. Held and T. McGrew (eds) *Modernity and Its Futures*, Cambridge: Polity/Open University Press.

Hall, Stuart (1996) 'Introduction: Who needs identity?', in P. du Gay and S. Hall (eds) *Questions of Cultural Identity*, London: Sage.

Harris, Anita (2008) 'Young women, late modern politics, and the participatory possibilities of online cultures', *Journal of Youth Studies*, 11(5): 481–95.

Harrison, Paul (2000) 'Making sense: Embodiment and the sensibilities of the everyday', *Environment and Planning D: Society and Space*, 18: 497–517.

Heaphy, Brian (2007) *Late Modernity and Social Change: Reconstructing Social and Personal Life*, London: Routledge.

Hearn, Alison (2008) '"Meat, mask, burden": Probing the contours of the branded "self"', *Journal of Consumer Culture*, 8(2): 197–217.

Heidegger, Martin ([1926]1962) *Being and Time* (trans. J. Macquarrie and E. Robinson), New York: Harper & Row.

Highmore, Ben (2004) 'Homework', *Cultural Studies*, 18(2): 306–27.

Hill, Miriam Helen (1985) 'Bound to the environment: Towards a phenomenology of sightlessness', in D. Seamon and R. Mugerauer (eds) *Dwelling, Place and Environment: Towards a Phenomenology of Person and World*, Malabar, FL: Krieger.

Hjorth, Larissa and Lim, Sun Sun (2012) 'Mobile intimacy in an age of affective mobile media', *Feminist Media Studies*, 12(4): 477–84.

Hochschild, Arlie (with Anne Machung) (1989) *The Second Shift*, New York: Avon Books.

Hochschild, Arlie (2011) 'Emotional life on the market frontier', *Annual Review of Sociology*, 37: 21–33.

Hodgetts, Darrin, Stolte, Ottilie, Chamberlain, Kerry et al. (2008) 'A trip to the library: Homelessness and social inclusion', *Social & Cultural Geography*, 9(8): 933–53.

Honneth, Axel (1995) *The Struggle for Recognition: The Moral Grammar of Social Conflicts* (trans. J. Anderson), Cambridge: Polity.

hooks, bell (1981) *Ain't I A Woman: Black Women and Feminism*, Boston, MA: South End Press.

Hopkins, Nick (2008) 'Identity, practice and dialogue', *Journal of Community & Applied Social Psychology*, 18(4): 363–68.

Ifekwunigwe, Jayne (1999) *Scattered Belongings: Cultural Paradoxes of 'Race', Nation and Gender*, London: Routledge.

Ingold, Tim (2000) *The Perception of the Environment: Essays in Livelihood, Dwelling and Skill*, London: Routledge.

Jackson, Michael (1983) 'Knowledge of the body', *Man*, 18(2): 327–45.

James, Alison and Curtis, Penny (2010) 'Family displays and personal lives', *Sociology*, 44(6): 1163–80.

Jayne, Mark (2006) *Cities and Consumption*, London: Routledge.

Jenkins, Richard (2000) 'Categorization: Identity, social process and epistemology', *Current Sociology*, 48(3): 7–25.

Jenkins, Richard (2008) *Social Identity* (3rd edn), London: Routledge.

Jørgensen, Anja (2010) 'The sense of belonging in new urban zones of transition', *Current Sociology*, 58(1): 3–23.

Kalberg, Stephen (ed.) (2005) *Max Weber: Readings and Commentary on Modernity*, Malden, MA: Blackwell.

Kennedy, Paul (2010) *Local Lives and Global Transformations: Towards World Society*, Basingstoke: Palgrave Macmillan.

Kramer, Anne-Marie (2011) 'Kinship, affinity and connectedness: Exploring the role of genealogy in personal lives', *Sociology*, 45(3): 379–95.

Krause, Neal and Wulff, Keith (2005) 'Church-based social ties, a sense of belonging in a congregation, and physical health status', *International Journal for the Psychology of Religion*, 15(1): 73–93.

Kroløkke, Charlotte and Sørensen, Anne Scott (2006) *Gender Communication Theories and Analyses: From Silence to Performance*, Thousand Oaks, CA: Sage.

Laing, Ronald David (1965) *The Divided Self: An Existential Study in Sanity and Madness*, London: Penguin.

Lakoff, George and Johnson, Mark (1999) *Philosophy in the Flesh: The Embodied Mind and Its Challenge to Western Thought*, New York: Basic Books.

Lamont, Michèle (1992) *Money, Morals, and Manners: The Culture of the French and American Upper-Middle Class*, Chicago, IL: University of Chicago Press.

Lasch, Christopher (1978) *The Culture of Narcissism: American Life in an Age of Diminishing Expectations*, New York: Norton.

Lash, Scott (1994) 'Reflexivity and its doubles: Structures, aesthetics, community', in U. Beck, A. Giddens and S. Lash (eds) *Reflexive Modernisation*, Cambridge: Polity.

Lawler, Steph (2008) *Identity: Sociological Perspectives*, Cambridge: Polity.

Leach, Neil (2002) 'Belonging: Towards a theory of identification with space', in J. Hillier and E. Rooksby (eds) *Habitus: A Sense of Place*, Farnham: Ashgate.

Lefebvre, Henri ([1947]1991) *Critique of Everyday Life*, vol. 1 (trans. J. Moore), London: Verso.

Lefebvre, Henri ([1961]2002) *Critique of Everyday Life*, vol. 2: *Foundations for a Sociology of the Everyday* (trans. J. Moore), London: Verso.

Levine, Donald (1971) 'Introduction', in D.N. Levine (ed.) *On Individuality and Social Forms*, Chicago, IL: University of Chicago Press.

Li, Yaojun, Savage, Mike and Pickles, Andrew (2003) 'Social change, friendship and civic participation', *Sociological Research Online*, 8(4) www.socresonline.org. uk/8/4/li.html.

Livingstone, Sonia (2008) 'Taking risky opportunities in youthful content creation: Teenagers' use of social networking sites for intimacy, privacy and self-expression', *New Media & Society*, 10(3): 393–411.

Lofland, Lyn (1973) *A World of Strangers: Order and Action in Urban Public Space*, New York: Basic Books.

Lofland, Lyn (1998) *The Public Realm: Exploring the City's Quintessential Social Territory*, New Brunswick, NJ: Aldine Transaction.

Lowenthal, David (1989) 'Nostalgia tells it like it wasn't', in C. Shaw and M. Chase (eds) *The Imagined Past: History and Nostalgia*, Manchester: Manchester University Press.

Lukes, Steven (2010) 'Prolegomena to the interpretation of Durkheim', in I. Strenski (ed.) *Emile Durkheim*, Farnham: Ashgate.

Lyon, Dawn (2007) 'Moral and cultural boundaries in representations of migrants: Italy and the Netherlands in comparative perspective', in L. Passerini, D. Lyon, E. Capussotti and I. Laliotou (eds) *Women Migrants from East to West: Gender, Mobility and Belonging in Contemporary Europe*, New York: Berghan Books.

Maconie, Stuart (2007) *Pies and Prejudice: In Search of the North*, London: Ebury Press.

McCracken, Scott (2002) 'The completion of old work: Walter Benjamin and the everyday', *Cultural Critique*, 52: 145–66.

McEachern, Charmaine (1998) 'Mapping the memories: Politics, place and identity in the District Six Museum, Cape Town', *Social Identities*, 4(3): 499–521.

McLaughlin, Caitlin and Vitak, Jessica (2011) 'Norm evolution and violation on Facebook', *New Media & Society*, 14(2) 299–315.

McNay, Lois (1999) 'Gender, habitus and the field: Pierre Bourdieu and the limits of reflexivity', *Theory, Culture & Society*, 16(1): 95–117.

McPherson, Miller, Smith-Lovin, Lynn and Cook, James. M. (2001) 'Birds of a feather: Homophily in social networks', *Annual Review of Sociology*, 27: 415–44.

Manzo, John (2005) 'Social control and the management of "private" space in shopping malls', *Space & Culture*, 8(1): 83–97.

Marcuse, Herbert (1964) *One-Dimensional Man: Studies in the Ideology of Advanced Industrial Society*, London: Routledge.

Marx, Karl ([1844]1970) *Economic and Philosophic Manuscripts of 1844* (trans. M. Milligan), London: Lawrence & Wishart.

Marx, Karl and Engels, Friedrich ([1846]1977) *The German Ideology*, Part One (ed. and intro. C.J. Arthur), London: Lawrence & Wishart.

Maslow, Abraham (1954) *Motivation and Personality*, New York: Harper & Row.

Mason, Jennifer (2006) 'Mixing methods in a qualitatively driven way', *Qualitative Research*, 6(1): 9–25.

Mason, Jennifer (2008) 'Tangible affinities and the real life fascination of kinship', *Sociology*, 42(1): 29–45.

Mason, Jennifer (2010) 'Knowing the in/tangible', plenary at Vital Signs 2, University of Manchester, 7–9 September.

Mason, Jennifer (2011a) 'Facet methodology: A case for an inventive research orientation', *Methodological Innovations Online*, 6(3): 75–92.

Mason, Jennifer (2011b) 'What it means to be related', in V. May (ed.) *Sociology of Personal Life*, Basingstoke: Palgrave Macmillan.

Mason, Jennifer and Davies, Katherine (2009) 'Coming to our senses? A critical approach to sensory methodology', *Qualitative Research*, 9(5): 587–603.

Mason-Schrock, Douglas (1996) '"Transsexuals" narrative construction of the "true self"', *Social Psychology Quarterly*, 59(3): 176–92.

Massey, Doreen (1994) *Space, Place and Gender*, Cambridge: Polity.

Mauthner, Melanie (2005) *Sistering: Power and Change in Female Relationships*, Basingstoke: Palgrave Macmillan.

May, Vanessa (2004) 'Narrative identity and the re-conceptualization of lone motherhood', *Narrative Inquiry*, 14(1): 169–89.

May, Vanessa (2008) 'On being a 'good' mother: The moral presentation of self in written life stories', *Sociology*, 42(3): 470–86.

May, Vanessa (2010) 'Lone motherhood as a category of practice', *Sociological Review*, 58(3): 429–43.

May, Vanessa (2011a) 'Self, belonging and social change', *Sociology*, 45(3): 363–78.

May, Vanessa (2011b) 'Introducing a sociology of personal life', in V. May (ed.) *Sociology of Personal Life*, Basingstoke: Palgrave Macmillan.

May, Vanessa (2011c) 'Personal life in public spaces', in V. May (ed.) *Sociology of Personal Life*, Basingstoke: Palgrave Macmillan.

May, Vanessa and Muir, Stewart (2011) 'Belonging as relationality: Capturing everyday belongings', British Sociological Association Annual Conference, London School of Economics, 6–8 April.

Mead, George Herbert (1934) *Mind, Self, & Society: From the Standpoint of a Social Behaviorist*, Chicago, IL: University of Chicago Press.

Meinhof, Ulrike and Galasiński, Dariusz (2005) *The Language of Belonging*, Basingstoke: Palgrave Macmillan.

Melucci, Alberto (1996) *The Playing Self: Person and Meaning in the Planetary Society*, Cambridge: Cambridge University Press.

Merleau-Ponty, Maurice ([1945]2002) *Phenomenology of Perception* (trans. C. Smith), London: Routledge.

Miller, Daniel (2008) *The Comfort of Things*, Cambridge: Polity.

Miller, Daniel (2010) *Stuff*, Cambridge: Polity.

Miller, Daniel (2011) *Tales from Facebook*, Cambridge: Polity.

Miller, Linn (2003) 'Belonging to country: A philosophical anthropology', *Journal of Australian Studies*, 27(76): 215–23.

Morgan, David (2009) *Acquaintances: The Space Between Intimates and Strangers*, Maidenhead: Open University Press.

Morgan, David (2011a) 'Conceptualizing the personal', in V. May (ed.) *Sociology of Personal Life*, Basingstoke: Palgrave Macmillan.

Morgan, David (2011b) *Rethinking Family Practices*, Basingstoke: Palgrave Macmillan.

Morrison, Ken (2006) *Marx, Durkheim, Weber: Formations of Modern Social Thought* (2nd edn), London: Sage.

Morton, Stephen (2007) *Gayatri Spivak: Ethics, Subalternity and the Critique of Postcolonial Reason*, Cambridge: Polity.

Münch, Richard (2011) *Understanding Modernity: Toward a New Perspective Going Beyond Durkheim and Weber*, London: Routledge.

Murphy, Michael (2011) 'The ties that bind: Distinction, recognition and the relational', *International Journal of Interdisciplinary Social Sciences*, 5(10): 103–16.

Nadkarni, Ashwini and Hofmann, Stefan (2012) 'Why do people use Facebook?', *Personality and Individual Differences*, 52(3): 243–9.

Nash, Catherine (2002) 'Genealogical identities', *Environment and Planning D: Society and Space*, 20(1): 27–52.

Nelson, Katherine (1989) 'Monologue as the linguistic construction of self in time', in K. Nelson (ed.) *Narratives from the Crib*, Cambridge, MA: Harvard University Press.

O'Byrne, Darren (1997) 'Working-class culture: Local community and global conditions', in J. Eade (ed.) *Living the Global City: Globalization as Local Process*, London: Routledge.

O'Neill, Máire Eithne (2001) 'Corporeal experience: A haptic way of knowing', *Journal of Architectural Education*, 55(1): 3–12.

Ortner, Sherry (2005) 'Subjectivity and cultural critique', *Anthropological Theory*, 5(1): 31–52.

Pahl, Ray and Pevalin, David (2005) 'Between family and friends: A longitudinal study of friendship choice', *British Journal of Sociology*, 56(3): 433–51.

Pahl, Ray and Spencer, Liz (2004) 'Personal communities: Not simply families of "fate" or "choice"', *Current Sociology*, 52(2): 199–221.

Pershai, Alexander (2008) 'Localness and mobility in Belarusian nationalism: The tactic of tuteisha', *Nationalities Papers*, 36(1): 85–103.

Personal Narratives Group (eds) (1989) *Interpreting Women's Lives: Feminist Theory and Personal Narratives*, Bloomington, IN: Indiana University Press.

Petö, Andrea (2007) 'Food-talk: Markers of identity and imaginary belongings', in L. Passerini, D. Lyon, E. Capussotti and I. Laliotou (eds) *Women Migrants from East to West: Gender, Mobility and Belonging in Contemporary Europe*, New York: Berghan Books.

Phillipson, Carl and Thompson, Paul (2008) 'Whither community studies?', *International Journal of Social Research Methodology*, 11(2): 87–91.

Plotz, John (2008) *Portable Property: Victorian Culture on the Move*, Princeton, NJ: Princeton University Press.

Poggi, Gianfranco (2006) *Weber: A Short Introduction*, Cambridge: Polity.

Popenoe, David (1993) 'American family decline, 1960–1990: A review and appraisal', *Journal of Marriage and the Family*, 55(3): 527–55.

Presser, Lois (2004) 'Violent offenders, moral selves: Constructing identities and accounts in the research interview', *Social Problems*, 51(1): 82–101.

Probyn, Elspeth (1996) *Outside Belongings*, New York: Routledge.

Putnam, Robert (2000) *Bowling Alone: The Collapse and Revival of American Community*, New York: Simon & Schuster.

Radley, Alan, Hodgetts, Darrin and Cullen, Andrea (2005) 'Visualizing homelessness: A study in photography and estrangement', *Journal of Community & Applied Social Psychology*, 15(4): 273–95.

Relph, Edward (1985) 'Geographical experiences and being-in-the-world: The phenomenological origins of geography', in D. Seamon and R. Mugerauer (eds) *Dwelling, Place and Environment: Towards a Phenomenology of Person and World*, Malabar, FL: Krieger.

Ribbens McCarthy, Jane, Edwards, Rosalind and Gillies, Val (2000) 'Moral tales of the child and the adult: Narratives of contemporary family lives under changing circumstances', *Sociology*, 34(4): 785–803.

Ries, Nancy (2002) 'Anthropology and the everyday, from comfort to terror', *New Literary History*, 33(4): 725–42.

Riesman, David (with Nathan Glazer and Reuel Denney) (1961) *The Lonely Crowd: A Study of the Changing American Character* (abridged edn), New Haven, CT: Yale University Press.

Riessman, Catherine Kohler (1993) *Narrative Analysis*, Thousand Oaks, CA: Sage.

Riessman, Catherine Kohler (2003) 'Performing identities in illness narrative: Masculinity and multiple sclerosis', *Qualitative Research*, 3(1): 5–33.

Rodaway, Paul (1994) *Sensuous Geographies: Body, Sense and Place*, London: Routledge.

Rogaly, Ben and Taylor, Becky (2009) *Moving Histories of Class and Community*, Basingstoke: Palgrave Macmillan.

Rooke, Alison (2007) 'Navigating embodied lesbian cultural space: Toward a lesbian habitus', *Space and Culture*, 10(2): 231–52.

Sandywell, Barry (2004) 'The myth of everyday life', *Cultural Studies*, 18(2): 160–80.

Sargin, Güven Arif (2004) 'Displaced memories, or the architecture of forgetting and remembrance', *Environment and Planning D: Society and Space*, 22(5): 659–80.

Savage, Mike, Bagnall, Gaynor and Longhurst, Brian (2005) *Globalization and Belonging: The Suburbanization of Identity*, London: Sage.

Savage, Mike, Warde, Alan and Ward, Kevin (2003) *Urban Sociology, Capitalism and Modernity* (2nd edn), Basingstoke: Palgrave Macmillan.

Sawchuk, Kim and Crow, Barbara (2012) 'I'm G-mom on the phone', *Feminist Media Studies*, 12(4): 496–505.

Sayer, Andrew (2005) *The Moral Significance of Class*, Cambridge: Cambridge University Press.

Schafer, Murray (1985) 'Acoustic space', in D. Seamon and R. Mugerauer (eds) *Dwelling, Place and Environment: Towards a Phenomenology of Person and World*, Malabar, FL: Krieger.

Scheff, Thomas J. (2006) *Goffman Unbound! A New Paradigm for Social Science*, Boulder, CO: Paradigm.

Scheibelhofer, Paul (2007) 'His-stories of belonging: Young second-generation Turkish men in Austria', *Journal of Intercultural Studies*, 28(3): 317–30.

Schutz, Alfred (1962) *Collected Papers I: The Problem of Social Reality* (ed. M. Natanson), The Hague: Martinus Nijhoff.

Schutz, Alfred (1964) *Collected Papers II: Studies in Social Theory* (ed. A. Brodersen), The Hague: Martinus Nijhoff.

Schutz, Alfred ([1932]1967) *The Phenomenology of the Social World* (trans. G. Walsh and F. Lehnert), Evanston, IL: Northwestern University Press.

Scott, Susie (2009) *Making Sense of Everyday Life*, Cambridge: Polity.

Seamon, David (1980) 'Body-subject, time-space routines, and place-ballets' in A. Buttimer and D. Seamon (eds) *The Human Experience of Space and Place*, London: Croom Helm.

Shaw, Alison (2000) *Kinship and Continuity: Pakistani Families in Britain*, London: Routledge.

Short, John Rennie (2004) *Global Metropolitan: Globalizing Cities in a Capitalist World*, London: Routledge.

Short, John Rennie (2006) *Urban Theory: A Critical Assessment*, Basingstoke: Palgrave Macmillan.

Shotter, John (1993) *Cultural Politics of Everyday Life*, Buckingham: Open University Press.

Silva, Elizabeth (2010) *Technology, Culture, Family: Influences on Home Life*, Basingstoke: Palgrave Macmillan.

Silverstone, Roger (2002) 'Complicity and collusion in the mediation of everyday life', *New Literary History*, 33(4): 761–80.

Simmel, Georg (1950) 'The field of sociology', in G. Wolff (ed. and trans.) *The Sociology of Georg Simmel*, New York: Free Press.

Simmel, Georg (1971a) 'Group expansion and the development of individuality', in D.N. Levine (ed.) *On Individuality and Social Forms*, Chicago, IL: University of Chicago Press.

Simmel, Georg (1971b) 'The metropolis and mental life', in D.N. Levine (ed.) *On Individuality and Social Forms*, Chicago, IL: University of Chicago Press.

Simmel, Georg (1990) *The Philosophy of Money* (2nd edn) (trans. T. Bottomore and D. Frisby), Routledge: London.

Skeggs, Bev (1997) *Formations of Class and Gender: Becoming Respectable*, London: Sage.

Skeggs, Bev (2004) *Class, Self and Culture*, London: Routledge.

Skey, Michael (2011) *National Belonging and Everyday Life: The Significance of Nationhood in an Uncertain World*, Basingstoke: Palgrave Macmillan.

Skifter Andersen, Hans (2003) *Urban Sores: On the Interaction Between Segregation, Urban Decay and Deprived Neighbourhoods*, Aldershot: Ashgate.

Śliwa, Martyna and Riach, Kathleen (2011) 'Making scents of transition: Smellscapes and the everyday in "old" and "new" urban Poland', *Urban Studies*, 49(1): 23–41.

Smart, Carol (2007) *Personal Life: New Directions in Sociological Thinking*, Cambridge: Polity.

Smart, Carol and Neale, Bren (1999) *Family Fragments?*, Cambridge: Polity.

Smart, Carol, Davies, Katherine, Heaphy, Brian and Mason, Jennifer (2012) 'Difficult friendships and ontological insecurity', *Sociological Review*, 60(1): 91–109.

Smith, Dorothy (1987) *The Everyday World as Problematic: A Feminist Sociology*, Boston, MA: Northeastern University Press.

Soja, Edward (2000) *Postmetropolis: Critical Studies of Cities and Regions*, Malden, MA: Blackwell.

Somers, Margaret (1994) 'The narrative constitution of identity: A relational and network approach', *Theory and Society*, 23(5): 605–49.

Southerton, Dale (2011) 'Consumer culture and personal life', in V. May (ed.) *Sociology of Personal Life*, Basingstoke: Palgrave Macmillan.

Spencer, Liz and Pahl, Ray (2006) *Rethinking Friendship: Hidden Solidarities Today*, Princeton, NJ: Princeton University Press.

Spivak, Gayatri (1999) *A Critique of Postcolonial Reason: Towards a History of the Vanishing Present*, Cambridge, MA: Harvard University Press.

Stacey, Judith (1993) 'Good riddance to "the family": A response to David Popenoe', *Journal of Marriage and the Family*, 55(3): 545–7.

Stafford, William (1989) '"This once happy country": Nostalgia for pre-modern society', in C. Shaw and M. Chase (eds) *The Imagined Past: History and Nostalgia*, Manchester: Manchester University Press.

Strathern, Marilyn (1982) 'The village as an idea: Constructs of village-ness in Elmdon, Essex', in A.P. Cohen (ed.) *Belonging: Identity and Social Organisation in British Rural Communities*, Manchester: Manchester University Press.

Stychin, Carl (1997) 'Queer nations: Nationalism, sexuality and the discourse of rights in Quebec', *Feminist Legal Studies*, 5(1): 3–34.

Taylor, Charles (1989) *Sources of the Self*, Cambridge: Cambridge University Press.

Thomas, William Isaac (1967) *Social Organization and Social Personality*, Chicago, IL: University of Chicago Press.

Thompson, John (1996) 'Tradition and self in a mediated world', in P. Heelas (ed.) *Detraditionalization: Critical Reflections on Authority and Identity*, Oxford: Blackwell.

Thorns, David (2002) *Transformation of Cities: Urban Theory and Urban Life*, Basingstoke: Palgrave Macmillan.

Tilley, Charles (1994) *A Phenomenology of Landscape: Places, Paths and Monuments*, Oxford: Berg.

Tomlinson, John (2007) *The Culture of Speed: The Coming of Immediacy*, London: Sage.

Tonkiss, Fran (2003) 'The ethics of indifference: Community and solitude in the city', *International Journal of Cultural Studies*, 6(3): 297–311.

Tonkiss, Fran (2005) *Space, the City and Social Theory*, Cambridge: Polity.

Tönnies, Ferdinand ([1887]1963) *Community and Society* (trans. and ed. C.P. Loomis), New York: Harper & Row.

Tönnies, Ferdinand ([1896]1972) 'A review of Émile Durkheim's *De la Division du Travail Social*', *American Journal of Sociology*, 77(6): 1199–200.

Trundle, Catherine (2010) 'Against the gated community: Contesting the "ugly American dream" through rural New Zealand dreams', in B. Bönisch-Brednich and C. Trundle (eds) *Local Lives: Migration and the Politics of Place*, Farnham: Ashgate.

Tseëlon, Efrat (1992) 'Is the presented self sincere? Goffman, impression management and the postmodern self', *Theory, Culture & Society*, 9(2): 115–28.

Tyler, Imogen (2008) '"Chav mum, chav scum": Class disgust in contemporary Britain', *Feminist Media Studies*, 8(1): 17–34.

Urry, John (2000) *Sociology Beyond Societies: Mobilities for the Twenty-First Century*, London: Routledge.

Varela, Francisco, Thompson, Evan and Rosch, Eleanor (1991) *The Embodied Mind: Cognitive Science and Human Experience*, Cambridge, MA: Massachusetts Institute of Technology.

Wacquant, Loïc (2008) *Urban Outcasts: A Comparative Sociology of Advanced Marginality*, Cambridge: Polity.

Walkerdine, Valerie, Lucey, Helen and Melody, June (2001) *Growing Up Girl: Psychosocial Explorations of Gender and Class*, Basingstoke: Palgrave – now Palgrave Macmillan.

Walther, Joseph, Slovacek, Celeste and Tidwell, Lisa (2001) 'Is a picture worth a thousand words? Photographic images in long-term and short-term computer-mediated communication', *Communication Research*, 28(1): 105–34.

Wang, Qi and Brockmeier, Jens (2002) 'Autobiographical remembering as cultural practice: Understanding the interplay between memory, self and culture', *Culture & Psychology*, 8(1): 45–64.

Warde, Alan and Martens, Lydia (2000) *Eating Out: Social Differentiation, Consumption and Pleasure*, Cambridge: Cambridge University Press.

Watson, Rita (1989) 'Monologue, dialogue, and regulation', in K. Nelson (ed.) *Narratives from the Crib*, Cambridge, MA: Harvard University Press.

Weber, Max ([1904]1992) *The Protestant Ethic and the Spirit of Capitalism* (trans. T. Parsons), London: Routledge.

Weber, Max ([1922]1968) *Economy and Society: An Outline of Interpretive Sociology* (ed. G. Roth and C. Wittich), New York: Bedminster Press.

Weedon, Chris (2004) *Identity and Culture: Narratives of Difference and Belonging*, Maidenhead: Open University Press.

Weeks, Jeffrey (1990) *Coming Out: Homosexual Politics in Britain from the Nineteenth Century to the Present* (rev. edn), London: Quartet Books.

Weeks, Jeffrey (1991) *Against Nature: Essays on History, Sexuality and Identity*, London: Rivers Oram Press.

Weeks, Jeffrey, Heaphy, Brian and Donovan, Catherine (2001) *Same Sex Intimacies*, London: Routledge.

Wemyss, Georgie (2006) 'The power to tolerate: Contests over Britishness and belonging in East London', *Patterns of Prejudice*, 40(3): 215–36.

Wemyss, Georgie (2009) *The Invisible Empire: White Discourse, Tolerance and Belonging*, Farnham: Ashgate.

Weston, K. (1991) *Families We Choose: Lesbians, Gays and Kinship*, New York: Columbia University Press.

Wiley, Norbert (1994) 'History of the self: From primates to present', *Sociological Perspectives*, 37(4): 527–45.

Williams, Raymond (1977) *Marxism and Literature*, Oxford: Oxford University Press.

Willis, Paul (1977) *Learning to Labor: How Working Class Kids Get Working Class Jobs*, New York: Columbia University Press.

Wilson, Sarah, Houmøller, Kathrin and Bernays, Sarah (2012) '"Home, and not some house": Young people's sensory construction of family relationships in domestic spaces', *Children's Geographies*, 10(1): 95–107.

Young, Anne, Russell, Anne and Powers, Jennifer (2004) 'The sense of belonging to a neighbourhood: Can it be measured and is it related to health and well being in older women?', *Social Science & Medicine*, 59(12): 2627–37.

Young, Iris Marion (1990) *Justice and the Politics of Difference*, Princeton, NJ: Princeton University Press.

Young, Iris Marion (2005) *On Female Body Experience: 'Throwing Like a Girl' and Other Essays*, Oxford: Oxford University Press.

Yuval-Davis, Nira (2011) *The Politics of Belonging: Intersectional Contestations*, London: Sage.

Zingaro, Linde (2009) *Speaking Out: Storytelling for Social Change*, Walnut Creek, CA: Left Coast Press.

Index

Bold numbers indicate Glossary terms